Literacy Practices of The Mumbai Dabbawalas, India

Writing an Ethnographic Case Study

Uma S. Krishnan

Literacy Practices of The Mumbai Dabbawalas, India

Writing an Ethnographic Case Study

PETER LANG

New York · Berlin · Bruxelles · Chennai · Lausanne · Oxford

Library of Congress Cataloging-in-Publication Data

Names: Krishnan, S. Uma, author.
Title: Literacy Practices of the Mumbai Dabbawalas, India: Writing an
    Ethnographic Case Study / Uma S. Krishnan.
Description: New York: Peter Lang, [2025] | Includes bibliographical
    references and index.
Identifiers: LCCN 2023041648 (print) | LCCN 2023041649 (ebook) |
    ISBN 9781433183133 (hardback: alk. paper) | ISBN 9781433183102 (ebook) |
    ISBN 9781433183119 (epub) | ISBN 9781433183126 (mobi)
Subjects: LCSH: Ethnography—Fieldwork—India. | Indigenous
    Peoples—India—Maharashtra—Social Life and Customs. |
    Literacy.
Classification: LCC GN635.I4 K755 2025 (print) | LCC GN635.I4 (ebook) |
    DDC 302.2/24408864795—dc23/eng/20231025
LC record available at https://lccn.loc.gov/2023041648
LC ebook record available at https://lccn.loc.gov/2023041649
DOI 10.3726/b20834

Bibliographic information published by the Deutsche Nationalbibliothek.
The German National Library lists this publication in the German
National Bibliography; detailed bibliographic data is available
on the Internet at http://dnb.d-nb.de.

Cover design by Peter Lang Group AG

ISBN 9781433183133 (hardback)
ISBN 9781433183102 (ebook)
ISBN 9781433183119 (epub)
DOI 10.3726/b20834

© 2025 Peter Lang Group AG, Lausanne
Published by Peter Lang Publishing Inc., New York, USA
info@peterlang.com—www.peterlang.com

Dedicated
To my loving parents, Sudarsanan and Kamala
for having so much faith in me!!
And
To my graduate student, KR, who asked me,
"Why can't you write a book on ethnographic case study,
that in many ways speaks to me and others like me, … it should be
more like having a conversation with you and not reading a text."

Epigraph

All eight billion on this planet, each individual, has a unique identity and
has been bestowed with a creative mind. Only when we tap and unleash the
unique creative genius within us, will we be happy. Our focus should always
be on being creative and bringing the highest value to any given situation.
—RATANJIT SONDHE (2021)

Given this thought process of Mr. Sondhe, this is my creative contribution
to the literacy paradigm.

Contents

List of Figures and Tables

Figures

Tables

List of Abbreviations

CITI	Collaborative Institutional Training Initiatives
CNS	Chakravarthi Narayana Sudarsanan
DB	Dabbawalas
FRQ	Framed Research Questions
IRB	Institutional Review Board
M.A.	Master of Arts
MMR	Mixed Methods Research
NLG	New London Group
PhD	Doctor of Philosophy

Prolegomenon

Brian Street (1996), in *Literacy in Theory and Practice*, begins his prolegomenon by discussing the established notions of literacy and illiteracy. He then proceeds to question the assumptions associated with them, including how these standards are used to frame literacy practices of native group members, their languages, and their ways of life. This allows him to reveal the "self-interested and ethnocentric" notions that exist in societies and the way some anthropologists, so-called objective scholars, have assessed ethnic and native groups in the past (p. x). He then discusses how he plans to "critique" the well-established autonomous models of literacy arguments and proposes an "alternative model" of literacy, by using his own fieldwork conducted in Iran in the 1970s (p. x). Reading the text, based on his observation and field notes of Maktab literacy, allows the readers to comprehend that literacy is ideological; it is the social context, milieu, language, and local culture that lead to a rich and robust native literacy practice, and why the "Western academic" technical approach to literacy cannot be used as a standard to assess indigenous or ethnic groups.

Following the footsteps of Brian Street, the literacy guru of the ideological model, this book provides its readers the design for conducting an overall ethnographic case study, methods to conduct such a study, gather and develop the research work, and practical application through the use of my own personal data findings, field notes, and observations—to reveal that literacy is indeed ideological. It also exposes to the readers how the autonomous model of labeling the Dabbawalas[1] as illiterates or semi-literates is based on ethnocentric and cultural biases of scholars studying such groups. Further, this book attempts to show that only when a researcher interacts with the participants continuously for months, and sometimes years, can they comprehend what it means to be in the field and what it means to conduct an ethnographic case study, leading to understanding natives or ethnic groups in their own environment and valuing their literacy practices on their own merit. Thus, the title:

Literacy Practices of the Mumbai Dabbawalas, India.

Note

1 Mumbai Dabbawalas—My ethnographic case study was based on studying the literacy practices of the Mumbai Dabbawalas, lunch carriers and deliverers, in the city of Mumbai, India. They are well known for their six-sigma business model and delivery; many universities including Ivy-league schools have conducted studies on their century-old sustainable business model. The Dabbawalas approach to their business, method of writing on the lunch boxes for pickup and delivery, and ways of delivering the food are not just unique but ingenious (although people think of it as very ordinary). Despite their success, these people have been called illiterates or semi-literates, and I was interested in knowing more about it and to see if they were truly illiterates or was there more to this definition than "what meets the eye." **My ethnographic case study proved that they are not only literate as per the ideological model of literacy, but there is a lot we can learn, as a society, from them. Indeed, after my study, I was in awe of these people, their philosophy, literacy practices, and their way of thinking and living.**

Foreword

The book you're holding, *Literacy Practices of the Mumbai Dabbawalas, India,* provides a richly annotated, instructive road map for qualitative research, ethnographic methods, a case-study approach, as well as dissertation and monograph writing in sociology, public policy, education, writing studies, and literacy studies. For those of us who work in rhetoric and writing studies, especially, Uma S. Krishnan's book offers us a step-by-step explanation for how to carry out qualitative research in our field. She takes us all from that murky initial step of trying to visualize a research project and working to focus on a critical question to designing the research framework, developing appropriate research methods and methodologies, wrestling with IRB protocols, and finally submitting the project to a dissertation committee or publisher.

Yes, the book is all that—and more. Krishnan demonstrates her research experience and expertise to showcase her own dissertation research on the quotidian literacy practices of an indigenous group of Indians whom many consider to be "illiterate." In this way, her how-to book on conducting a rich and complex research project is also a book about a multifaceted popular literacy, an unofficial multimodal code-switching literacy neither constrained nor regulated by the formal, schooled expectations of a reading-and-writing literacy that relies solely on the eye and hand. By bounding her research within the Mumbai Dabbawalas, Krishnan decolonizes literacy studies in ways that Brian Street, Jack Goody, Ian Watt, James Gee, Courtney Cazden, and so many others in the New London Group would applaud.

Krishnan has packed a great deal of information into her book, all of which she has successfully organized into four manageable divisions: "Dream," "Design," "Develop," and "Demonstrate." She includes all the "stuff" we researchers need to *know* and *know how to do*, so much of which has for too long remained unspoken, implied, expected but never articulated, let alone explained.

With meticulous care, then, Krishnan takes the reader's hand (she addresses the reader as "you"), walks you through each step of the research and writing process, and advises you about what must be done and why. Take the section on "Choosing the Dissertation Director," for example. When was the last time anyone explained to graduate students how to choose a dissertation director? Too many graduate students are under the mistaken belief that they're bound to the professor(s) they (as undergraduates) mentioned in their application to the graduate program or to the professor who claims them as "their" advisee. Instead, Krishnan asks you to consider a list of questions that will guide *you* in choosing the mentor/director that best suits *you*, questions that include that person's expertise and experience; their timely and substantive (or not) response to drafts; their in/attentiveness to students' frustrations, questions, insecurities; their in/ability to support and motivate; and any biases they might hold. Krishnan challenges you to talk to your peers before making such an important decision. After all, you should choose your director (and your committee), not the other way around!

She goes on to explain not only the Citi Test and IRB procedures but also how to write a research proposal (a prospectus), one of those documents you have never written before but that you're already "supposed" to know how to do or intuit how to do. She breaks the proposal down into sensible categories of (1) The Critical Question: what *single* question is propelling your research? (2) The Significance of the Project: why your topic is worthy of investigation, how it holds significance; (3) The Conception and Definition of the project, which Krishnan astutely refers to as "bounding" in terms of dates, geography, place, and space; (4) The Scholarly Conversation that your research project is entering and extending, a scholarly/cultural/professional conversation that involves leading spokespeople and researchers, as well as the main currents of thought (agreements and disagreements); (5) The Methods[1] and Methodologies[2] you will be using to carry out your project; (6) Your Rationale for Subject Selection, which requires specific reasons for your selections of people, medium, ideas, time span, or sites of research; (7) The Plan of Work, a timeline of due dates; and, of course, (8) Bibliography. Who could possibly put together a usable prospectus without the kinds of help Krishnan offers?

From the prospectus to the research design, from coding to deciphering that coding, from conducting an ethical ethnography to defending your research, Krishnan illuminates the arduous process that is qualitative research. She wrote this book and compiled a stupendous bibliography with *only* you in mind. Like many first academic books, *Literacy Practices of the Mumbai Dabbawalas, India* is based on Krishnan's dissertation project. Translating a dissertation into a book is a commonplace activity, but Krishnan's book transcends that dissertation, becoming an entirely new enterprise with extraordinary significance to researchers. Perhaps even more important than the research findings of her original dissertation on the popular literacy of the Mumbai Dabbawalas is Krishnan's ability to explain research practices and protocols that can be applied across many academic and public-sphere disciplines. Uma Krishnan wrote this book for *all* of you.

Cheryl Glenn
Distinguished Professor of English, Emerita
Penn State University

Notes

1 The concrete techniques of collecting information, methods include library and archival research, online research, interviews, ethnographic or naturalistic research, personal experience and observation.

2 The underlying theories you're using to interpret that information, methodologies provide a theory or lens through which you experience, read, or interpret your research, such as various feminist, rhetorical, critical-race, postcolonial, historiographic, literary, literacy, translingual, and queer theories. Methodologies usually feature leading theorists.

Preface

Recently, I read a book, *The Power of Optimism,* by Alan Loy McGinnis (1990), not because I wanted to read it but because the preface intrigued me. Like all book lovers, the first thing that crosses my mind whenever I pick up a book to read is what is this book all about and what am I going to gain from reading it? As a reader, I have always turned to the preface to see if the author addresses the who, what, why, when, where, and how questions. Even if they are not related to my field, if the information in the introduction interests me, then I will purchase and read it. And, I can say this is the same experience for many readers who are browsing and looking for a book in their field of study. With this background in mind, in this preface, I address almost all the "W" and "H" questions superficially, but I answer them in detail in the book and provide information on how this book contributes to the field of literacy and indigenous studies. I also provide researchers a path to understand and emulate research methods and methodologies like ethnography, ethnographic case study, qualitative methods, grounded theory (and coding), and showcase pathways to working with them, using my dissertation research and experiences as an example.

Why is it Titled Writing an Ethnographic Case Study? And When was the Data Gathered?

When I commenced my doctoral research, I used case study methodology to study the Mumbai Dabbawalas. This was mainly due to three reasons: (1) I felt case study was the most appropriate methodology that would enable me to answer my research question, (2) I had, initially, only a week to ten days to study my participants in a foreign location, and (3) I knew this was a pilot study. What I was unaware of, at that time, was that I would end up visiting the Dabbawalas in my initial year of study in 2011, during different times of the year over many weeks to repeat my case study methods. Interestingly, I repeated the same methods over a period of three years from 2011 to 2014. It is only during my third visit to India, I realized that I was conducting an ethnographic study using case study protocols; but in my dissertation, I refer to using only case study methods as per the decision of my committee members. *So, the question that still haunts me till today is why didn't I refer to my methodology section as an ethnographic case study?* This is probably one of the reasons that led me to write this book, as I wanted to address this and many other aspects to future researchers and ethnographers—you—who will be crossing the path that I have crossed and to inform that you can rewrite the research question/s and methodology, even after they have been bound and framed, provided you have a clear and valid rationale to support the reframing. Thus, this book, based on my own dissertation research and writing, is designed to guide graduate (and in some cases, undergraduate) students to successfully complete their terminal degree. Therefore, the subtitle: *Writing an Ethnographic Case Study.*

Although I might be criticized, after my audience read the book, for not being present continuously with my participants for a lengthy period of six months to one year to observe their literacy practices and thus not qualified or entitled to call my study ethnography, I realized while completing my thesis, and later, that my dissertation had all aspects of ethnography. This was because I was constantly in touch with my participants on and off the field, in India and in the United States, during the three years of my writing the dissertation from 2011 to 2014. And as the Dabbawalas[1] mentioned during my 2015 visit, after my defense, "*Didi*[2] (sister), you have been a constant feature in our lives for the past three years. You visit us and then go, but it is always a pleasure to see you back and so often; and of course, we talk to you many times over the phone." Such comments helped me to see that visiting the Dabbawalas, continuously for days and intermittently between months and making phone calls to converse with them, enabled me to write from an emic[3] perspective and strengthen my analysis from an etic[4] perspective. Further, etic and emic perspectives provided me ample time to reflect on different aspects of what I had observed and written down and to seek clarification from my participants to get a better understanding of their practices. Based on the ideological[5] model of literacy, this approach also allowed me to analyze the collected data and code them in an objective way and theorize the Dabbawalas literacy habits and ways of life.

Further, my argument for calling this book "Writing an ethnographic case study" is based on Fretterman's (2010) argument that ethnographic research conducted in one's own culture does not require as much time to reach a certain point of understanding, as ethnographic work takes in a foreign culture. This is mainly due to the researcher's familiarity with language and customs; in some ways, the researcher is already an insider in many respects. Fretterman (2010) further suggests that although this familiarity is good, it can become an issue when everything the participants are practicing appear to be too normal and things that are to be observed and noted, go unnoticed. The best way to avoid such pitfalls is by recording everything for later viewing and to observe the participants through these recordings and reflect on their activities. In many ways, it provides the researcher new pathways to use the methods to his/her advantage and answer the research question in a holistic way. And in many ways, it also reaffirms what Street (2004) refers to in the *Futures of Ethnography of Literacy* that as the field of social science expands and as we observe our participants' practices, so do the methods and methodologies. Generally, the methods refer to the way we gather and collect information in a specific manner and methodologies refer to the way we interpret the gathered information in a systematic way to later build theories. These, in turn, allows the researchers to approach and understand these out-of-school literacies, like the Dabbawalas literacy, in multimodal ways and view them in their own context, location, and environment.

What Can Readers Expect from This Book?

This book takes the readers on an informative and narrative journey on *how I used ethnographic case study and methods to study my participants, while providing future researchers an opportunity to see how ethnographic case studies are conducted—in real life—in global settings.* After reading the book, you can emulate some of these methods and add your own flavoring or perspective to the methods section like a cooking recipe.

You can also use this book:

1. As a template/model to study any ethnic or indigenous group or use it to study any subject matter or a community in general. This could range from studying the workings of Wall Street trends to observing the shifting nature of political groups. I say this as once doctoral students complete their qualifying or comprehensive exam, they are on a journey to choose the appropriate topic for their dissertation from/in their field. It is during and after the transition phase of changing status from **doctoral student to doctoral candidate**, this book really comes in handy as it enables the reader to approach the next phase of their journey in a methodical way. I must add here that some departments want their doctoral students to write the proposal first and then take the qualifying exams. Although the timing of writing the qualifying exams might be different, this book will still act as a guide during that phase and during the whole research process.

2. As a way to organize your data in a systematic fashion. By using my own observations, interactions, recordings, interviews, field notes, focus-group discussions, transcriptions, and translations with the Dabbawalas, I provide a complete picture of (a) how to conduct a step-by-step ethnographic case study, (b) how to conduct it in an organized way from the beginning to end, and (c) how to think about factors/challenges a researcher might face (that are

never mentioned) while conducting a research study in a foreign country. I provide personal narratives, mainly for two reasons: as it will help the readers to see the challenges an ethnographer faces on and off the field, and to overcome different issues while writing the dissertation. These narratives, personal and professional, allow the readers to see how the process of "involvement and detachment" work at the same time (Powdermaker, 1966).

Although Powdermaker's book was written in 1966, it is still pertinent as it refers to the ways the observer gathers different types of data streams, sometimes messy data, and organizes it. Before I read this book, I was perplexed at the amount of data I had gathered over my visits to India and meeting with my participants. Although all the materials I gathered were organized, I still felt they were too complex and was unsure of how I was going to unpack them and make sense of the materials. Reading Powdermaker made me realize data gathering, especially in such large amounts, can be confusing and complex. The author suggests that mistakes and accidental stumbling upon pieces of information that a researcher discovers, as serendipitous information, are often not showcased in their work, which leaves the people following their work confused and unsure about the findings. Therefore, the author suggests a level of transparency, including showcasing pitfalls in the research, such as what happens if the field researcher decides to be too rigid or too committed to a particular hypothesis or has personality issues (pp. 10–11). So, in some ways, this book is also about stumbling and learning.

3. As a text to refer and understand the format and structure of writing field notes and comprehend the importance of using field notes to answer research questions. This book also showcases what Emerson et al. (1995) in their discussion of writing field notes explain as the process of "understanding how an observer/ researcher sits down and turns a piece of her lived experiences into a bit of written text in the first place" (p. vii). As Sanjek (1990) suggests, I recommend that although writing about field notes varies from person to person, it is important for a researcher to

keep all the writing that materializes from the observation—from scratch notes, personal notes, emails, and thoughts written on pieces of paper—as valid resources. These resources, especially if the researcher is conducting an international study, *will really help to vicariously feel the sounds, smell, mental images of being there and relive through the past moments during the final stages of writing.* Further, this book highlights what it means to be an ethnographer, recording and observing an ethnic group and taking notes of their professional and personal lives. Thus, it provides a glimpse into the everyday life of the Mumbai Dabbawalas—their business and personal literacy practices.

4. As a sample study to see how triangulation works in an ethnographic case study and why it is an integral part of a qualitative study. Triangulation keeps the dilemma of subjective interpretations at bay that ethnographers face while transcribing, coding, and writing about their data findings. Behar (1996) refers to it as a dilemma, as researchers become vulnerable to what they are observing and become subjective. At certain moments of reporting and writing, they are unable to maintain objectivity and unsure on how the world will read their text in case they become too subjective. Therefore, triangulation and the three-way association provides the ethnographer tools for real-time interpretations and cross-examination leading to findings that are valuable resource materials not just for one field but across many fields.

What is the Format and Outline of the Book?

Many years ago, when my husband and I wanted to build our first house, we went to meet my father to inform him of our plans. My dad hearing our plans reacted to us by writing four words in block letters in different colors and gave it to me by saying: "Everything in life begins with a design, what is yours?" The four words were:

"Dream, Design, Develop, and Demonstrate."

It is fascinating to note that this is applicable in every sphere or field in our lives. We all know that dreams are amorphous and translucent unless they are harnessed and pinned down into concrete workable plans. In many ways, realized dreams are like a metamorphosis of thoughts changing from a cocoon to a butterfly. The translucent thought that exists in our mind as questions during the research phase, change into decipherable shapes once they are defined to form well-established designs, which in turn allows the researcher to develop and find answers to their questions.

Although my father used these words for building a house, my research study literally started with this very amorphous thought or question in mind. I say this based on my everyday journal writing from the year 2009 that reflect my monologues. It appears that for many days, I have repeated the same questions: Why am I so interested in literacy? Why am I considered literate and others, not schooled, as illiterate? Is it because of just receiving school and college education? But what about kids who go to school for a few years or my own grandma who went to school till second grade and dropped out? Would she be considered illiterate, although multilingual? Why are people, especially some, in ethnic groups called illiterates? How do people define illiteracy? Will I be able to meet people who are illiterate? Will I be able to study an indigenous or ethnic group? Is it even possible? How do I find answers? Have people studied indigenous groups in the past? How did they do it? Were they successful?

These myriad questions bothered me so much that I started intensely reading about it. I found that scholars in the field were able to direct me on a literacy quest, and I could view their study in terms of how they conducted their research work; but what I realized was that I could not emulate their research methods or experiments. Mainly due to the authors not providing templates or a framework that I could use to conduct my own study. Also, I could not refer to the other researchers due to the ethnic group I had chosen and the subject matter I was planning to research and explore: *The Mumbai Dabbawalas literacy practices.* What it also meant was I had to study my group, as an individual with an open mind, and figure out a design that would help me uncover the truth behind this indigenous groups' literacy practices and lifestyle. I also realized that only toward the end of the study would I be able to make the "judgmental call" and decide if my participants were "literates or illiterates." I must say, to this day, I feel very fortunate to have come across the Mumbai Dabbawalas and was able to study their literacy practices and their secret recipe for success.

With this thought in my mind, in the following sections, I trace how I identified my research topic, defined my research questions, designed my study to be developed and executed, and finally, demonstrated by presenting and publishing my research work to the committee and others later. Thus, each part in this book, using my dissertation research, I showcase the step that a researcher will need to take to reach the end of their journey.

Part I: Dream

In this part, I provide the rationale for visualizing a project, choosing a certain topic, narrowing, and writing a detailed rationale for the topic. I then move on to discussing the importance of choosing a dissertation director, working with the director in selecting a committee, developing a rough sketch of the methods section, writing the IRB, and preparing the prospectus or proposal for submission to the committee.

Part II: Design

In this part, I focus on the importance of understanding the methodology and logistical issues that need to be addressed from choosing the location and participants to chalking out the future (plans)in minute details including writing field notes. Every aspect needs to be considered from arriving at the location to transportation, from venue of meeting the participants to interacting with the group. I also address how to cross the language barrier, how to explain the research work to participants and seek their (IRB) approval. This in many ways paves the road for how to be on the field, work around participants schedules, learn their everyday routine, record all the information, and yet, be unobtrusive.

Part III: Develop

In this part, I showcase how to unpack all aspects of the field notes in an organized manner, as longitudinal study notes, based on research questions. I reveal how I used *only* my pilot study data for this book, although during later visits it was more of the repetition of the same methods. The developing plan also includes how to transcribe and translate the data for interpretation. This is also the first step toward coding and recognizing the complexity and beauty behind it and recognizing that coding and writing have to be cross-checked constantly, every step of the way, to ensure that ethical practices are being maintained. I also share personal narratives of my joy at discovering all the information while analyzing the coded material leading to findings and what Nabokov terms as *Upsilamba*.

Part IV: Demonstrate

In this part, I address steps that need to be taken before the researcher sends the chapters to the committee. I explain how and why addressing and reviewing the rhetorical aspect of the thesis is very important, and why you need to involve your thesis director heavily at this stage. I also address the importance of discussing the format for the defense with the director, as it differs in every field and university, and the importance of preparing potential questions and answers. I provide suggestion on how to prepare a PowerPoint or other forms of presentation for the defense and how to develop confidence in defending your brainchild. I conclude with why congratulating oneself on a job well done is very important and necessary, and how to submit the thesis for national repository based on the format, requirements, and embargo followed by the researcher's university. I end this section and book by discussing how this research of mine, a small pillar, adds to the large field of literacy.

Who Can Read This Book and Use it?

In many ways, this book is applicable to all readers, especially students conducting qualitative research work, students interested in following a path to write their dissertation or thesis and students who want to know about coding. This book can also be used by instructors who are planning to teach qualitative mixed method research work in any field, to those who want to know about the Dabbawalas' literacy, just out of curiosity, and to readers who are interested to understand what it means to define literacy in a global setting. The data gathered through ethnographic qualitative case study methods will be of great interest to different audiences: businessmen, professionals, educators, non-profit institution administrators, historians, literacy and rhetoric graduate students, and undergraduate students across field. It will be useful to all of them, as it provides many valuable life lessons and reveals how group dynamics and peripheral participation are important tools in learning new skills, let it be in a classroom or in a formal business setting. The information provided in this book can be used by business schools to broaden their understanding of how entrepreneurship and multilingual practices work in a service industry, given the concept of the flat world and global markets (Friedman, 2005), and the type of economic strategies these Dabbawalas use to maintain their century-old business industry. Further, it provides researchers and professors an opportunity to view how translation and transcriptions are used in international studies and to discuss that in their graduate courses.

Few Notes to My Readers

Note 1: An important aspect that I want to address in this book is repetition. You will find in many places that I repeat some aspects of research; it is not due to oversight on my part but purposeful. As Dr. C. N. Sudarsanan, my mentor would say, "Mention the research question or pivotal points of interest at crucial junctures. Readers tend to forget them while they are reading, and you can't expect them to be flipping back to page 6 or whichever page that you provided key information or suggested some important points. It is necessary to weave it, so that it becomes one narrative." Therefore, dear readers, if you find places where there are some repetitive points or perspectives, it is because they provide context to my argument or explanation.

Note 2: Another important aspect to be noted is that I did not consider the Mumbai Dabbawalas an indigenous group, till they addressed themselves as one. When I started my study, I considered them as an ethnic group, but it is only after I met my participants and how they described themselves, I termed them as indigenous and ethnic. Please see my rationale for why I refer to them as an indigenous group in Chapter 2.

Further, I have capitalized the "Dabbawalas" throughout the book, as my participants mentioned that each dabbawala, tiffin carrier, was an owner, having his own franchise belonging to the Nutan Mumbai Dabbawala Association, and therefore, should be referred to as "Dabbawala—as a proper noun" and not as just a "dabbawala—tiffin carrier." We are known as "Mumbai Dabbawalas, so what if there is No Mumbai prefix to our identity. We are one of a kind and that is our name. In Hindi, we don't have to worry about uppercase or lowercase but in English ..." Also, we are a team or group of members, "We are the Dabbawalas, in plural form."

Also, some of their references on literacy are based on how the business started during the colonization period and the assumptions people had on definition of literacy and what does it mean to be a *unpad*[6] or illiterate.

Note 3: I use analogies throughout the book, maybe due to my teaching profession, that my students have pointed out as being helpful. Therefore, you will see quite a few references to painting, architecture, construction, etc. As I have taught a wide variety of courses, my references and examples vary throughout the book.

Note 4: I use "you" in many areas in the text to directly address my readers—the graduate and undergraduate students and readers conducting research. Also, as my graduate student, Kyle, R., suggested, "Can you please make it conversational, so that I feel you are talking to me and guiding me?"

Note 5: Further, you might find some chapters to be very short and some too long; this is because my focus is on helping you, the student, accomplish one task at a time. Please refer to the appendix as it provides a table on how to keep track of your thesis or dissertation journey.

Note 5: Sometimes you will find words have quotation marks and there are no citations for them. This is mainly because they are considered common knowledge in the academia and some words/quotes are from interviewing my participants.

Note 6: This book is based on my dissertation research and only parts of the thesis have been showcased to guide and enable you to reach your final goal.

Notes

1 My participants are from two different groups who were assigned to me, specifically for this study, by the group president.

2 Hindi is one of the national languages of India; "didi" is a common word used for sister—I spoke to the Dabbawalas in Hindi during my visits, with a few English words.

3 Emic here refers to the researcher providing a perspective by describing the language, practices, and culture of the Dabbawalas as an insider and as a native of that country.

4 Etic perspective here refers to how I viewed the Dabbawalas practices in an objective way, by wearing a researcher's lens.

5 Ideological model of literacy—A model that posits that literacy is rooted in social practices, contexts, and situations, and differs from autonomous model—as literacy in and by itself will not and does not—have an effect on other social and cognitive practices (Street, 1984, 2000).

6 *Unpad—In Hindi, it means to be uneducated or illiterate.*

References

Behar, R. (1996). *The Vulnerable Observer: Anthropology that Breaks Your Heart.* Beacon Press.

Emerson, R. M., Fretz, R. I., & Shaw, L. (1995). *Writing ethnographic fieldnotes.* The University of Chicago.

Fetterman, D. M. (2010). *Ethnography: Step-by-Step guide* (3rd ed.). Sage Publishing.

Friedman, T. L. (2005). *The World Is Flat: A brief history of the twenty-first century*. Farrar, Straus, and Giroux.

McGinnis, A. L. (1990). *The Power of Optimism*. Harper & Row.

Powdermaker, H. (1966). *Stranger and Friend: The Way of an Anthropologist*. W. W. Norton & Company.

Sanjek, R. (Ed.). (1990). *Fieldnotes: The Makings of Anthropology*. State University of New York Press.

Street, B. (1984). *Literacy in Theory and Practice*. Cambridge: Cambridge University Press.

Street, B. (2000). Literacy Events and Literacy Practices. In M. Martin-Jones & K. Jones (Ed.), *Multilingual literacies: Comparative perspectives on research and practice* pp. 17–29. Amsterdam: John Benjamin's.

Street, B. (2004). Futures of the ethnography of literacy? *Language and Education, 18*(4), pp. 326–330 (published online in 2010). https://doi.org/10.1080/09500780408666885

Acknowledgments

As I write this acknowledgment, the first thought that enters my mind is Newton's well-known belief that standing on the shoulders of giants only helps us to look further and see what lies ahead of us. For me, these giants or scholars in the field are the people I refer to in this book, people I met who helped me during my study and during the process of writing this book, colleagues who made recommendations, and reviewers I couldn't thank due to the review process being anonymous. Although this book has no resemblance to my dissertation, I have used many aspects of my research work and references, so that you, too, can benefit from these scholars' point of view. Indeed, I am truly thankful to them as their knowledge helped me to *provide my own flavoring* to my dissertation work and this book.

With this frame of mind, I proceed to express my sincere and heart-felt gratitude to a distinguished scholar, writer, and mentor, Dr. Cheryl Glenn. I am indebted to her for her willingness to write the foreword for my book. Having admired and quoted her extensively in many of my work, I decided to email her but was unsure of her response and unsure of her schedule. When she agreed, my first reaction was disbelief as she has been an invisible guru to me, with some of her books being my bedside companion, especially *Rhetorical Feminism and This Thing Called Hope*, and *Rhetoric Retold*. Every day, I salute her for providing us with books and articles that have profoundly impacted many of us with our teaching of rhetoric and writing in the classroom. I feel blessed.

In addition to Dr. Glenn, I am also extremely grateful and thankful to Dr. Beverly Moss, Dr. Tarez Graban, and Prof. Mechenbier who were willing to endorse this book. I am indebted to them for taking the time out of their busy schedule to read the book and provide their recommendation. I feel humbled.

Further, I am indebted to my parents, spouse, children, and my siblings for their support throughout my dissertation journey and while writing this book. They were my pillars of strength. I am also grateful to Dr. Brian Huot, Dr. Pamela Takayoshi, and Dr. Iswari Pandey for their guidance during the dissertation process, and Dr. Cunningham during the prospectus stage. My heartfelt thanks to Dr. Joanne Dowdy for always being there like a sister, motivating and supporting me through my quests. Special thanks to Dr. Agrawal for sharing his knowledge on the Dabbawalas business model with me during many of my visits and for always willing to talk to me. In addition, I am truly thankful to the Peter Lang Publications team, who were very patient with me as I wrote, rewrote, and revised my drafts and for their help in getting this book published.

Finally, my heartfelt thanks and gratitude to the Dabbawalas, my participants, for all their help and patience, so that I could complete my research work and study. I feel indebted to them.

While working on this book, there were many changes happening in the United States and across the world due to the pandemic, Covid-19. Everyone was affected including the Mumbai Dabbawalas. Their business came to a halt or there was minimum delivery, as their clients' businesses in Mumbai and the railway transportation system was shut down and people had to return to their villages. Post-Covid, things have recovered and they are back to their normal routine, continuing their century-old business and providing opportunities for researchers to see their amazing work.

Part I

Dream

I argue that an ethnographic perspective offers two major contributions to this debate: (1) that ethnographic perspectives and an understanding of literacy practices as multiple and culturally varied, can help avoid simplistic and often ethnocentric claims regarding the consequences of literacy based on one-dimensional and culturally narrow categories and definitions and (2) that an ethnographic perspective can sensitise us to the ways in which the power to name and define is a crucial component of inequality.

—Brian Street (2011)

In this part, I provide the rationale for visualizing a project, choosing a certain topic, narrowing, and writing a detailed rationale for the topic. I then move on to discussing the importance of choosing a dissertation director, working with the director in selecting a committee, developing a rough sketch of the methods section, writing the IRB and preparing the prospectus or proposal for submission to the committee.

Chapter One

Visualizing the Research Topic

It is not what you look at that matters, it's what you see.

—Henry David Thoreau

"See your topic in your inner eyes before you define and speculate on a particular aspect of your research work" was a comment made by Dr. C. N. Sudarsanan (CNS),[1] when I first thought about pursuing a dissertation study on the Mumbai Dabbawalas, India. His rationale was that seeing comes before words and clearly visualizing a topic in the "inner eye" will allow me to explore the topic further. His suggestion was I must meditate on the topic for a few days to a few weeks, as it will enable me to define and speculate on a particular aspect of the Dabbawalas business instead of exploring all aspects of their business model. He explained that "looking" addresses the conscious mind, but "visualizing deeply" addresses the subconscious and conscious mind, allowing human beings to develop certain perspectives and "act on a subject matter with greater introspection." He referred to Peale's (1961) idea of visualization, imaging and mental engineering, and explained that "although it is from 1960s, the idea is still the same" that looking is superficial while visualizing is analytical and in-depth, and it activates the mind to think and processes information a certain way; thus, allowing the researcher or "you, in this case" to align and systematically work on a certain topic of your choice. He explained, "Shifting the focus from just looking to seeing and visualizing and focusing on a certain aspect of your research allows you to perceive the topic in different light and makes you become cognizant of new aspects that you might want to explore, which you might have been overlooked earlier."

To be honest, I was very skeptical about his advice but quietly listened and decided to visualize this picture of my study in my head. My first few attempts led me to view the Dabbawalas, their way of life, and their work. This picturization was based on the research I had conducted on them to comprehend why they were famous. Later attempts allowed me to sketch superficially what and why I was deeply interested in studying this group. Mulling constantly over my inner thoughts led to the conviction that I wanted to literally follow, observe, and study the Mumbai Dabbawalas' everyday practices and to understand why they were being termed as illiterates or semi-literates, despite having a successful supply-chain business practice. In hindsight, I can now testify that envisioning led me to shift my focus from studying the Dabbawalas management practices to studying their literacy practices and led to the successful completion of my dissertation.

Once I had visualized my project, I started framing my study and as per CNS's suggestion, "penciling it down." His suggestion led me to create a set of questions, which is applicable to all researchers. One can always add to these questions, but the key is to explore each aspect of the topic thoroughly and write about it, so that it grounds your thoughts on the subject matter. Thus, begin by asking yourself:

- What or who do I want to study?
- What is my purpose in conducting this study?
- Who or what is my subject matter?
- What and which aspect do I want to pursue about the topic?
- How passionate am I to pursue this topic and why?
- How much do I know about my subject matter?
- How do I plan to develop my study?
- What do I want to accomplish by pursuing this study?

And, pencil the following lines at the end:

Once I answer the above questions to the best of my abilities, I will decide tentatively on the most appropriate methodology for studying and investigating my subject matter/s!!

In my case, before visualizing the topic, I had never thought of asking myself these questions as I was very busy identifying the topic and focusing on methodology. What I didn't realize was that these questions are the initial "writing" steps that need to be addressed *in detail* as a researcher, before starting any part of the dissertation journey. I mention this, as the chosen topic should bring a smile to your face even after a decade of the final defense and you should be able to write about the topic for many years to come. Thus, the initial penciling is very important as it paves the way for the student-researcher to become a scholar down the road. As my director would say, "You are a researcher while you are writing your dissertation but once you defend—you should start publishing your work and contributing to the field." The common belief in academia is that once you become knowledgeable in the area of your research, you need to develop expertise in that specific field, and start contributing to peer-reviewed journals and texts to join the field of scholarly writers. Further, one of the interesting shifts that happens in the academic circles *after your defense* is the committee members refer to you as a colleague, as you have crossed "the researcher threshold" and entered the realm of doing independent and scholarly work leading to the change in status. Therefore, my suggestion to all students, who are planning to write their thesis at the undergraduate, graduate, or doctoral level would be that they should be very committed to the topic and take the time to think about their research, by visualizing and penciling their thoughts, before delving into it—as it impacts the individual's career goals, short-term and long-term.

Note

1 Dr. CNS had worked for the Indian Government and is well-known for his books and talks on performance budgeting and for inspirational lectures, research

methods, and thesis writing. I also interviewed him as he had used the Dabbawalas services during his residence in Mumbai, India.

Reference

Peale, N. V. (1961). *The Tough-Minded Optimist*. Prentice Hall.

Chapter Two

Narrowing and Providing a Rationale for Choosing a Specific Topic: Illiteracy and Indigenous Group

One of the keys to writing a successful thesis and completing it on time is to write a detailed rationale for your study. The more grounded it is, the more passionate you become; and this will help you to trudge through the writing and rewriting, despite the hardships lined in your pathway instead of giving up halfway through.

—Joanne Dowdy

Once the project has been envisioned, the next step to be taken in the research journey is to work on the scope of the study. A few years back, one of my students wanted to write her master's thesis on the British colonization of India and when I asked her if this was a ten-year project, as she will need go through close to 250 years of history, she appeared confused. At that point, I informed her about the difference between a wide and narrow scope by providing an analogy of painting her whole house verses painting a wall, and then painting a wall verses a canvas that has certain strict dimensions. I also explained to her that instead of suggesting how she wanted to write on British colonization in general (whole house), she could focus on a specific time period and conduct research on the effects of colonization on a group (one wall), or the impact of colonization during a specific time period on the Indian political system, or the role of certain/ specific leaders and their group dynamics in gaining independence for India (canvas), etc. As I was explaining, she understood why choosing a specific topic from the field is important and why the topic should be narrow and manageable, so that it can be explored within a span of few semesters to few years.

Therefore, as a researcher, it is important to measure and limit the scope of one's study and ensure that the research questions are focused and answer a certain aspect of the researcher's quest. Another suggestion that I usually provide my students is to conduct an in-depth study, especially if they are going to be gathering data for many months, as this will enable the researcher to establish solid roots and in turn strengthen their study. In her email to me after her defense, she wrote, "I am thankful for all your guidance, but I will never forget what you said when I was unsure about narrowing the scope of my project and about going longitudinal by referring to your favorite painter analogy."

You said:

It is like asking a painter to paint your whole house verses asking an artist to paint a piece of art for your living room. The house painter will paint the house as per your color specification. Although both are artists, the focus of the house painter is on providing a uniform look across all the walls of your house. On the other hand, the artist, also a painter, specifically chooses a frame, a specific size, a pattern, then envisions a drawing, visualizes a design, then carefully weighs in the placement of each and every aspect of that painting to provide the necessary impact. Thus, choosing a topic for your thesis needs to be focused, specific, and narrow. The scope of painting the house is large and broad, rather two-dimensional while a canvas painting in many ways is three-dimensional, as it has length, width and depth. You asked me why is Mona Lisa so famous, after all it is just a painting?

Dr. Krishnan, what you said made so much sense that I not only changed the period of my investigation to one decade, but also remained focused on the impact of nationalist movement and leadership during that time. What is further interesting is that my investigation on just focusing on one decade of the movement was itself 150 pages long. To be honest, I know there is more research that needs to be added to my thesis and when the other committee member asked me to cut it short to 100 pages, I was heartbroken and upset. And ... this is despite narrowing the scope and working for more than 15 weeks on this topic. Thank you for providing the insight.

On a similar note, when I initially chose my dissertation topic, I was like my students and was interested in focusing on all aspects of the Mumbai Dabbawalas and wanting to view every aspect of their business model and their literacy. What I didn't realize was that the scope of my study was too broad, given the time that I could spend with my participants. But after conducting research on the Dabbawalas and the process of visualization, I decided to narrow my scope *to only their literacy practices* as there was a sizable amount of literature on their business model and nothing on their literacy practices, other than calling them illiterates or semi-literates.

Further, given the time schedule and length of 200–250 pages required for the dissertation, I decided to shift my focus and delve into the literacy aspect. In addition, I had two other reasons to pursue this topic: first, research had not been conducted on viewing their work from the literacy angle, and second, my desire was to add new literature to the literacy paradigm, especially on non-Western rhetoric, based on my research methods. Although I had narrowed my topic, I had nagging doubts about data gathering, which led to a discussion with the director, "What happens if I am unable to gather enough material on the Dabbawalas' literacy? Will I have to expand my study again and redo the whole process?" His response was that I should "start the journey and see things falling into place." What I didn't realize when I started my study was that I would have to reduce 6,600 pages of work into 660 pages and then produce a final draft of 210 pages for my dissertation.

Rationale for Choosing the Topic: Why is it Important?

In the following paragraphs, I showcase and provide the rationale for choosing my topic on two different levels:

- Rationale for choosing to investigate the literacy aspect of the Dabbawalas
- Rationale for focusing on Illiteracy and why indigenous group?

The question that often arises among graduate students is why is it important to write a detailed rationale for choosing a certain topic. Council of Graduate Schools (2014) pilot study suggests that there are many factors that contribute to student "completion or attrition" in STEM Master's Program. The most disturbing information from 2019 research suggests that doctoral student attrition remains at "50% over the past 50 years" (Sverdlik & Hall, 2020). The reasons attributed to students not completing the program vary from *losing interest in the program, lacking the motivation to continue the subject matter, advising and relationship with supervisor to lacking an understanding of "departmental structures and socialization efforts"*.[1] Students after three semesters or sometimes after three years of working on a project suddenly lose interest on the topic and discontinue their studies (Bair & Haworth, 2004; Bitzer & Wilkinson, 2009; Litalien & Guay, 2015; Mason, 2012; Rigler et al., 2017).

On the contrary, based on research investigation, scholars found what keeps the others motivated to complete the program ranges from having a good rationale for pursuing the graduate program, achievement of personal goals, job placement, to academic contribution. Hardre and Hackett (2015) argue that there is a clear gap between what graduate students expect from their study and institution to what they experience as a researcher, in terms of pursuing their agenda and how it impacts their motivation and perseverance on the project. Recommendations made by scholars in the field suggest that providing a clear rationale for choosing a topic for the final research work/ study should be the second step that is essential to map out for all graduate students; the first step being choosing the topic and narrowing the scope. Further, providing a detailed, clear, convincing, and long-winded rationale on the topic, keeps the researcher motivated till the end of their seminal work; it moves them from inertia to action stage. Dowdy, in one of our conversations, when I asked her about how she wrote so many books and how she motivated so many of her students to graduate said, "… And, sometimes, I feel that we have topics ingrained in some part of our mind; and at the right time, the morphological grooves that hold information they appear and goad us into taking action and completing it at a certain time. This is the same for writing books and same for enabling our students to think about topics they are passionate about. "

This is true as I have witnessed it within me and within my students. Few years back, a student in my Argumentative Prose class had chosen a topic and titled it, "Calling someone a retard equals to you being retarded!!" I was amazed at the rationale she had provided in her proposal on why she was extremely interested in researching this specific topic, why psychology was her major, and why the rationale was based on three appeals. In the pathos section, she started with her family background and then wrote:

> I am sick and tired of people calling others retard as I have heard it for 18 years of my life. I have a brother, who is 21 but thinks like a six-year-old. He is incapable of understanding anything at his age level as his brain isn't developed. As a child, when parents would bring him to school and drop him off at special classes, I would hear other students calling him a retard and it would make me feel sad, but I moved on, as my parents counseled me. While I was in middle school, the comments really started bothering me as it became personal. One day, while I was in a math class, I didn't respond to a question correctly and someone from the back commented, "She, too, is a retard like her brother." I came home and cried myself to sleep that night and many other nights. I also couldn't share this anguish with my parents, as they had to deal with this situation in their own ways. Interestingly, as I moved on to high school, it didn't bother me as this was the norm—to call everyone a retard. I also realized that fighting back with other people and providing explanation was unimportant, as I could not change the world other than change my attitude and my thought process. But thanks to my brother and to all the comments I heard, I have become passionate about pursuing psychology and cognitive science as my major to see why some people have mental growth challenges—a topic that has bothered me from childhood; and any chance I get to write and educate other people, like I am doing with this project about the word retard, I am the first in line.

I have provided this student's narrative as it reveals that somehow this topic was repressed in some part of her mind and resurfaced when an opportunity arose for her to clarify and address the word "retard" to others. When I dreamt of my own topic of following the Mumbai Dabbawalas, my intentions moved from passion to obsession that I was determined to pursue it, and I never considered the issues and challenges that I might face conducting the study. What I realized at that point was that there is always a reason of why we want to investigate a particular subject matter. This could be something from our past or something related to our environment; it could range from a traumatic relationship, comments, or criticism to an experience that has bothered us but remained dormant for a long period of time, to suddenly resurface at a given time (Boag, 2006; Freud, 1915). In my case, it certainly resurfaced while I was undertaking a course on literacy.

Rationale for Choosing to Investigate the Literacy Aspect of the Dabbawalas and Why?

I hope the reasons I provide, in the following pages, *acts as a template* to write the rationale for your prospectus. The focus is on understanding why the chosen topic intrigues you, what is your justification for working on it, what relevance does it have from the past to the present, and how will this topic hold your interest for a long time. In my case, there were four distinct categories, and I am showcasing these categories, as an example, as many of my graduate and undergraduate Honors students have used this to build their own rationale for their thesis:

- Illiteracy and Irritability
- Illiteracy and Perplexity
- Illiteracy and Ingenuity
- Illiteracy in Literacy Studies and Choosing a Specific Topic

After I selected my topic, for one week, I mulled over the topic and wrote down all the reasons associated with *why* I wanted to specifically work on this subject matter. What I realized after writing my rationale that I was passionate about this topic because of what I had read, seen, and heard from different sources as a young child and adult. Further, as a doctoral candidate, I realized that illiteracy and literacy had been analyzed extensively over the years by scholars, but I still felt there were some unanswered questions that needed personal observation to grasp the truth behind what it means to be *truly literate*.

At this point the question arises, as my student asked, "So, how does all this relate to my work?" And the response is that by providing the following rationale I showcase the invisible aspect of conducting research and to inform the audience that behind the curtains, the beginning of research work is very confusing and no one bothers to inform the researcher what they should be prepared for—in terms of what does it mean to begin researcher work? Further, I want to reveal how important it is to organize the information that a researcher might have gathered from the past to the present and weave those life experiences in a way that makes sense. It is like the hoarder trying to declutter materials/information from a long time, including memories on the topic that the researcher wants to pursue. Things have to be viewed from a new angle, based on the researcher's interest on a topic, and then decisions have to be made to look for materials/data that are pertinent to that subject matter. In addition, I want my readers to use this information as an example to create their own personal rationales to reach their final goal.

Illiteracy and Irritability: The term illiteracy used to bother me from a young age when I would read history or other social science books. The references in the books to India would be that it was a poor country, where most of the people lived below the poverty line and most of the people in the rural areas were either illiterate or semiliterate. Further, many of these books rationalized the poverty as being prevalent from ancient times and showcased the British colonization in positive light, arguing that they were instrumental in providing education to the colored masses. Interestingly, the references to the ancient civilization, inventions, languages, customs, traditions, alternative medicines, literature, and discoveries made by Indians were mentioned in passing and not as something that should be showcased on the world stage. What was even more appalling was that all the texts almost or never provided a rationale for why most Indians were considered illiterates or poor; there was/is never any reference provided on the systematic plundering and looting by different colonizers: Mongols, Mughal rulers, and later by the British, all over a period of three to four centuries; and there was/is never a mention about how they had "raped the continent" of all its riches over the centuries (Durant, 1930). On the contrary, it was about how these conquerors loved India and how they had brought great reforms in every field ranging from political, social, civil, and education to other fields. What bothered me the most about these writings was the generic use of the word "illiteracy" to refer to the masses in general and the aspect of innate bias existing in some of the Western scholarly texts.

Illiteracy and Perplexity: On another level, as a child, I would come home from school reading about poverty and illiteracy and find my grandmother, considered to be "illiterate" as per the definition of literacy, as she had attended school only till second grade, fluently speaking in four different languages to our neighbors. She was extremely proficient in reading and writing in Tamil, Telugu, Kannada, Grantha, Hindi, and Sanskrit. In addition, she could understand and speak broken English. She had read the Indian Epics in Tamil and would converse with us on a wide range of topics from literature to religion and from cooking to Karma philosophy. She had herbal cures for many of our physical ailments, that often after consuming these Ayurvedic medicines we found there was no need to visit an allopathic doctor. When questioned about it she would respond with a nod saying, "This is all passed down information from one generation to another." When I would question her about her knowledge of the unique language, Grantham, and how she had learned it, she would respond by saying, "There are certain things that were taught to us as young children. We never questioned the adults about what they were teaching us, we would just follow." She continued by suggesting, "This includes everything from learning to speak to writing to cooking to practicing many aspects of our culture. You can learn everything as a young child and practice it; but as adults, you can choose to lose them or retain them, the choice is yours." Probably, it was this fascination and confusion that was deeply entrenched in my mind that I wanted to understand what really constitutes as illiteracy.

Illiteracy and Ingenuity: On a different level, another fascinating aspect that intrigues me till today is how the local vegetable vendor or the carpenter or rickshaw (three-wheeled taxi service) driver in India can calculate numbers in their heads and speak different languages. I refer to these groups specifically based on a graduate study[2] and on my findings that: (a) many of these people come from poor families having almost no exposure to even primary school education, (b) relocate to new places forsaking their hometowns, communities, or villages to find new opportunities in cities, and (c) although their native language is often different from what is spoken in the new place they have migrated to, they acquire or learn the local dialects so that they can communicate with the local population to conduct business and survive. And what is further fascinating is that these people were/are capable of intertwining their speech with English phrases, philosophy, and myth as part of their everyday conversation. Pandit Nehru (India's first Prime minister after gaining independence from the British rule) refers to this aspect that he discovered during his travels across India in *The Discovery of India* (1946):

> The old epics of India, the Ramayana and Mahabharata and other books, in popular translations and paraphrases were widely known among the masses and every incident and story and moral in them was engraved on the popular mind and gave a richness and content to it. Illiterate villagers would know hundreds of verses by heart, and their conversations would be so full of references to them or to some story with a moral, enshrined in some old classic. Often, I was surprised by some such literary turn given by a group of villagers to a simple talk about present day affairs. I realized that even the illiterate peasant had a picture gallery in his mind, though this was largely from myth and tradition and epic heroes and only very little from history. Nevertheless, it was vivid enough.

Although, his reference to "illiterate peasant" bothered me, I was more fascinated with the ingenuity of these people and how these "illiterates had a picture gallery in their mind." What perplexed me as a graduate student was that these vendors could calculate complex arithmetic mentally, speak different languages, and comprehend the rhetoric of the situation to make a livelihood for themselves and their families in new environments. This probably was another reason that navigated me to my study.

Illiteracy in Literacy Studies and Choosing a Specific Topic: In addition to the above reasons, studying a course on literacy studies, during doctoral coursework, provided the surety, rather the fuel, required to study an ethnic group. My journey with illiteracy, mystification, and indigenous group started when I was reading Kathleen Gough's (1968) study on the implications of literacy in India and her ethnographic work in Kerala, India. Her essays were considered for a very long time to be one of the best in literacy studies, especially related to India during the post-independence period from the British. What I failed to comprehend was how did she arrive at certain conclusions about the ethnic group she was studying, *The Nayars*, and what was her strategy for measuring their literacy rates? Did she observe them every day? Did she write notes? How was it measured? How did she code them? What methods did she use to rationalize her findings? How did she measure their language capacity? Was her research based on responses to their native tongue, Malayalam or Sanskrit or both? I had too many questions but no answers. My professor in India mentioned that as far as she knew there were no records to showcase Gough's coding work, no records of her thesis being published, and asked me to refer to Mencher's article from 1993.

If that was the case, the unanswered question remained, what were Gough's research questions that allowed her to suggest that Indians' (in general) approach to literacy, writing, and myth in *Literacy in Traditional China and India* lacked "dearth of historical records." This phrase was disturbing to note for me, given the fact that her own dissertation was never published (p. 74) and given that she must have been aware that great universities like Nalanda[3] were burned and destroyed by the colonists in the previous centuries. I mention this, as history notations reveal that Nalanda was the greatest center of learning in the ancient times, having a renowned and vast library that it took months for all the texts to be burned to cinders. As a professor mentioned, "This not only revealed that texts, maybe from different languages, were an intrinsic part of Indian culture, but also showcased how the colonizers manipulated and deleted aspects of local culture, history, and traditions. Further, what is fascinating is that almost all the temples in Kerala, have written scripts/inscriptions on the temple walls; so, the question remains, 'What did Dr. Gough mean about Indian's literacy practices?' "

But what is interesting here is that many scholarly works like hers, conducted in India, have never been questioned, as they have become mystified over a period of time. Berger (1972/2002) terms this placid acceptance of information by the elite or scholarly class as mystification; it is the process of explaining away what might otherwise be evident. He uses paintings to explain that when the meaning of a painting or situation is obscured, and when the real politics is kept out, the focus then shifts to the aesthetics of technique and not the message itself that is glaring in front of us.

Although Berger (1972/2002) in his well-known essay *Ways of Seeing* uses paintings to question and explain the process of assumptions, per-spectives, and mystification, I feel it applies to all aspects of life, espe-cially pertaining to research, where the process behind the scenes is left invisible for the readers to assume and construe. In some cases, Western scholars' writing on other ethnic groups provide no appendix or footnotes to showcase how their research was conducted and how the data was assembled and coded. To a certain extent, I was scared of questioning these figures of authority and felt maybe I was the one at fault in not comprehending their approach. It was only when I met my professor in India, read Brian Street's (1984) book on *Literacy in theory and practice* and had long conversations with CNS and Dowdy that I felt it was normal to question some aspects of research work. And in that vein, I am sure there will be researchers who will question my writing and my way of observation. And, hopefully, I will be able to respond to these queries in an email and provide validity by showcasing the recordings or pictures that I took with my participants.

As I continued my questioning, I realized that statements made by such well-known scholars on other ethnic or indigenous groups create an opinion or bias in the reader's mind due to the inaccurate information provided as facts by the writer (Nakata, 2007). This could also be considered as an aspect of erroneous interpretation. The read-ers fall into the writer's trap and soon their own beliefs are tainted subjectively or objectively based on mystification. *The writer's views and the reader's assumptions about an ethnic group soon become a judg-mental collective reality.* In Gough's case, as there was not much data to showcase her research work—her observation approach, analysis, and contradictions—it only added to my questions on the role of a researcher. Her argument that India was a great civilization was jux-taposed with comments based on the autonomous model of literacy focusing on how oral literacy was more prevalent than written. Further, she would discuss at great length Indian's understanding of astronomy but would then contradict that by citing another scholar suggesting "cyclical conceptions of time … are primitive, since they do not require records of the notion of chronology" (p. 75). I was fascianted to read about her findings on one level and perplexed that she would refer to the Indian concept of time as being "primitive." So, I again interviewed one of the professors from India and his comment was that "Gough must have been aware of the *Sutras* from ancient times and the writings on cosmology, astronomy, time interpretations related to calendars, including advance predictions of eclipses and other aspects related to astrology; but the question remains why, after knowing all this information, she would call our literacy and conceptions of time primitive... Maybe there were errors in interpretation as the ancient texts were all written in Sanskrit? Language barrier can sometimes be a hindrance to a research study, especially when conducting research abroad, and one must be aware of that ..." (Professor Das).

On the flip side, I was in awe that she had wanted to research an ethnic group in the southern part of India. In my journal I have referred to it as: I am unaware of how the author produced her work and how she started her work? Why did she choose this topic that, too, in a different country far away from Britain? Why southern part of India? Why a foreign land? Why choose this method? Why is everything not explained? I wish I could access her writing and find answers to a lot of my questions.

What I realized from reading many such ethnographic texts was that I wanted to read and use a text where the author could help me understand every aspect of their research, so that I could refer to it and follow it; indeed, I was looking for a book titled *Ethnographic Case Methodology for Dummies Sans Mystification*. What I understood was that ethnographic studies conducted in India and in other third world countries on ethnic or indigenous groups during the early nineteenth and twentieth centuries were all accepted at face value and the results usually never questioned. This was probably due to the effects of colonization and the assumption that Britishers, then rulers of the country, were literate unlike the locals and their approach to literacy was viewed as the norm, in terms of the autonomous model.[4] This soon led to ethnocentric research writings and publications. It is only after the New Literacy Group in the 1980s recognized the limitations in the autonomous model (Goody & Watt, 1963) that people started questioning some of these assumptions or mystification in the writings of many Western scholars (Behar, 2003; Denzin et al., 2008; Street, 1999). In some ways, this was another key aspect that provided me the grounding to pursue a study on ethnic group and their literate practices.

Rationale for Focusing on Illiteracy and Indigenous Group: Why Indigenous Groups?

We are a unique group of people, our ancestors belonged to the nearby regions of Mumbai and shifted locally to become part of the Dabbawala group. We have maintained our ethnic and religious identity. We have also maintained our professional and personal identity. We have our own business practices that we pass on from one generation to the next. We are not "adivasi tribes" but we have our own community sentiments like we don't recruit people outside our community for our business. We are all from the Warkari community ...
—Chacha, Senior Member of the Dabbawala group[5]/[6]

Based on this definition of Chacha, one of the senior members of the *Nutan Mumbai Tiffin Box Suppliers Charity Trust*, I refer to the Mumbai Dabbawalas as being indigenous and ethnic group. Based on dictionary, scholarly references and my own fieldwork, it refers to a community of people who are native to a certain geographical region and have their own cultural and literacy practices (Coates, 1999; Cobb, 2004; Corntassel, 2003; Fast et al., 2017) Although these groups are influenced by their external environment and societies around them, they adapt only to some degree to their outside community, while remaining loyal to their traditions and heritage. Their rationale for preserving their cultural practices, despite modern amenities being available to them, is that they innately believe that their traditions will be lost if they join the mainstream "of modernism." They also believe that it is only by passing on these traditions from one generation to another "these practices will remain alive" and will allow the group members to maintain their unique-core identity. The Mumbai Dabbawalas are one such indigenous group as International Labor Organization (ILO) suggests, "Indigenous and tribal peoples have their own cultures, languages, customs and institutions, which distinguish them from other parts of the societies in which they find themselves." Thus, if the question arises are Dabbawalas identifiable in Mumbai as being unique and different, then the resounding response is "Yes, they are." They are indigenous, ethnic, unique and literate—as per the ideological model of literacy.

When I first started my research, many people were surprised that I would choose an indigenous group in India and wanted to travel across continents, but this was my way of creating the "borders" of my quest, as a woman, and to explore shadowy regions of literacy, where roads would not " run off the edge off the paper" and "drop away at sharp angles" (Glenn, 1997, p. 3). As Glenn suggests, I felt that "for years we had ignored the borders of our map (non-Western literacy)...we had assumed some areas were barren territories" like illiteracy in India, and had accepted these phrases and terms at face value. Maybe, it was the unwillingness to accept the assumptions associated with illiterates as savages (Goody and Watt, 1964) that forced me to my research work and to decolonize words "illiterates and semi-literates" in terms of indigenous and ethnic groups in India.

When I expressed to everyone that I will be conducting my research in India, some of my friends informed me that Mumbai (location of my research work) was not New Delhi, given that I grew up in the Northern part of India. They were concerned that I will be living in an unfamiliar place, in another state with different language and cultural practices. Some family members were disturbed that I wanted to leave my family and children to pursue something that I was clueless about and directionless. But one thing that really turned my passion into action was to understand the stigma associated with illiteracy and the stereotypical association made with this indigenous groups. What bothered me then and still bothers me are the judgmental and sometimes pejorative statements like, "The Dabbawalas despite their illiteracy are successful" or "They didn't go to school but are very smart" or "These poor people don't know their alphabets but are very good in their business model." It is lugubrious to note that as humans we are judgmental about others' literacy when we ourselves are not literate in all subject matters. So, the question remained, who are these indigenous people; how does our society frame such people; why study them, their cultural and literacy practices? What can we learn from them?

Such questions have been eloquently addressed by Wade Davis (1998), well-known scholar and anthropologist, in *Shadows in the Sun.*

His research studying indigenous groups across the world allowed him to see that "Just as landscape defines a people, culture springs from a spirit of place" (p. 241). He suggests that anthropology allows us to understand that the social order that we live in today is basically due to the adaptations—intellectual and spiritual choices—our fore-fathers and we have made, over a period, as members of a society. It is these conscious decisions that have led us to become a successful modern society. He then suggests that this also doesn't mean that we view other cultures in a derogatory way; rather we need to respect and recognize that they also have equal claim on this reality:

> ... they are not simply failed attempts to be us, failed attempts to be modern. They are by definition unique answers to fundamental question. What does it mean to be human and alive? When asked that question, myriad of cultures from our world would respond with seven thousand different voices, which collectively comprise the human repertoire for dealing with complex chal-lenges that will confront us as a species in the coming millennia. Every cul-ture deserves a place at the council of wisdom and knowledge ... all people ought to have the right to choose the components of their lives. (pp. xi–xiii)

Davis argues that although we want to preserve the biosphere, preserv-ing the ethnosphere is also very important. He defines ethnosphere as "the sum total of all thoughts and dreams, myths, ideas, inspirations, intuitions, brought into being by human imagination since the dawn of consciousness. It's a symbol of all that we are, and all that we can be, as an astonishingly inquisitive species."[7] Davis suggests that studying these groups provides us with a "polychromatic world of diversity," but if we allow the crude power of domination to take over our ethno-sphere, then we will all be living in a "monochromatic world of monot-ony" and soon we will be wondering if there were even other ways that humans could have lived. He argues that these groups existed—way before humans decided to merge into present-day living—and might have many solutions to the problem humans might face in the future.[8]

Ruth Benedict (1934) appropriately suggests, "The human cultural heritage, for better or worse, is not biologically transmitted ... we must accept all the implications of our human inheritance, one of the most important of which is the small scope of biologically transmitted behavior, and the enormous role of the cultural process of the transmission of tradition" (pp. 14–15). If traditions were and are transmitted, we might, as Davis believes, "... have all the answers for all the challenges that will confront us in the ensuing millennia" (Ted talk).

Further, studying these groups allows us to see, understand, and learn about how they interact with the nature around them, what are their unique practices, what can we learn from them, and how can we use some of their practices to enhance our own lifestyle. Maybe this is what I was searching for, as my diary suggests from April 14, 2009, "... that's it. I am going to India and doing this research on the Dabbawalas, but how? I have not thought about the logistics but for sure I am going; rationale provided by Davis is worth my journey and all the hardships that I will face but at least I would have tried. If I succeed in this journey, I will be grateful for the knowledge I gain. If I fail, at least, I will not be upset with myself that I didn't try. Either way, I have nothing to lose! So, I need to have faith and take the next steps."

The above rationale goaded me into action and helped me to stay on course as it revealed my passion and intrinsic motivation to work on this project till my defense. Further, I used to refer to these notes, as a form of reiteration for the work I wanted to conduct, whenever I was unmotivated or frustrated about the workload.

Notes

1 Council of Graduate Schools (2014).
2 Graduate study conducted on a population of vegetable vendors, autorickshaw drivers, and laundry/ironing laborers.
3 Nalanda University was well-known as a learning center during the fourth century and was well-known for having a library with various texts; currently a UNESCO World Heritage site.
4 Autonomous model of literary—According to Street (2000), this model works under the assumption that literacy in itself—autonomously—impacts the social and cognitive practices of an individual and thereby, the community.
5 Chacha—a senior member of the group who had been part of the Dabbawala community for more than 32 years was well respected and revered among the Dabbawalas. He was a wise man and spoke in many languages including English. Sadly, during one of my visits, I came to know he had passed away due to poor

health. I owe my gratitude to him for providing valuable information and allowing me to record him many times, and specifically when he spoke and read in English. His video, with his permission, was used and showcased during my dissertation defense.

6 Chacha's words translated from Hindi to English.

7 Davis (Dreams from endangered cultures TED talk 2003 https://www.ted.com/talks/wade_davis_dreams_from_endangered_cultures/transcript?language=en).

8 Davis statements and comments actually made me think differently about indigenous groups and in one of my journal entries, I pose this question: Could some indigenous group somewhere be making their own medicine that could save us from the deadly pandemic. After all, my grandmother did save me from the first malarial attack when I was eight years old *without* the use of Chloroquine (medicine used to treat malaria). Of course, in terms of scientific discovery and quantitative analysis, it is pure speculation if this could be possible, and I will be mocked for thinking in such terms.

Again, the nagging question appears, in ancient India, only Ayurveda and Yoga were used to cure many ailments, does this mean there is a possibility that indigenous groups might have answers to some of the modern-day diseases. Further, centers like World Indigenous Studies (CWIS), a think tank of activist scholars, write "traditional medicine is the 'mother' of all medicine ... and more than 80% of the world's population uses a form of traditional medicine to treat primary health. The intimate connection between life on earth and the living universe has formed the foundation for virtually all systems of healing for millennia." And, maybe indigenous and ethnic groups have a lot to teach other groups and maybe knowledge sharing can enable humanity to overcome diseases that have taken millions of lives in the form of pandemic.

References

Bair, C., & Haworth, J. (2004). Doctoral student attrition and persistence: A meta-synthesis of research higher education. In J. C. Smart (Ed.), *Higher education: Handbook of theory and research* (Vol. 19, pp. 481–534). Kluwer Academic Publishers.

Behar, R. (2003). Ethnography and the book that was lost. *Ethnography*, 4(1), pp. 15–39.

Benedict, R. (1934). *Patterns of Culture*. Houghton Mifflin Company.

Berger, J. (2002). Ways of Seeing. In D. Bartholomae & A. Petrosky (Eds.), *Ways of Reading: An Anthology for Writers* (6th ed., pp. 104–138). Before/St. Martin's. (Original work published 1972)

Bitzer, E. & Wilkinson, A. (2009). Higher education as a field of study and research. In E. Bitzer (Ed.), *Higher Education in South Africa: A Scholarly Look Behind the Scenes* (pp. 369–408). SUN MeDIA. https://doi.org/10.18820/9781920338183/17

Boag, S. (2006). Freudian Dream Theory, Dream Bizarreness, and the Disguise-Censor Controversy. *Neuro-Psychoanalysis*, *8*(1), pp. 5–16. https://doi.org/10.1080/15294 145.2006.10773503

Coates, K. (1999). Being Aboriginal: The cultural politics of identity, membership and belonging among first nations in Canada. In Behiels, M. (Ed.), *Futures and identities* (pp. 23–41). Association for Canadian Studies.

Cobb, C. R. (2004). Archaeology and the "Savage Slot": Displacement and Emplacement in the Premodern World. *American Anthropologist*, *107*(4), pp. 163–174.

Corntassel, J. (2003). Who is Indigenous? "Peoplehood" and ethnonationalist approaches to rearticulating Indigenous identity. *Nationalism & Ethnic Politics, 9*, pp. 75–100.

Council of Graduate Schools. (2014). Graduate enrollment and degrees: 2003 to 2013. Retrieved from http://www.cgsnet.org/graduate-enrollment-and-degr ees-2003-2013-0

Davis, W. (1998). *Shadows in the Sun*. Island Press.

Denzin, N. K., Lincoln, Y. S., & Smith, L. T. (Eds.). (2008). *Handbook of Critical Indigenous Methodologies* (1st ed.). Sage.

Durant, W. (1930). *The Case for India*. Simon and Schuster.

Fast, E., Drouin-Gagné, M.-È., Bertrand, N., Bertrand, S., & Allouche, Z. (2017). Incorporating diverse understandings of Indigenous identity: toward a broader definition of cultural safety for urban Indigenous youth. *AlterNative: An International Journal of Indigenous Peoples, 13*(3), pp. 152–160. https://doi.org/10.1177/117718011 7714158

Freud, S. (1915). *Repression* (Standard ed., Vol. XIV). Hogarth.

Glenn, C. (1997). *Rhetoric Retold: Regendering the Tradition from Antiquity Through the Renaissance* (p. 3). Southern Illinois University Press.

Goody, J., & Watt, I. (1963). The consequences of literacy. In E. R. Kingten, B. M. Kroll, & M. Rose (Eds.), *Perspectives on Literacy*, pp. 3–27. Southern Illinois University Press.

Gough, K. (1968). Implications of literacy in traditional China and India. In J. Goody (Ed.), *Literacy in traditional societies*, pp. 132–160. Cambridge University Press.

Hardre, P. L., & Hackett, S. (2015). Defining the graduate college experience: What it "should" versus "does" include. *International Journal of Doctoral Studies, 10*, pp. 57–77. Retrieved from http://ijds.org/Volume10/IJDSv10p057-077Hardre0 665.pdf

Litalien, D., & Guay, F. (2015). Dropout intentions in PhD studies: A comprehensive model based on interpersonal relationships and motivational resources. *Contemporary Educational Psychology, 41*, pp. 218–231.

Mason, M. M. (2012). Motivation, satisfaction, and innate psychological needs. *International Journal of Doctoral Studies, 7*, pp. 259–277. Retrieved from https://ijds. org/Volume7/IJDSv7p259-277Mason0345.pdf

Mencher, J. (1993). Katheleen Gough and Research in Kerala. *Anthropologica, 35*(2), pp. 195–201. https://doi.org/10.2307/25605731

Nehru, J. (1946). *The Discovery of India*. The Signet Press.

Nakata, M. (2007). The Cultural Interface. *The Australian Journal of Indigenous Education*, *36*, pp. 7–14. https://doi.org/10.1017/S1326011100004646

Rigler, K. L., Bowlin, L. K., Sweat, K., Watts, S., & Throne, R. (2017). Agency, socialization, and support: A critical review of doctoral student attrition. *Paper presented at the 3rd International Conference on Doctoral Education*, University of Central Florida.

Street, B. (1984). *Literacy in theory and practice*. Cambridge University Press.

Street, B. (1999). The meanings of literacy. In A. W. Wagner, R. L. Venezky, & B. V. Street (Eds.), *Literacy: An International Handbook*, pp. 34–40. Westview Press.

Sverdlik, A., & Hall, N. C. (2020). Not just a phase: Exploring the role of program stage on well-being and motivation in doctoral students. *Journal of Adult and Continuing Education*, *26*(1), pp. 97–124. https://doi.org/10.1177/1477971419842887

Chapter Three

Choosing the Dissertation Director

If education is always to be conceived along the same antiquated lines of a mere trans-
mission of knowledge, there is little to be hoped from it in the bettering of man's
future.

—Maria Montessori

Whenever the word director comes to mind, it reminds me of Dr. Maria Montessori. She believed that a teacher should play the role of a director or directress in a classroom (Standing, 1984). Their presence is only to provide guidance to the child and direct the child in a way that he or she self-discovers the workings of a subject matter, ranging from learning mathematical operations to word building; and, as the child develops, the adult teacher presents the materials in a nuanced way that the young adult is constantly experimenting and applying the tools in unique ways to gain knowledge of the subject matter. In many ways, this is what the dissertation director does while engaging with his/her graduate student.

Thus, choosing a dissertation director requires a lot of deliberation, as this person will be the researcher's mentor and adviser for the next few years till the dissertation is complete. It is like hiring a well-known builder to construct your house, who can advise, guide, and critique your well-self-designed plans. The goal of the builder is to construct the best house in your neighborhood as it becomes a referral home to showcase the construction and quality of his/her work. On this point, a colleague once commented, "How many times have you seen that all graduate students want the same professor in their committee? It is not because the other professors are not knowledgeable, but two factors dictate student choices: expertise in the field that they will be researching and working on and the person's working relationship with students as a director." Therefore, it is very important that you choose a person, whom you trust, respect, and believe, who will guide you to the end. Many students choose their thesis or dissertation directors based on the seminars they studied/attended under this person, or because they like the professor's approach to the subject matter, or they are impressed by the way they interacted in class. But, before choosing a director, research and talk to peers who have worked with this person. Although it might sound clinical, having a checklist, and noting down the responses to the following questions might help:

- What is his/her expertise?
- How do they interact with their undergraduate and graduate students?
- How does this person react to drafts?
- What type of feedback does he/she provide?
- How often are they willing to meet/text/email, when you need advice or simply need to talk on the phone as you need guidance?
- What type of guidelines do they provide students, while conducting research?
- Will they motivate you to write better?
- Does this person have gender bias?

Again, you, as a researcher, need to be aware of this person's attitude, as it is common to hear horror stories of the same director working well with some individual while treating others as pariahs. As CNS suggested with a smile: "You want a mentor who can advice, guide, and discuss your topic and prod you to think about it in a way that invigorates you to get back to writing; also keep in mind, your topic is your new partner in this case, as you will be married to this subject matter for the next few years till you complete your dissertation." He further suggested that having faith in your director is important as they always have your "best interest" at heart. At times the researcher might not see or feel that way, but it is essential to trust this person. He continued, "Therefore, if you feel strongly about this person, you must approach the professor and start the discussion." He suggested that deciding on the main adviser for your dissertation committee is like "choosing the location of your house and the builder of your choice (topic and director); you need to move to the next stage." Once the director has been selected, work with this person to choose the other members of the committee and ensure that they can all work together as a unit. Sometimes, when the committee consists of members who disagree with each other, it will lead to different kinds of issues as time progresses. The ideal thing would be to ask the director to suggest names of other team members, who can work in a congenial fashion, as a group, to enhance the study. In many ways, this is a better approach as the director will have their own resources and network of people who can provide the expertise to the given topic. Once the adviser suggests the names of the other committee members "try to research and get to know" these people and their work. If possible, approach these members in person to provide information about the research study and the tentative approach you will be taking toward the subject matter.

Reference

Standing, E. M. (1984). *Maria Montessori: Her life and Work*. Plume, a member of Penguin Putnam.

Chapter Four

Formatting the Research Question

Still, all writing is about stuff—sometimes imaginary stuff or conceptual stuff or obscured stuff—but always about stuff, evoking some meanings, thoughts, representations, calculations, or feelings of the reader. The quality of the writing is often centrally evaluated on what it tells us about the world and how compellingly and persuasively.

—Charles Bazerman

All writing is about stuff, as Bazerman (2019) suggests, and interestingly, it mostly begins with a question. In a dissertation, formatting the research question is the central and most crucial part of the study. Rather it is the central aspect of most research-based studies, like the conductor of a concert, as it directs all aspects of the study from the beginning till the end. Especially in an ethnographic study, it allows the researcher to focus on the purpose, select the group or community that he/she wants to observe, geographical location, length of time required for observation, participants to be observed, and the approach to be taken to study the subject matter. At a later stage, it enables the researcher to construct theory behind their observation. It also allows the investigator to understand and realize the potential limitation/s to their study due to various reasons, and why they might need to frame their study from the beginning.

Framing using research questions, at the outset, is necessary to conduct an ethnographic study as it allows the researcher to become focused on the qualitative aspect of their study and dig deeper; a phrase I often use with my students to suggest "go vertical than horizontal." I mention this, as my case study forced me to interview many new participants and have a detailed focus group discussions on the same topic. This, in turn, provided me the opportunity to gather different perspectives on the same topic and produce replicable data. It is like informing ourselves to answer who, what, when, why, and how questions for our research *repeatedly*.

Another key aspect that I learned through my research was having open-ended (Bazerman, 2019; Charmaz, 2006; Corbin & Strauss, 2008; Dey, 2008) questions, as they provide multiple opportunities for the researcher to gather and triangulate data from different sources. This doesn't mean that one should refrain from having closed-ended questions. My suggestion to researchers would be to create subject-related open-ended questions. Often, when researchers pose why and how questions to the participants, it allows the participants the opportunity to speak about the subject matter in great length, which in turn provides relevant and supplementary data for writing. Also, it is important to discuss the number of research questions that one wants to frame for the study with the adviser, as the questions will be developed and data discussed as one of the dissertation chapters.

Based on this, my initial research questions were:

- What are the literacy practices of the Dabbawalas in general?
- How and what type of literacies do they use in their daily lives to maintain their business practices?
- How and why do they write the scripts in English without being schooled in it?
- How do they interpret the codes and translate it in their minds?

During the data collection, *what* questions enabled me to gather and organize the different practices that the Dabbawalas used. The *how and why* questions provided me the depth of knowledge to understand, code, and write in a comprehensive way about the different literacies that the Dabbawalas used to make their supply-chain delivery practice successful. Thus, the purpose of this chapter was to specifically draw attention to the importance of the research questions, RQs, and learn how to frame them, as data collection is dependent on them.

References

Bazerman, C. (2019). Inscribing the World into Knowledge: Data and evidence in Disciplinary Academic Writing. In C. Bazerman, B. Gonzalez, D. Russell, P. Rogers, L. Pena, E. Narvaez, P. Carlino, M. Castello, & M. Tapia-Ladino (Eds.), *Conocer la Escritura: Investigación más allá de las Fronteras; Knowing writing: Writing research across borders*, pp. 279–294. Universidad Javeriana.

Charmaz, K. (2006). *Constructing Grounded Theory. A Practical Guide Through Qualitative Analysis*. SAGE Publishing.

Corbin, J., & Strauss, A. (2008). *Basics of Qualitative Research. Techniques and Procedures for Developing Grounded Theory* (3rd ed.). SAGE Publishing.

Dey, I. (2008). *Grounding Grounded Theory. Guidelines for Qualitative Inquiry*. Emerald Publishing.

Chapter Five

Developing a Rough Sketch of Methods Section

If you can't explain it simply, you don't understand it well enough.
—Albert Einstein

One of the key aspects for writing this book was based on my observation over the years, that graduate and undergraduate students are often unsure of the research methodology to choose from when they begin their research for their senior undergraduate or graduate thesis or dissertation, based on the topic they want to pursue. Although students have taken courses on research methods, there is a sense of nagging uncertainty when it comes to choosing the methods section for their seminal work. This stems from various reasons, but the main reason being, as one of my student's said, "All that we have theorized has to be practically applied and there is this gut feeling within me that says what if I don't succeed in my findings?" The student continued to suggest that "added to this uncertainty, there are no templates or examples available for all of us to follow that specifically relates to what we are pursuing." And interestingly, I was in that position when I started my dissertation research.

In the following narrative, I reveal the conundrum I was in and why we should not be hasty about choosing a methodology; and in case it takes time, we should not assess it as a failure on our part. In some ways, reviewing different methodology provides us the opportunity to study the different methods and what is the most suitable one for our study. After I chose my dissertation topic to study the Mumbai Dabbawalas and their literacy practices in India,[1] I met with my director many times and suggested many methods. At the beginning of every meeting, I would explain that I was unhappy with the previous method suggested and wanted to change it. My methodology section underwent many changes that I was nervous at one point and unsure on how to proceed. It went from quantitative to qualitative to both, from grounded theory to feminist approach to narrative approach to case study to all of the above but never ethnography. What was most disturbing was that at every meeting I would convince my adviser that the methodology I had chosen was the best. He humored me and listened to me and one day after four meetings on methodology suggested that it was very important that I decide on the methods sections, even before I think of writing my prospectus. I was upset that as my director he was unable to help or guide me with choosing a methodology that would work for my topic. But, looking back, I am glad that he left me to fend for myself as it forced me to explore all the different methods and methodologies that were available to me as a researcher and allowed me to see the nuances and beauty in collecting data and framing them around my research question.

After two months of deliberating, in a moment of frustration, as I was not progressing, I asked him if I could discuss my methodology section with Dr. Pamela Takayoshi.[2] As I had already attended seminar course on research methods with her, I was comfortable discussing my options with her. Takayoshi after a few meetings asked me to rationalize and articulate clearly why I was choosing a certain methodology and suggested, "Think in terms of what methods can I use to study the Dabbawalas? How am I going to apply the methodolgy that will enable me to showcase my data and later use it to write my dissertation?" Her suggestion, after our initial meeting, was that I must explore qualitative methods in further detail and then meet her. I viewed that as a setback but reviewed other methodologies and wrote my rationale of why I had finally chosen grounded theory and shared it with her. As we were discussing, I realized that grounded theory alone would not be enough to study my participants and this, once again, sent me back to the drawing board.

What I discovered was that when we mull over and meditate upon a subject matter by reading extensively about it, answers sometimes appear on their own. The reason for my dissatisfaction with the earlier methodologies stemmed from the fact that the group I was going to be studying was unique and ethnic and in some ways required an approach that would showcase the participants and their literacies—the way they are—without interpretations. I realized I needed to follow an anthropological way to study them, similar to what literacy scholars had done in the past, and felt ethnography was the best methodology.

But somehow, the gut feeling of uncertainty remained as I kept thinking that an ethnography is used for conducting research over a lengthy period, for months and sometime years, and my trip to India could not be extended beyond two weeks. This was mainly due to my leaving behind my family with young kids and a fulltime job. So, I went back, once more, to look at my research question and to mull over what was best suited for my investigation. This, in turn, led to a realization that before I could start anything I needed to clearly understand and define the key difference between the terms—method/s and methodology. According to OED,[3] a methodology is:

> Originally: the branch of knowledge that deals with method generally or with the methods of a particular discipline or field of study; (*archaic*) a treatise or dissertation on method; (*Botany*) †systematic classification (*obsolete rare*). Subsequently also: the study of the direction and implications of empirical research, or of the suitability of the techniques employed in it; (more generally) **a method or body of methods used in a particular field of study or activity.**

A method is:

> a procedure used for attaining an object; more generally: a way of doing anything, esp. according to a defined and regular plan; a mode of procedure in

any activity, business, etc. A special form of procedure or characteristic set of procedures employed (more or less systematically) in an intellectual discipline or field of study as a mode of investigation and inquiry, or of teaching and exposition.

Based on these definitions, it was clear that many methods could be and are used to create the methodology that guides and enables the researcher to find answers to their research questions. Thus, the whole process of combining different methods from primary and secondary information to collecting data, organizing them to understanding and interpreting the research question/s, analyzing, cross-examining, coding, writing the findings, and arguing a certain point of view becomes the methodology. In the end, my methodology consisted of integrating many methods to find answers to the research questions and to theorize them.

Once I knew that my methodology would be ethnography, I knew my methods were going to be a mix of qualitative, grounded theory, and case study. I met with Takayoshi and explained my methods as being a qualitative case study. She agreed that case study would be most appropriate as the timeline of my research consisted of being with my participants for only a week to ten days. She further suggested that I should first begin by reading all the scholarship related to case study methods and start thinking about the research process, from start to finish, in terms of flow diagrams "as every step in the process is crucial to gathering data."

Note: What I didn't realize at that point was that I would continue studying the Dabbawalas for three more years after my first visit. I collected all my initial data for my dissertation in 2011, but I was in touch with my participants over the phone and later visits for many months after my return back to the United States. Every visit after the first one was a repetition of the case study methods using the same format and some of the same questions, sometimes with the same or some new participants. Further, even after I finished my dissertation in 2014, I went back to see my participants every year from 2015 to 2018. Any data that I gathered between 2015 through 2018 was maintained as post-dissertation observation and research. I also realized that in order to gain a holistic perspective, especially when studying an indigenous group or a unique subject matter, piloting the project as a qualitative case study is the easiest and best way to begin the research process.

Notes

1 Mumbai Dabbawalas—detailed reference provided in the early parts of the book.
2 Dr. Pamela Takayoshi was one of my dissertation advisers.
3 OED—Oxford English Dictionary—OED.com.

Chapter Six

Passing the CITI Test and Writing the IRB: What is IRB? Why IRB?

In law a man is guilty when he violates the rights of others.
In ethics he is guilty if he only thinks of doing so.

—Immanuel Kant

Usually once the methodology section has been decided and approved by the committee, graduates are requested to complete the research ethics and compliance training, commonly referred to as CITI[1] test, and complete the Institutional Review Board (IRB) research protocols and requirements. Every project associated with research on human subjects, irrespective of the level, undergraduate or graduate study, needs to be approved by IRB. This board is instrumental in protecting the rights and welfare of all the study participants and in many ways ensuring that ethical practices are maintained throughout the research work.[2]

Important aspects to keep in mind while completing the IRB:

- it needs to be as thorough as possible, including completing all aspects of the appendix/ces

- it needs to address the different aspects of the research work that will be conducted
- it takes time
- it needs to be detail-oriented; and in some cases explanations should include information about the references that will be used and information about speaking a different language other than English.

Completing the IRB is one of the first steps the researcher takes toward developing the data collection. Before completing the IRB forms, it is necessary to undertake the CITI test, which provides the researcher the rationale on how to conduct ethnical and objective research and how "not to coerce" participants into a study. The test is very informative and allows the researcher to think about their future approach to their study, more in terms of maintaining ethical practices on and off the field. In my research study, given that it was a long-term international project and given that my participants would be speaking different languages, I wanted to ensure that it was as thorough and as complete as possible, including the part about "not" coercing or subjugating my participants to any type of trauma or forced decisions. I am glad that I was very meticulous in completing the IRB as there were incidents on the field that made me realize how participants can get coerced, and why it is important for the researcher to recognize the ethics behind it, so that they can clearly explain the aspect of coercion to the participants when required.

During my initial visit, there were days when participants would speak in a focus group discussion and next day they would return and say, "I want you to delete what I said yesterday" or they might say, "I don't want you to use my name." At that point, I had to respect their wishes and agree with their sentiments and remove their comments and names in front of them. I also had to follow the same protocols on all the backup materials. Although a tedious process, this was a key aspect that allowed me to gain their trust and respect. In my later visits when I asked some of my participants about what made them change their mind, their responses ranged from, "I don't want my name in public" to "I don't think my family will like me to say things" or "this is not my true feeling and in a heated moment, I spoke when others were speaking." But what is amazing is none of their comments—that they wanted me to exclude—were in any way or form unworthy of mentioning or unclear or vicious or negative of another person, it was rather remorseful or self-deprecating.

On the other hand, they were some comments that were made by a few Dabbawalas that were philosophical and meaningful that I had to seek their permission to use them in an anonymous way and use pseudonyms to refer to their comments. For example, one of the participants discussed literacy in such length that I was shocked and amazed that he had such a thorough understanding of what literacy really meant in an everyday life situation and how it is used in a business setting. After I took my field notes, I went back to my participant and asked him if he would allow me to use a pseudonym for him or suggest one. He was very happy that I had not misconstrued or misunderstood his remarks and that I appreciated his candid opinion. He was also surprised that I would go the extent of asking him for his permission to use a different name and use it in my thesis. This situation required that I gather additional signatures from the participant, as he had already signed the initial IRB with his original name. I asked him to choose a new name and handwrite it under the pseudonym section as shown below.

Original Name:
Pseudonym:

I mention this as a well-documented IRB needs to be thoughtful and thorough and should take many diverse aspects into consideration.

My advise to all the students applying for IRB has been that rushing to complete and submit the IRB without providing all the necessary documents will only lead to frustration, as it will be considered incomplete and sent back for further scrutiny. I must also mention that depending on the university, the review board members meet only certain times of the year; and sometimes this means that an IRB can be delayed or pushed back for the next meeting, which could be a few months, if the researcher isn't diligent about completing all the formalities or all aspects of the form in a thoughtful manner, although things are changing due to technology interfaces.

Usually, the IRB forms take time to be reviewed as board members from different fields of study evaluate every aspect of the study that is to be conducted in the near future and deliberate over issues that might arise from it. As a researcher, I am truly grateful for their work as many of them are not compensated but still do the work, as they want other researchers to succeed in their data-driven work. It took me close to three months to have my IRB completed as there were many changes that were necessary and many formalities to be completed, before I could even book my tickets to India. Thus, it is very important to realize that IRB takes time from a few weeks to a few months; and in case it is delayed, a word of advice to all researchers, be patient and prepared.

Another key aspect to consider while completing the IRB application is to "place yourself in your participants shoes" in every section and "feel everything that they might feel and be sensitive to their environment; respect them for who they are and not what you want them to be." I always ask this question to my students, "Would you like to be coerced into participating in a survey or respond to something that you don't want to part of and someone using your name without your permission?" In a similar way, the participants, specifically ethnic groups, are very sensitive about how people view them and write about them. Some of my students have informed me that while completing the IRB interview questions section, they were reminded of "what if this was me syndrome" and it has allowed them to become more sensitive to what and how their participants might feel during face-to-face interviews. My experience also taught me that empathizing and being ethical allows for trust and mutual respect to be developed between the researcher and participants, as they feel that if they share information with you it will not be misused or misrepresented. Rather, they recognize that you are genuinely interested in showcasing their literacy, culture, ways of everyday living, and other practices "as they are" and not in a pejorative way and that you will not manipulate the information for your readers.

A note for all researchers that once they complete the CITI test, it is important to meet with the director before and while completing the IRB forms, to ensure that all parts of the IRB have been reviewed thoroughly including the appendices.

Notes

1 Collaborative Institutional Training Initiatives (CITI Program).
2 https://about.citiprogram.org/en/homepage/.

Chapter Seven

Writing the Prospectus or Proposal for Submission to the Committee

Remember Toni Morrison's famous quote, "If there's a book that you want to read, but it hasn't been written yet, then you must write it." Now where is yours?
—Sudarsanan

Writing a proposal or prospectus, depending on the department requirements, is one of the initial steps to be undertaken by a researcher to *define their topic or subject matter*. Often, this step is initiated after the completion of the IRB formalities and having an IRB number assigned to the research work. The prospectus lays the foundation for the research study. In many cases, this is used as the first chapter of the final dissertation with some edits. The general format of the proposal consists of five parts or sections: Background or introduction ending with research question/s, Literature Review, Methodology, Time Schedule, and Conclusion ending with tentative suggestion as to how the study will add to the field and to the researcher's future quest.

Anytime a student wants to write a thesis proposal, I always use the analogy of how painters, as artists, choose a surface and medium to paint on, such as a canvas or charcoal paper or cloth or wall, and how this allows them to choose the type of paint they want to use on that surface material. I inform them about how initial choices shape the quality of painting that is going to be drawn and exhibited, and how important it is to be selective on the purchase of the base materials. In a similar way, the chosen topic when combined with the five parts mentioned above, act as the rough sketch drawn on the canvas or dissertation topic. This provides the framework of the scope of work that is to be undertaken. My students laugh at my analogies, but they always come back to inform me that it worked and how it is embedded in their mind.

The proposal as the word suggests is a "**proposal or prospectus**," which is presented to the members of the committee to seek their approval and commitment for the next few semesters or years. Therefore, this **rough sketch** needs to inform the committee of what you, as a serious researcher, are planning to engage in or paint, a portrait or landscape or still life and the list goes on. This helps the committee and the researcher to stay focused on that path and not digress from the scope of the study. I have provided a sample of my own prospectus to showcase how it can be written and formatted.

Introduction

The Introduction consists of providing the readers information about (a) what the topic is all about, (b) why the need for this study on a specific topic based on a problem or a gap that you observed after reviewing the literature materials from the past and present, and (c) what are the research questions that will frame the study.

NOTE: I have showcased only parts of the prospectus, as this is meant to be used as an example. Therefore, you will find the absence of a complete bibliography.

Just as Pandit Nehru was fascinated with illiterate villagers quoting thousands of verses from the Indian epics, the "illiterate" Dabbawalas, too, in recent times, have intrigued the world by establishing a six-sigma business status. The same fascination that Pandit Nehru had for the "illiterate peasants having a picture gallery" has now been replaced with the "illiterate Dabbawalas," having a *script* gallery in their minds. Much of this amazement between the educated Western and Eastern reporters, journalists, and researchers stems from certain assumptions about the nature of literacy in general and specifically, with the practices of the Dabbawalas. This has led to production of many written texts discussing the successful business and management module of the Dabbawalas. However, the reference to their literacy and literacy practices has been pejorative, belittling the accomplishments of the Dabbawalas, because they do not exhibit traditionally valued literacy skills.

Instead, the Dabbawalas are referred to as "illiterates" or "barely literate and barefoot delivery men," or as "illiterates, who use color codes and boxes marked with letters and numbers to deliver food." These references to their literacy practice as color-codes not only misrepresents the Dabbawalas' ability to use a complex symbol system to solve important and complicated problems but also confirms the fundamental ethnocentric notions of literacy that still exists in our societies today. These notions of literacy have been characterized as situations where literacy is an independent use of powerful symbol system, perhaps even raising one's consciousness (Goody & Watt, 1963; Ong, 1982). Such notions have been challenged by many New Literacy Scholars successfully and led to new approaches to literacy (Branch, 2004; Graff, 1986; Heath, 1983; Lave & Wenger, 1991; Scribner & Cole, 1981; Street, 1984) and workplace literacy (Cope & Kalantzis, 2000; Deephouse & Suchman, 2008; Engestrom, 2008; Goodwin & Goodwin, 1996; Heath & Luff, 2000; Hutchins, 1995; Lave & Wenger, 1991; Seth & Lave, 1993). Though the idea of literacy as being situated within a specific set of human behaviors is well established in academic circles, this understanding has yet to become commonplace and deserves more attention from scholars in other fields and from journalists writing about literacy practices of a community. There still seems to be an assumption by people in general that successful businesses must employ a workforce with traditional literate skills (Graff, 1986). For example, in businesses, to achieve six-sigma status employees must be educated and well versed with academic, Western, preferably English literacy. Combined with this notion, there is another assumption that accumulation of wealth and economic progress are part of literate and civilized societies (Farrell, 1983; Goody & Watt, 1963; Greenfield, 1972; Hildyard & Olson, 1978; Ong, 1982).

Based on what we know about literacy, symbol systems, and the Dabbawalas, this dissertation assumes that a key to achieving a successful business model lies in the effective use of material and symbolic tools. Therefore, alphabetic literacy is but one set of symbolic tools, purposeful, pervasive, and well-known but not unique or irreplaceable. In some ways, the computer field reminds us that computer-functional language cannot function or exist through alphabetic literacy as we see in languages like JAVA programs and others. There is a need for accuracy, brevity, and conciseness for coding information—a language that the machine can comprehend and act upon. In some ways, accuracy, brevity, and being cryptic, as in the case of the Dabbawalas, allows for the message to be understood and interpreted correctly (Hartley & Buckmann, 2001; Kuiper & Clippinger, 2013). In the Dabbawalas case, the efficiency allows for productive work and eliminates excessive paperwork.

The Problem

This part should state what is the gap that you are interested in investigating, and why do you find it to be a problem that needs addressing.

Extensive research on communication and literacy has offered many new ways to understanding literacy among different social classes and literacy practices (Barton et al., 2007; Branch, 2004; Brandt, 2001; Bruch et al., 2004; Finnegan, 1999; Levin, 1985; Ogbu, 1983). Most researchers believe that the technical and narrow approach to viewing literacy practices continues to influence the field in general, and there needs to be a growing call to approach literacy that rigorously incorporates the realities of its situated dimension (Brandt, 2001; Glenn, 2004; Moss, 2013). Brandt (2001) argues, "From a contextual perspective, literate abilities originate in social postures and social knowledge that begin well before and extend well beyond words on a page" (p. 4).

In the global context of this dissertation, Brandt's call takes on a new meaning in terms viewing literacy in a global framework and in "contextual and contextualizing dimensions" (p. 4) to receive a just and successful view. It brings to light that little research has been done about comprehending the literacy practices of an ethnic group and how they conduct business using scripts of their own for their day-to-day operations (Lave & Wenger, 1991; Scribner & Cole, 1981; Street, 1984), especially how scripts can be viewed as literacy events (Heath, 1982), even if the employees are only elementary school educated as in the case of the Dabbawalas.

This research addresses what it means to conduct a cross-cultural literacy study based on geographical location, ethnicity, culture, and traditional background. This provides a new paradigm to the field of literacy, in terms of—what defines a meaningful literacy script that is appropriate for business. My attempt to explore the above issues will be driven by the following research questions:

- What are the literacy practices[1] of the Dabbawalas in general?
- How and what type of literacies do they use in their daily lives to maintain their business practices?
- How and why do they write the scripts in English without being schooled in it?
- How do they interpret the codes and translate it in their minds?

These questions situate my research within the literature on literacy *in the last three or more decades*. In addition, I will also refer to scholarship from the field of business management and workplace literacy to view the different aspects of communication.

The Scope of the Problem

This part should provide details about your research limitations and scope. In this section, the focus is on showcasing how the research is being framed and how some information is beyond the scope of purview. Also, please note there are no reference (years) provided other the names *as this is an example* provided for the viewers.

The assumptions and beliefs informing many current notions about literacy and the Dabbawalas' low literacy rates are supported by the Great-Divide theory proposed in the late 1960s and early 1970s, lauding the accomplishments of alphabetic literacy and the cognitive advantage alphabetic literacy gives its users (Farrell, 1983; Goody, 1968; Havelock, 1986; Ong, 1982). The Great-Divide theory assumes that effective business practices, like any other complicated literacy are best practiced through alphabetic literacy (Goody & Watt, 1963). Complicating the claim for the cognitive and material benefits of alphabetic literacy is the fact that the Western World, during certain time periods, were the most advanced in technology, business, etc. ...

To study the cognitive effects of literacy, Scribner and Cole (1978) conducted a comprehensive study in northern Libya and found people to be literate in three scripts: Vai, an indigenous script; Arabic, used mostly for religious purposes; and English, the official language of the country. Employing psychological field-tests as well as an ethnographic study on a small community, Scribner and Cole categorically denied the existence of any special cognitive effects on the acquisition or use of literacy. One of the field tests that they refer to showcases the cultural, functional, environmental and host of other assumptions inherent in the Great-Divide theory ...

Half a decade after Scribner and Cole published their book-length study, Street (1984) defined traditional notions of literacy, including those held by the great-divide theorists as being an autonomous ...

Street offers another definition of literacy, which he terms ideological where literate practices cannot be understood outside of the culture that produce and sustain them. An ideological model of literacy research that focuses on the literacy practices of the indigenous people, in their own context, can lead to a movement towards a better theoretical and methodological understanding of literacy (p. 96). Street (1984) thus offers the following principles, *which this study aspires to follow* for studying the literacy practices of the Mumbai Dabbawalas, in terms of the ideological model of literacy:

- As being dependent on the social institution in which it is embedded
- Literacy can only be known to us in forms that have political and ideological significance and cannot be separated from them and treated as autonomous

- The particular practices of reading and writing that are taught in any context depend upon such aspects of social structure as stratification and the role of educational institutions
- The process whereby reading, and writing are learned are what construct the meaning of it for particular practitioners
- Refer to literacies in that community than to literacy (p. 8).

The scope of my study responds to Street's call for research that exposes the underlying theoretical assumptions and contradictions about the material circumstances, thought, language, culture, and customs of indigenous groups and their unique literacy practices. Within the local conditions, it's important to understand that the Dabbawalas complex symbol system works because of the way the city of Mumbai is designed (the central aspect to developing and maintaining a specific literacy practice) as well as the connection of this design to the extensive rail system they use (for transportation and communication). Further, studying a cross-cultural successful workplace literacy like the Dabbawalas answers Street and Brandt's recent calls about the need for studying diverse workplace literacies within a globalizing (Brandt, 1990) and fast capital (Gee, 1990; Hull, 1999) economic climate.

Methodology

This section must include an outline of the methods and methodology that will be used in the field, and how you are planning to gather data based on the preliminary reaction from your participants or others involved in the project.

To investigate the literacy practices of the Dabbawalas, employing a case study design methodology (Yin, 2002) works best as it will be a pilot project. Mainly due to two important factors: as a researcher doing a qualitative study: (1) I have no control over my participants' behavioral patterns and responses, and (2) it is a study of contemporary issues.

Although the Dabbawalas have existed for a century, their recognition for six-sigma rating and the association with il-literacy is recent. Further, as the research is bounded mainly focusing on the "What, How, and Why" factors of the Dabbawalas literacy practices, case study will allow me to procure data on both, primary and secondary levels.

Data Collection and Sampling (Tentative)

The data gathered will be based on observing one set of unit members actively working in the field. They will be interviewed while they are working and during lunch breaks or while traveling. The focus group discussion will be in the evening after the Dabbawalas return back to their meeting place, after performing a whole day's work of picking and delivering food packages to their respective places. To acquire primary sampling and to maintain ethical practices, IRB-approved consent form has already been sent to the President of the Nutan Mumbai Dabbawala Association or organization, Mr. Medge, and the aspect of selecting participants for my study has been discussed. As per his recommendations, the interview/s with the individual participants begins once I arrive in Mumbai, India. Though I would like to interview many members of the organization, from every level, as portrayed in their online website, I have to follow the recommendations of the head of the organization ...

The hierarchical structure of the Dabbawala organization includes—President, Vice President, General Secretary, Treasurer, and nine Directors. The above members also act as directors. Then, there are Mukadams/supervisors (800) and 5,000 members. The groups that I am planning to observe, interview and interact with—consist of the following members: President, Director, Supervisor and Members. Mr. Medge pointed out that the organization is more horizontal than vertical, "as we all deliver food, you will benefit more from interviewing two groups that deliver food to two different locations in Mumbai" (Phone Interview—June 12, 2011).

Data Sources

As per Mr. Medge's suggestion, the sampling will be based on acquiring interviews from two groups that deliver food to different regions and from focus groups consisting of members from group I and II in Mumbai. The textual data will be obtained through transcribing the participants' interviews, writing gathered in the form of field notes from observing the Dabbawalas while working, and from texts the Dabbawalas use, and other sources that will shed light on their literacy practices. In addition, documents related to their everyday literacy practice, as provided by the Dabbawalas, will be used to corroborate my study.

Once all the data is compiled, it will be analyzed and classified based on certain categories. The corpus of materials will be coded to ascertain features that have already been researched in the field of literacy and to discern new information and pattern, which can happen through coding and reduction of the information into categories (Spinuzzi, 2008).

Contribution to the Field

This section is again hypothetical but provides the researcher "a kind of authority" as they have to write about how their research will add to the field.

The Dabbawala case study contributes to the literacy and writing field in three specific ways:

First, as research is yet to be conducted on the Dabbawalas' literacy and their literacy perspective, it adds to the cross-cultural linguistic perspective in the world of literacy studies. It rejects the autonomous model and grounds the Dabbawalas practice as ideological, adding to the new literacy paradigm that both orality and literacy are ideological constructions ...

Second, the study can easily be transferred and used as a model in our classrooms, where writing instructors can change and tune their students' mental models and writing samples by effectively comprehending the world that students belong to (instead of dismissing it as non-academic) and facilitate their transition to academic writing ...

Third, this study adds a new dimension to supply-chain management studies and provides a new basis for managers and workers ...

Organization of the Dissertation

This part addresses the layout of the TOC (Table of Contents) of the final dissertation. It is important that the researcher refers to the format used by their school/department and follow that template.

Chapter I—Scope of the Problem and Framing the Research Purpose and Questions

Chapter II—Literature Review

Chapter III—Methodology

Chapter IV—Field Notes, Interpretations, Discussion, and Findings

Chapter V—Conclusion, Recommendations and Need for Further Research

Timeline for Completion of Project

This is the most important part of the proposal as the researcher has to commit to a time schedule and follow that as closely as possible.

Tentative Dates: Work to be completed (2012–2013)

- May–June 2012: File Prospectus
- July 2012: Be on the field and collect data
- August–September 2012: Transcribe Collected data Chapter II—Write the Literature Review
- September–October 2012: Write Chapter III—Methodology and Revise

- October–November 2012: Write Chapter IV—Textual Analysis and Revision
- November–December 2012: Write Chapter 1—Revisit Scope of the Problem and Revise
- December–January 2013: Final Chapter V—Contribution to the Field and Revise
- February–May 2013: Revisions and Defense

Note

1 When I refer to literate practices, I am referring to all the activities that involve texts (written, symbols, codes, etc.) reading of texts (in groups or as individually and interpreting it), discussing the text (oral communications among groups or interpersonal one-on-one as trainer to trainee) and handling the text (interpreting, picking up, delivering and return pick up).

References

Barton, D., Ivanic, R., Appleby, Y., Hodge, R., & Tusting, K. (2007). *Literacy, Lives and Learning*. Routledge.

Bazerman, C. (1989). Introduction: Rhetoricians on the Rhetoric of Science. *Science, Technology, & Human Values, 14*(1), pp. 3–6. https://doi.org/10.1177/016224398901400101

Branch, K. (2004). In the Hallways of the Literacy Narrative. In B. Huot, B. Stroble & C. Bazerman (Eds), *Multiple Literacies for the 21st Century*, pp 1–12. Hampton Press.

Brandt, D. (1990). *Literacy as Involvement: The Acts of Writers, Readers, and Texts*. Southern Illinois University Press.

Brandt, D. (2001). *Literacy in American Lives*. Cambridge University Press.

Bruch, P. L., Marback, R., & Kinloch, V. (2004). Neither distant privilege nor privileging distance: Literacies and the lessons of the Heidelberg project. In B. Huot, B. Stroble, & C. Bazerman (Eds.), *Multiple Literacies for the Twenty-first Century*, pp. 277–293. Hampton Press.

Cope, B., & Kalantzis, M. (Eds.). (2000). *Multiliteracies: Literacy Learning and the Design of Social Futures*. Routledge.

Deephouse, D. L., & Suchman, M. C. (2008). Legitimacy in Organizational Institutionalism. In R. Greenwood, C. Oliver, K. Sahlin, & R. Suddaby (Eds.), *The SAGE handbook of organizational institutionalism*, pp. 49–77.

Engeström, Y. (2008). *From Teams to Knots: Activity-Theoretical Studies of Collaboration and Learning at Work*. Cambridge University Press. https://doi.org/10.1017/CBO97 80511619847

Farrell, T. (1983). IQ and Standard English. *College Composition and Communication, 34(4)*, pp. 470–484.

Finnegan, R. (1999). Sociological and Anthropological Issues in Literacy. In A. Wagner, R. L. Venezky, & B. Street (Eds.), *Literacy: An international handbook*, pp. 89–94. Westview Press.

Gee, J. (1990). *Sociolinguistics and Literacies: Ideologies in Discourse*. Falmer Press.

Glenn, C. (2004). *Unspoken: A Rhetoric of Silence*. SIU Press.

Goodwin, C., & Goodwin, M. H. (1996). Seeing as Situated Activity: Formulating Planes. In Y. Engeström & D. Middleton (Eds.), *Cognition and communication at work*, pp. 61–95. Cambridge University Press.

Goody, J., & Watt, I. (1963). The Consequences of Literacy. In E. R. Kingten, B. M. Kroll & M. Rose (Eds.), *Perspectives on literacy*, pp. 3–27. Southern Illinois University Press.

Goody, J. (Ed.). (1968). *Literacy in traditional societies*. Cambridge University Press.

Gough, K. (1968). Implications of literacy in traditional China and India. In E. R. Kingten, B. M. Kroll, & M. Rose (Eds.), *Perspectives on literacy*, pp. 44–56. Southern Illinois University Press.

Graff, H. J. (1986). The Legacies of Literacy. In E. R. Kingten, B. M. Kroll, & M. Rose (Eds.), *Perspectives on literacy*, pp. 82–91. Southern Illinois University Press.

Greenfield, P. M. (1972). Oral or written language: The consequences for cognitive development in Africa, the United States and England. *Language and Speech, 15*, pp. 169–178.

Hartley, P., & Bruckmann, C. (2001). Business Communication: Rethinking your professional practice for the post-digital age (1st ed.). Routledge. https://doi.org/10.4324/9780203930045

Havelock, E. (1986). Orality, Literacy and Star Wars. *Written Communications, 3*, pp. 411–420.

Heath, S. B. (1982). Protean Shapes in Literacy Events: Ever-shifting oral and literate traditions. In D. Tannen (Ed.), *Spoken and Written Language: Exploring Orality and Literacy*, pp. 91–117. Ablex.

Heath, S. B. (1983). *Ways with Words: Language, Life, and Work in Communities and Classrooms*. Cambridge University Press.

Heath, C., & Luff, P. (2000). *Technology in Action*. Cambridge University Press.

Hildyard, A., & Olson, D. (1978). Memory and inference in the comprehension of oral and written discourse. *Discourse Processes 1*, pp. 91–117.

Hull, G. A. (1999). What's in a Label?: Complicating Notions of the Skills-Poor Worker. *Written Communication, 16(4)*, pp. 379–411. https://doi.org/10.1177/0741 088399016004001

Hutchins, E. (1995). *Cognition in the Wild*. The MIT Press.

Kuiper, S., & Clippinger, D. A. (2013). *Contemporary Business Reports* (5th ed.). South-Western, Cengage Learning.

Lave, J., & Wenger, E. (1991). *Situated learning: Legitimate peripheral participation.* Cambridge University Press.

Levin, K. (1985). *The Social Context of Literacy.* Routledge.

Moss, B. J. (2003). *A Community Text Arises: A Literate Text and a Literacy Tradition in African-American Churches.* Hampton Press.

Ogbu, J. U. (1983). *Literacy and Schooling in Subordinate Cultures: The Case of Black Americans.* In D. Resnick (Ed.), *Literacy in Historical Perspective,* pp. 129–155. Washington, DC: Library of Congress.

Ong, W. J. (1982). Some Psychodynamics of Orality. In E. R. Kingten, B. M. Kroll, & M. Rose, (Eds.), *Perspectives on Literacy,* pp. 28–43. Southern Illinois University Press.

Scribner, S., & Cole, M. (1978). Literacy Without Schooling: Testing for Intellectual Effects. *Harvard Educational Review, 48,* pp. 448–461.

Scribner, S., & Cole, M. (1981). *The Psychology of Literacy.* Harvard University Press.

Seth, C., & Lave, J. (1993). *Understanding practice: Perspectives on activity and context.* Cambridge University Press.

Spinuzzi, C. (2008). *Network: Theorizing Knowledge Work in Telecommunications.* Cambridge University Press.

Street, B. (1984). *Literacy in theory and practice.* Cambridge University Press.

Yin, R. K. (2002). *Case Study Research: Design and Methods 4.* Sage.

I have showcased only parts of the prospectus as this was meant to be used as an example. Therefore, the absence of complete bibliography.

Note: Be mentally prepared when the timeline starts shifting during the writing process, as it is dependent on personal and professional situations. Also, as a doctoral candidate, it is necessary to factor in the time commitment of the committee members and their schedule to provide the necessary feedback at the right time.

In my case, I had a setback in completing my dissertation by one whole year as I lost two of my close family members. I was emotionally drained and just focusing on the everyday routine, taking care of my family and work provided me the time to heal. What kept me going during this phase was that every day I would transcribe and translate a very small portion of my data. I just dated them and never checked on the page numbers. I would work 30–45 minutes every day. At the end of close to one year, I hadn't realized that I had transcribed and translated about 6,000 pages. It was a huge stack. When I showed this to my director, he called it the "data dump—DD," as it was still in a raw form and had to be assembled and coded in a way that it could be presented to the audience in a meaningful way.

The reason tentative dates are required is that it enables the researcher to stay on course; but in my case, I completed my seminal work and defended 13 months later than I had planned to defend. And, yes, there were times when I wanted to give up on my dissertation, but every time I would have that feeling, I would revisit my rationale for choosing this project and view my notes on why I wanted to undertake *only* this project and nothing else.

Part II

Design

> ... *But qualitative research is not meant to have a lot of structure or rigid approach to analysis. It is an interpretive, very dynamic, free-flowing process, and unless researchers understand the basics of what they are trying to do, they lose the aspects of analysis. Their research becomes superficial and fails to provide the novel insights into human behavior that give qualitative research its dynamic edge.*

—CORBIN AND STRAUSS (2015)

In this part, I focus on the importance of understanding the logistical issues that need to be addressed, from choosing the location and participants to chalking out the future plans in minute details—including writing field notes. Every aspect needs to be considered from arriving at the location, transportation, venue of meeting the participants, language, dress code, cultural interactions and introductions to interacting with group members. I also address the aspect of how to cross the language barrier, how to explain the research work to participants, and how to seek their (IRB) approval. This in many ways paves the road for field work, scheduling work with participants, learning their everyday routine, recording all the information, and most importantly, learning to be unobtrusive.

Note: Further, I want to begin this part by using the analogy of the painter to showcase why a thorough understanding of the design or methodology is very important, before beginning any data collection. It is very similar to a painter, who before beginning to paint a subject matter, envisions the placement of certain aspects or objects in his/her painting, so that it can be methodically constructed. For example, when you are following a tutorial of Bob Ross, a very well-known artist, one of the first things that is discussed is the overall picture or design, if it is going to be a landscape, rustic or rural, or if it is going to be rep-resentation of a season. Once that is decided, the next aspect that is considered are the placement of trees, mountains, streams, etc. Ross in his tutorials also poses many questions, as it allows the audience to think through their own design and positioning of the forms/shapes in certain places on their canvas. Similarly, designing a methodology is asking yourselves questions about every aspect of your method and constructing it in such a way that when all the parts come together, it appears as one complete picture. It is important to note that the parts cannot be placed haphazardly; they need to be individually analyzed and positioned appropriately. In this design section, my intention is to showcase that it is a step-by-step development, and it all begins with understanding the methodology. In the following chapters, I showcase how ethnography (landscape) was my large frame, and how case study protocol and methods were the forms positioned in certain places to develop and enhance the landscape-spaces on the canvas. The methods provided the colors and hues to my painting. Each stroke of the brush added value to the study or picture. There were many times when cer-tain places on the canvas had to be repainted and reworked or touched up to provide the necessary effects, what we, as investigators, refer to as "stimulated recall."

Chapter Eight

Understanding
the Methodology

Perseverance is not a long race; it is many short races one after the other.
—Walter Elliott

In most cases, the methodology section provides the necessary and appropriate tools for conducting research study. It reminds me of what CNS said, "Methodology section is like digging homegrown peanut pods from underground; you must use appropriate tools or methods to loosen the soil around the roots where the pods are and uproot them above the ground to view the harvest (here it will be considered interpretation of gathered data) And, usually, as there are many peanut pods growing from different pegs, you need to be patient and meticulous during the digging process; only then will you be able to gather all the pods from the ground. Although technology has revolutionized the way we gather the pods in large fields, I am here referring to only what is home grown " Similarly, as researchers, the information or data we need to uncover in the field depends on the tools we use and the diligent digging process we employ to uncover and unpack the information and bring in to the forefront by coding, analyzing, interpreting, and writing about it as findings. Therefore, every method used needs to be meaningful and accounted for in different ways.

In my case, I started the research with the three-pronged approach:

1. *Framed Research Questions (FRQ):* These questions kept me focused on my quest: What was I truly looking for?
2. *Case study tools and process used to answer the FRQ:* These methods helped me gather data: How do I find answers to my questions?
3. *Repetitive research leading to Ethnography, Anthropology, and theory building:* Literature guided me to theorize data in terms of what are scholars saying and how do I write about it?

1. Framed Research Questions (FRQ): I need to mention here that researchers sometimes repeat the FRQ in different chapters because it keeps them focused on their quest; they are like blinders that one wears to stay concentrated on a subject matter and not inadvertently shift to writing about aspects that one might have observed and seen during the field visit. I used the word *inadvertently* as there were many times when I digressed from my topic and wrote about other practices of the Dabbawalas that were unrelated to the focus of my study. I vividly remember, I once got carried away while writing my fourth chapter on findings and had written about 20 pages on Dabbawalas' philosophical approach to life to realize that it was irrelevant, specifically to my literacy study, especially based on the questions I was trying to answer. So, I had to shorten it to showcase that these participants were way more philosophical in their approach to life than expected, "allowing them to be happy" with what they earned and be content, rather than fall into "depression and drugs" (Dabbawala Interview).

On the other hand, I also recognized after I had collected all my data that my FRQs were limited in some ways. This was based on the comments from some of the interview questions and focus group discussions the Dabbawalas were making on literacy. I felt that it was crucial to add the new information to my study as it would contribute to the literacy paradigm. But I was unsure if I could add another question to the framed set of questions, as I had already completed most of the coding. It was reassuring to know that this is a common concern, as researchers are often worried about adding new questions or rephrasing their old questions, once they have framed their initial set of questions for the prospectus or while writing the dissertation. It is important to know that although the questions are framed to keep the researcher on track within the scope of the study, new questions can be added to the initial set of questions. This happens mainly due to three reasons:

(a) while being in the field, the researcher observes or views something that adds a new dimension to their quest and requires additional question/s

(b) while interpreting the data, the researcher finds aspects that fail to fit or answer the questions posed earlier, and

(c) while writing the final thesis, there are gaps in the coding of information and in the way it can be written as findings.

Thus, when additional questions are posed or added to the initial set of questions, they provide a clarity to the audience about what was observed and why there are references to it. Further, it clarifies the findings and allows the researcher to theorize concepts that are an integral part of the qualitative study. Geertz (1973) suggests that reporting just primitive facts from faraway places is not enough; it is more important that the ethnographer is able to clarify and provide clear and detailed information "about what goes on in such places, to reduce the puzzlement—what manner of men are these?" (p. 16). Therefore, adding a few more open-ended questions or reframing the research questions after they have been bounded, only adds to the process of understanding the interactions among the participants, comprehending the relationships and power dynamics among the group members, and the myriad interaction that unfold in front of you while you are observing (Creswell, 2007, p. 43; Strauss, 1987, p. 6). When I initially started data collection, I had four research questions but while coding, based on certain statements that my participants were making and based on certain practices that they were repeating, I realized I needed to add another question.

1. What are the literacy practices of the Dabbawalas (in general)?
2. What type of literacies do they use in their daily lives to maintain their business practices?
3. How and why do they write the scripts in English without being schooled in it?
4. How do they interpret the codes (scripts written on the lunch boxes) and translate it in their minds?

The fifth question I added was:

5. Although the Dabbawalas consider themselves literate, *they feel* others who observe them *think* they are illiterate. Why?

Therefore, in all the different fields, researchers usually begin their quest with FRQs that either need some minor or major adjustment/ modification.

Further, in fields relating to science, generally speaking, reality exists in nature in the form of facts and therefore hypothesis is created leading to data collection and validation as proofs. On the other hand, social sciences, considered as soft science, are based more on human behavior, their psychology, social norms, attitudes and other related matters, where data is collected based on assumptions, leading to validation and theorization (empirical evidence) to prove if the judgment calls are correct or incorrect or both. Thus, this is what I wrote down for myself as I started my methodology section.

Sciences: facts exist (nature/truth) > theorize → Data gathered to prove and validate

Social Sciences: Assumptions exist theoretically > replicable, aggregate, and data-supported research tools used to collect information to prove > theorize and report

In some ways, the more answers the researcher seeks from the FRQ, the easier it is to observe, write, repeat, and validate the observations and the better it is for the case that is being studied, as it helps with the RAD[1] approach (Haswell, 2005). Further, if the pilot case study is well constructed with all the necessary questions, where the researcher seeks to gather "facts and conclusion" for that particular case through different methods, then it is considered to be very helpful on two levels: it enables the researcher to replicate the pilot study data and it enables future researchers to replicate the same study over a period of time (Yin, 2009, p. 56).

2. Case Study Tools and Process Used to Answer the FRQ (Framed Research Questions): When I started my study, I didn't realize that I would continue studying the Dabbawalas for three more years after my initial visit. As I assumed my first would be my last visit and assuming that their business model was non-replicable,[2] I collected all my data in 2011. Further, I knew case study was the right methodology to understand the Dabbawalas' literacy practices as it was based on influential authors who had used case study in their own research and publications like Merriam (1998), Yin (2009), and Stake (1995 & 2010). These scholars advocated that a non-replicable aspect in any study manifests itself in physical, cultural, ethnic, and in many other contextual ways or issues or practices. Based on this notion, my initial rationale was:

(1) Case study will allow me to represent my experience with these people in a study, through descriptive use of language of the "incidents and settings" providing the audience an opportunity "to vicariously experience what was observed" (Merriam, 1998).

(2) Case study would allow me to showcase why the Dabbawalas business model is non-replicable to be emulated in other cities—even within India: (a) due to the specific layout of the city and the design of the railway services in Mumbai, and (b) the exclusive way the community members interact and participate in making this practice unique and inimitable.

(3) Case study will allow me to represent my experience for one week or more by sharing my schedule of observing, shadowing, and interviewing the Dabbawalas.

(4) Case study will provide me the opportunity to research a single group or multiple groups of individuals using literacy practices in similar ways, and to "contribute to our knowledge of individual, group, organizational, social, political, and related phenomena" (Yin, 2009, p. 4).

(5) Case study design has been used in many disciplines, such as psychology, sociology, political science, anthropology, social

work, business and marketing, public administration, public health, and education, helping social scientists evaluate, design, conduct, and investigate a research issue (Yin, 2009).

(6) Case study methods allow the investigators to retain the holistic and meaningful characteristics of real-life events by viewing "small group behavior, organization; and managerial processes, neighborhood change, school performance, international relations, and maturation of industries" (Yin, 2009, p. 4). Also, the holistic picture of a practice is obtained when a group viewing includes in-depth interviewing, continual participant observation of a situation, and capturing how people describe and structure their world around them (Creswell, 2007).

Interestingly, case study provided me all of the above and the much-needed flexibility to observe the literacy practice of individual members and group members at different—spaces, times, days, and years—to gather data across continents in longitudinal ways. Also, using different methods to study the literacy practices of the Dabbawalas over the years made me realize that the repeated observation of this group provided me an in-depth measure of their culture and literacy practices, which became key identifying markers that are often used in ethnographic studies.

This was because:

- I had repeated the same observation with another group and interviewed them and gathered the same data I had during my first visit.
- I was studying and describing the Dabbawalas' practices in greater detail, after every visit, based on observing individual and group practices.
- I was constantly addressing the value system they shared within the group members.
- I was observing and providing different examples of the writing patterns the participants used for writing their complex codes.
- I realized that based on my work other researchers could repeat these methods and arrive at the same conclusions.

Further, all my scholarly and myriad references were from the field of anthropology and sociology, beginning with the definition of ethnography. Based on this, as I mention in the preface, *the question that still haunts me—till today—is why didn't I refer to my methodology section as an ethnographic case study? Well, I made the mistake, and I don't want my fellow researchers to make the same mistake.*[3] This is probably one of the reasons that led me to writing this book as I wanted to address this to my readers, who will be crossing the path I have crossed and to inform them that "… you can reframe your research question after they have been bounded, and reframe your methodology, provided you have a clear and valid rationale to support the reframing" (interview with graduate student)

3. Repetitive Research Leading to Ethnography, Anthropology, and Theory Building: Ethnography according to the Oxford English Dictionary[4] is considered in the field of social sciences to be "a systematic study and description of people, societies, and cultures." The second definition that is provided suggests that it could include, "The ethnic character or constitution of a place, people, sphere of human action, etc." The dictionary also refers to the time when it was first used in the year 1811 to as recently as 2009 when it was used to study the workings of Wall Street. Based on this definition, the question arises: (1) how can ethnography be used in different fields including Wall Street, and (2) why and how do we study the culture of a society or a group of people from different communities, indigenous or ethnic, as it is abstract and opaque in many ways?

Street (2009) provides the answer to this in *The Future of Social literacies*, where he argues that research allows us to change the opaque and invisible to become visible and to reveal "the complexity of local, every day, community literacy practices" by challenging "the dominant stereotypes and myopia" (p. 22). To make the opaque literacy practices of indigenous groups transparent, research in the field of literacy studies has often been in the form of anthropological studies (Lave & Wenger, 1991; Scribner & Cole, 1981; Street, 1984), where researchers have spent extensive periods of time with their subjects to understand their oral and literacy practices. The research conducted by these scholars has provided us with different perspectives on studying and understanding how humans develop as individuals, how individuals behave in groups to create a community, and how humans collaborate and create a society. These scholars have allowed us to further comprehend:

(1) how these group cultures interact within themselves to create certain group identities,
(2) how these cultures contribute and add value to larger societies, and
(3) how they contribute to societal framework and functioning (as a whole unit).

Although, there have been wide-ranging research conducted on indigenous groups and their practices in the latter part of the nineteenth and early part of the twentieth century, I found some of them to be biased toward their subjects as they were rooted in ethnocentric notions. Street (2009) refers to his own study and experience of how the outside world viewed the Iranian villagers as illiterates and what he observed:

> I noticed that not only was there actually a lot of literacy going on but also there were quite different practices associated with literacy: Those in a traditional Qur'anic school, in the new State schools and amongst traders using literacy in their buying and selling of fruit to urban markets. If these complex variations in literacy, happening in one small locale, were characterized by outside agencies (e.g. state education, UNESCO, literacy campaigns) as illiterate, might this be the case in other situations, too? I have kept this image in mind as I have observed and investigated literacy in other parts of the world such as urban Philadelphia, South Africa, India, and the United Kingdom. In all of these cases, I hear dominant voices characterizing local people as illiterate (currently media in the UK are full of such accounts, cf. Street 1997); while on the ground, ethnographic and literacy-sensitive observation indicates a rich variety of practices. (Barton & Hamilton, 1998; Heath, 1983)

Street (1984) through his ethnographic study in Iran was able to construct the ideological model of literacy that led to a shift in perceptions from treating ethnic groups as primitive and non-literate to unique and ideological. Thus, the important takeaway for me was to view and unpack the culture of a group on their own merits and not compare them with other groups or our modern society. To be honest, this was another important factor that led me to study the Dabbawalas. I wanted to know how they were "illiterate yet successful" despite their non-adherence to following the Western cultural and literacy practices, and how did they survive so long by maintaining their century old practice. I also thought the Dabbawalas way of life was being discredited:

1. due to existing assumptions on literacy based on late nineteenth and early twentieth century scholars from cultural anthropology, including some armchair[5] anthropologists, who were biased about the literacy practices of their subjects, and
2. due to people writing about them, based on established autonomous model scholars' views from the field of literacy.

And, this study provided me a platform to prove that the above assumptions were subjective and derogatory. Although I had all these perspectives and information, I was unsure where to start with my cultural anthropology research, especially from the late nineteenth century, and it was sheer coincidence that led me to Sir Edward Taylor.

Anthropology method, as per Sir Edwards Tylor (1871), provides us an understanding of, "Culture, or civilization ... is that complex whole which includes knowledge, belief, art, law, morals, customs, and any other capabilities and habits acquired by man as a member of society" (p. 13). Further, Sir Edwards Taylor along with Sir James Frazer and Lewis Henry Morgan in the eighteenth and nineteenth centuries were instrumental in developing a model of cultural evolution that suggested cultures usually evolve from lower to higher forms of thinking over time. This basically translated to placing all non-Western people at a "primitive" stage and Euro-American culture as being civilized (Miller, 2017, p. 9). They further assumed that these non-Western cultures would die out due to lack of cultural (and literacy) practices and progression, as it was contrary to what was evident in Western cultures. Unfortunately, such studies were only instrumental in developing ethnocentrism in the later centuries and in creating the perceptions that non-literate cultures were primitive and savage.

This same perception on many levels was expressed by Goody and Watt (1963) in *The Consequences of Literacy* based on their anthropological study of the Tiv and Gonja Tribe. They concluded that due to lack of written material, oral non-literate groups have little perception of the past except in terms of the present (p. 311). Their argument was that due to lack of written records, the group members merge myth and history into one; thus, there is no clear demarcation between fact and fiction, leading to the group members forgetting their past cultural heritage and replacing it with new vocabulary, genealogies, and myths, "unaware that various words, proper names and stories have dropped out, or that others have changed their meanings or been replaced" (p. 311) Goody and Watt's claim only reestablished the ethnocentric notion that cultures with writing technology were instrumental in creating Western advanced societies due to their way of abstract thinking and growth of individuality. On a parallel note, during that time, this way of thinking was accepted by some scholars and challenged by others in the world of cultural anthropology.

Interestingly, cultural anthropologists like Leslie. A. White (1947) defended and explained that it was inappropriate to compare one culture to another, as men don't have any control over their culture, and it varies from one to another. White suggested that although there are different sciences to make us understand the physical, psychological, and spiritual aspects of human behavior, what provides us the grounding for such theories is the culture of a group, "Customs and institutions, culture traits in general, constitute a distinct class of phenomena. As such, it may be treated as a closed system." White by referring to R. H. Lowie (1917) was able to state, "Culture can be explained only in terms of culture" (p. 192). White argued that at the epicenter of all these gamut of theories lies culturology. He argued, "... culturologist knows fully well that culture traits do not go walking about like disembodied souls interacting with each other." He recognized that he could explain "cultural phenomena *as a cultural phenomena*" only when treated *"as* if they had a life of their own, quite apart from the glands, nerves, muscles, etc., of human organisms. The remarkable thing about this argument is not that it is revolutionary, but that it should be necessary to defend it" (p. 204). It is this deep understanding and the wish to defend the culture of ethnic groups that probably led him away from psychology and sociology to anthropology.

Further, Malinowski's (1922) functionalism, Frank Boas (1888) cultural relativism, and Margaret Mead's (1934) cultural constructionism theories, and later Brian Street's (1984) ideological model of literacy proved that each culture is unique and should *not be* judged by the standard of another (Miller, 2017). Geertz (1973) approach added to this thought process by suggesting that culture is "a system of inherited conceptions expressed in symbolic forms by means of which men communicate, perpetuate, and develop their knowledge about and attitudes toward life" (p. 89).

Indeed, my three-pronged approach enabled me to see that cultural anthropology is considered to be the study of living people and their cultures; this includes their shared beliefs, learning and knowledge building and the changes they make to create their environment. To observe and study these groups and their different practices from within, as a group member, anthropologist often had to spend a long time in the field, ranging from six months to one year to many years. Although anthropologists study different topics or aspects by being part of an ethnic group what is common to all of them is the methodology, which is ethnography. The commonality is due to this methodology providing people the interpretive tools to study culture or the complex whole that makes humans form groups or communities to maintain a social order. It provides scholars an opportunity, as many anthropologists suggest, to make the strange familiar and familiar strange. Hammersley and Atkinson (1995) suggest that the reason researchers use ethnography is mainly due to two reasons: first, it allows them to focus on the perspectives of the people who are being observed, and second, it allows them to view the work of the participants in real time. Baillie (1995) also suggests that ethnography allows researchers to study an unexplored aspect or area without bias and allows them to gather data, record information in natural setting, within the context of the community.

Also, when I started my data collection, it was interesting to observe that a systematic approach to studying the literate practices of specific ethnic groups, like the Mumbai Dabbawalas, did not exist as such in the literacy field. This is surprising, given the central role the literacy practices of nonmainstream groups provided in the first main debate on literacy studies (Goody & Watt, 1963) and the response of other studies repudiating the earlier thinking, encouraging new ways to studying nonmainstream and ethnic cultures use of literacy (Heath, 1982; Scribner & Cole, 1981; Street, 1984). What I also discovered was that researchers in the past decades had faced challenges of being unable to study ethnic and indigenous groups due to cultural barriers, language, and physical locations. This made me realize that any appropriate methodology that is used needs to consider the practical, theoretical, cultural, linguistic, and ethical issues that researchers may face in the field. This also made me realize why scholars in the field had expanded the options for doing qualitative research using new theoretical frames and methods to investigate the social and literacy practices of indigenous groups in their own environment (Lecompte, 2002).

In the past decade alone, researchers have found new ways to observe their participants and write about their practices in different ways using mixed techniques. For example, Charmaz (2006) suggests that researchers use qualitative methods but gather extensive data by memoing. Green and Bloome (1997) suggest adopting an ethnographic perspective if researchers are constrained due to lack of time at the site of investigation or research. Heath and Street (2008) suggest that researchers when they begin their study clearly list the choices about performing their fieldwork to establish ethnographic authority. They suggest that "sometimes one individual or situation may be just as good as another for satisfying the ethnographer's urge to learn about a particular phenomenon" (p. 49). The focus of these different approaches, as developed by literacy scholars, is to allow the researcher opportunities to gather data in ways that enable them to better understand indigenous or other groups and their practices in their environment (Bazerman, 2011). Further, these scholars allowed me to see how beautifully researchers can interweave aspects of "case study + ethnography + grounded theory," all in one study, and provide richness to the data that a researcher gathers on the field and uses it to code and theorize the information. Thus, my suggestion to my graduate students has been to decide on a certain methodology as their main framework and then choose and combine methods that will enable the researcher to gather data in multifarious ways.

Notes

1 RAD—Developed by Richard Haswell (2005) and stand for replicable, aggregate, and data-supported research tools that can be used for developing evident supported best practices in the field of composition and classroom research and can also be used across qualitative and quantitative fields.

2 Non-replicable in terms of the Dabbawalas lineage—they are unique in their ancestry and their business model but what is replicable to observe are their supply-chain methods, literacy practices, and delivery system coding.

3 As I mention in the preface, this book is about emulating and learning from my mistakes. Therefore, I have tried to be as candid as possible.

4 OED definition for ethnography.

5 Armchair anthropologists were dependent on the research conducted by others and formulated their opinions on others' experience in the field. These anthropologists would view another culture from their armchair instead of being on the field and collecting data, and compare it to their own culture, leading to coining of this term and leading to ethnocentric notions—of their own culture being superior to other cultures. In fact Lienhardt (1964) criticized Sir James Frazer of his assumptions and conclusions by saying, " … he thought that he could understand very foreign beliefs quite out of their real contexts simply by an effort of introspection. He and others of his time had something of the approach of Sherlock Holmes" (p. 27).

References

Baillie, L. (1995). Ethnography and nursing research: A critical appraisal. *Nurse Researcher, 3*(2), pp. 5–21. https://doi.org/10.7748/nr.3.2.5.s2

Bazerman, C. (2011). Standpoints: The disciplined interdisciplinarity of writing studies. *Research in the Teaching of English, 46*(1), pp. 8–21.

Charmaz, K. (2006) *Constructing Grounded Theory: A Practical Guide Through Qualitative Analysis*. SAGE Publications.

Corbin, J., & Strauss, A. (2015). *Basics of Qualitative Research*. SAGE Publications.

Creswell, J. W. (2007). *Qualitative Inquiry and Research Design: Choosing Among Five Approaches* (2nd ed.). SAGE Publication.

Geertz, C. (1973). *The Interpretation of Cultures: Selected Essays*. Basic Books.

Goody, J., & Watt, I. (1963). The Consequences of Literacy. In J. Goody (Ed.) *Literacy in Traditional Societies*. Cambridge University Press.

Green, J., & Bloome, D. (1997). Ethnography and Ethnographers of and in Education: A Situated Perspective. In J. Flood, S. B. Heath & D. Lapp (Eds.), *Handbook of research on teaching literacy through the communicative and visual arts*. Routledge Publishers.

Haswell, R. H. (2005). NCTE/CCCC's recent war on scholarship. *Written Communication, 22*(2), pp. 198–223. https://doi.org/10.1177/0741088305275367

Hammersley, M., & Atkinson, P. (1995). *Ethnography: Principles in Practice* (2nd ed.). Routledge.

Heath, S. B. (1982). Protean Shapes in Literacy Events: Ever-shifting Oral and Literate Traditions. In D. Tannen (Ed.), *Spoken and written language: Exploring orality and literacy*, pp. 91–117. Ablex Publishing.

Heath, S. B., & Street, B. (2008). *On Ethnography: Approaches to Language and Literacy Research*. Teachers College Press.

Lave, J., & Wenger, E. (1991). *Situated Learning: Legitimate Peripheral Participation*. Cambridge University Press.

LeCompte, M. (2002). The transformation of ethnographic practice: past and current challenges. *Qualitative Research*, 2(3), pp. 283–299.

Lienhardt, R. G. (1964). *Social Anthropology*. Oxford University Press.

Merriam, S. B. (1998). *Qualitative Research and Case-Study Applications in Education*. Jossey-Bass.

Miller, B. (2017). *Cultural Anthropology* (8th ed.). Pearson Publication.

Scribner, S., & Cole, M. (1981). *The Psychology of Literacy*. Harvard University Press.

Street, B. (1984). *Literacy in Theory and Practice*. Cambridge University Press.

Street B. (2009) The Future of 'social literacies.' In M. Baynham & M. Prinsloo (Eds.), *The Future of Literacy Studies*. Palgrave Macmillan.

Strauss, A. L. (1987). *Qualitative Analysis for Social Scientists*. Cambridge University Press. https://doi.org/10.1017/CBO9780511557842

Stake, R. E. (1995). *The Art of Case Study Research*. Sage Publication.

Stake, R. E. (2010). *Qualitative Research: Studying How Things Work*. The Guilford Press.

Tylor, E. (1871). *Primitive Culture: Research Into the Development of Mythology, Philosophy, Religion, Art, and Custom*. J. P. Putnam's Sons.

White, L. A. (1947). The expansion of the scope of science. *Journal of the Washington Academy of Sciences*, 37(6), pp. 181–210. http://www.jstor.org/stable/24531942

Yin, R. K. (2009). *Case Study Research: Design and Methods* (4th ed.). SAGE Publication.

Chapter Nine

Choosing the Location and Participants

Ethnography for me was a journey back into my birthland to unravel the intricate history, culture, and group dynamics that exists among the Dabbawalas.

—Krishnan

Once ethnography is chosen as the methodology, ethnographers are often asked to choose the exact location and participants to conduct the research study. But there are exceptions to this rule, where the committee members have asked the researcher to provide information about the location and participants while formatting the research question or even before writing the IRB, especially if it involves conducting a cross-cultural study abroad; the rationale being it provides the researcher more time to plan all aspects of the study.[1] Once the location has been identified, it is essential to ensure that the researcher has enough financial, physical, psychological, and digital-technological support every step of the way. Of course, problems do occur even when everything has been meticulously planned, but it becomes manageable if the researcher is well prepared to address the issues. Below, I present a general checklist that will help researchers, who are planning to conduct a cross-cultural ethnographic study abroad:

Table 1. Aspects to Consider before Conducting a Cross-cultural Study Abroad

Aspects to consider for conducting a cross-cultural study (abroad)	Detailed Notes/ Responses
Physical aspects to consider—location—Geography	
• Region—where the study will be conducted? Foreign location—provide information about the town or city, state, country, etc.	
• Weather conditions given the time period of the study	
• Plane travel and visas—days required	
• Local travel and logistics and approvals from local authorities, if needed	
• Dress code, if any	
Financial aspects to consider—specific days	
• Plane travel—to and fro	
• Local transportation	
• Hotel and accommodation	
• Food and other expenses	
• Fees required or volunteer donations to pay the organizations/ groups/community members	
Psychological aspects to consider	
• Language barriers, if any	
• New location and acculturation	
• Weather issues—physical and mental well-being	
Digital-Technological aspects to consider	
• Internet and access to email	
• Telephone and other communication coverage	
• Camera and uploading	

After every aspect of the above list has been addressed in detail, the researcher should move on to the participants list:

Table 2. Participants and Group Dynamics to be Considered before the Trip

Participants and Group dynamics to be considered	Detailed Notes / Responses
• How to recruit participants?	
• Is there a president or CEO or high-ranking official I need to meet and require permission before beginning the study?	
• What are the best methods/ways to recruit them, given the type of indigenous/ethnic group and the group dynamics/ hierarchy that exists within the members?	
• How many participants can I interview, specifically how many in number?	
• How to engage with the participants?	
• How to provide my participants the IRB and acquire signatures?	
• How will I maintain the data, such as IRB, in a safe location?	
• How to interview them individually?	
• Will I be speaking to them in English?	
• If not, in what language will I speak to them?	
• How will I transcribe and translate them?	
• What type of routes/ driving or walking will I undertake to be on the field?	
• How to record the multimodal ways of expression: written, oral, gestures, etc.?	
• How to ensure that video recordings can be done properly and repeatedly?	
• Are their procedures to record participants, during a certain time of day or at a certain location, as per the laws of the organization/ group?	
• How to record audio and keep them safe?	
• How to record focus group sessions?	
• What are the times/dates/days when focus group sessions can be done?	
• How many participants can be involved in the group sessions?	
• How to record these sessions unobtrusively yet add to the conversation?	
In some cases, city laws and regulations need to be considered	
• Are there any city rules for foreigners to follow to acquire data/ pictures/videos, etc.?	
• Is there a requirement to meet with city officials and receive permission before beginning the study?	

Once these steps are well planned, it becomes easy to move on to the next stage of planning. But what I failed to address in my excitement about my onward journey to India was that I had forgotten to make arrangements for my children. As my husband's job required traveling, I had to make arrangements for them to stay with relatives, so that I could be away for ten days to collect the data in India. Further, as part of the planning process, it is necessary for the researcher to inform family members of their location abroad, provide them with all hotel information, contacts, and other details, including embassy information.

Note: A word of caution—it is advisable to have a few printed copies of the IRB, audio, video forms and other aspects of the study, before entering the field, as the participants might request for a hardcopy of the forms they are going to sign. In some locations, while abroad, accessing a photocopying machine can be difficult and the participants might refuse to sign the IRB, till you provide them a copy of it. In case, the researcher is on a strict timeline, it is possible to lose one whole day because of being unprepared and lose out on interviewing the participants and focus group discussion.

Note

1 Interview with Prof. Lal, "Once the methodology is decided, the director often will ask you to start working on the data collection steps immediately, as it is an international study, and they don't want you to waste your time in a foreign land." In my case, as I knew even before my qualifying exams what I wanted to work on, I started gathering data about the Dabbawalas, in terms of their location, their services, and other aspects related to their business.

Chapter Ten

Chalking Out Other Aspects of the Research in Minute Details: Including Writing Field Notes

... Some of the tensions are those that exist in the field of composition (and literacy) studies. These tensions led me to resist any easy or set conclusions and, instead, to call for more self-conscious acknowledgment and examination of the competing roles any researcher must face in pursuing issues as those involving community literacies.
—Beverly J. Moss

One of the most important tensions (Moss, 2003) that I faced very early in my journey, even before traveling to Mumbai as a researcher, was "what if I am unable to ..." This thought haunted me for many days, as I knew I was taking a big risk by taking this journey across continents. But, what really helped me through the process was the role of checklists. From experience, I can now vouch that having a checklist of information and chalking out the myriad aspects of fieldwork, before traveling abroad, really helps, as it speeds up the research process once arriving at the location. Being unprepared leads to many unwarranted issues and researchers often lose precious time in the process, leading to frustration and anxiety. Keep in mind, "Field work usually means living with and living like those who are studied" (Maanen, 2010, p. 2), which means every aspect of living like/with the participants is

important and worth noting down. Some of these aspects include pay-
ing attention to:

- Time period
- Research's role
- Dress code
- Language to be spoken

Time Period: Few weeks before my departure, I chalked out a time
period by creating a table for myself with the days/dates and activities,
so that I could carry the tools needed for recording information and
writing field notes.

For each day, I had folders and subfolders that were categorized
based on dates and other information, such as: Main folder marked
June 25, 2011, and had three subfolders within it marked: Arrival in
India, Interview with Mr. Medge, Memo/observation. Similarly, for the
next day, it was: Main folder marked June 26, 2011, with subfolders
marked—IRB, Memo/observation, Individual interview notes, etc. The
work schedule of observing, shadowing, and interviewing was written down and discussed with Mr. Medge, before he assigned me the

Table 3. Time Period of My Initial Pilot Study

Days spent	Activities
June 25, 2011	Arrive at Mumbai. Appointment set up for 26th morning with Mr. Medge
June 26, 2011	Interview with Mr. Medge and Interview Dr. Pawan Agrawal
June ...	Field Observation, Interviews, and focus-group I discussions—Day I
June ...	Field Observation, Interviews, and focus-group discussions—Day II
June ...	Field Observation, Interviews, and focus-group I/ II discussions—Day III Second Interview with Mr. Medge and Mr. Sawant
July ...	Meeting with the focus group members I again, Interview with Dr. Agrawal, and Final reflections ... Evening—Departure from Mumbai

groups and introduced me to the supervisor of the groups, who, in turn, introduced me to the participant members.

Researcher's Role: Before starting the study, I was fully aware that cross-cultural studies have often been challenging for women due to gender bias (male versus female researcher based on context of the study), race, language, location, weather, or contextual barriers, where the researchers were treated as outsiders and information not made accessible to them (Barton & Hamilton, 1998; Gross, 1995; Heath & Street, 2008; Johnstone, 2008). I was also aware that qualitative study can be affected due to the following reasons: (a) lack of trust between the researcher and the participants, (b) the community members uneasiness with discussing work information with an outsider; (c) participants' use of a local language that is unfamiliar to the researcher; (d) participants change the subject when the researcher arrives; (e) participants refusal to answer certain questions, or to purposefully move away from the researcher to talk out of ear shot; or (f) not allowing the researcher to see some of their practices, leading to the researcher being unable to observe many of the practices; thus, hindering the outcomes of the study in many ways (Schensul et al., 1999, p. 17).

Further, Gross (1995) suggests that cross-cultural researchers must adopt a self-conscious and critical stance throughout their study. His suggestion allowed me to realize that there were two major self-related, personal, cross-cultural issues in conducting this study. First, I was a female researcher in a business site where every member, or Dabbawala, on the site was a male. Second, I didn't want the participants to think of me as an American, an outsider, due to my citizenship. Therefore, to downplay gender-specific uneasiness and nationality issues while on site with the Dabbawalas, I had to decide on how I should present myself, in terms of dress code, in front of my participants so that they would feel comfortable interacting with me.

Dress Code: As I had researched the Dabbawalas online before reaching India, I decided to wear the traditional Indian dress of *Salwar-Kameez* for two reasons. It shifted the attention away from my status as an outsider and as a woman, and it was the dress the other members in their community, such as their mothers, sisters, daughters and even their grand-children would wear.

I was also aware of the Dabbawalas dress code and their usage of "Gandhian topis," a hat, symbolizing their principles and adherence to a traditional way of life. Mr. Medge elaborated on this during one of the interview sessions and said that they all wear "white kurta and pajama (similar to shirt and pant)" and "white topis (cap)" on their head as:

These topics are used by the Dabbawalas for four reasonss:

(a) Identification: what we stand for, our principles, and in case there is an accident, we know who was affected.
(b) Advertisement: so that people immediately recognize that Dabbawalas deliver food in this route and can use their services.
(c) Substitute and accuracy: If someone is sick or not able to deliver, they call upon others just by seeing the white cap and continue to deliver the food on time.
(d) Computer cover: The mind or memory—CPU is covered—from heat, rain, and weather in general (Krishnan, 2014).

Language to Be Spoken: Sanjek (1990) mentions that a researcher doing qualitative, ethnographic fieldwork makes a series of choices, including the language to converse with the participants. I made my choice of speaking in Hindi based on what was best suited for the site and for the study. This assumption was appropriate as all the Dabbawalas felt comfortable from day one and none of them exhibited any discomfort during my shadowing them, or while traveling with them on the train, or even while I was recording them during interviews. On the last day, my assumption was validated when Chotu, one of the participants, on behalf of the other Dabbawalas, commented that despite being educated and living in America for more than two decades, "Sister, you are very Indian in your ways. We all liked the fact that you spoke to us in Hindi and thought of us as your brothers" (*Didi, aap bahut Bharti hain. Humsab ko acha laga ki aapne Hindi mein hamaray saath baath kiyay aur hum sab ko apna bhayee samjaa*). We feel you are "A lady carrier or a Dabbewali." My everyday memo, another method used as part of case study, reveals my reaction to this comment: "I feel somehow happy that I got this title, unsure why? Probably because they felt that I respected them or thought of them as equals, but I feel, 'I am the illiterate in their business world.'" I was also happy that they didn't think of me "as a dull visitor, meddlesome busybodies, hopeless dummies, social creeps, anthrofoologists ..." (Van Maanen, 2011, p. 2).

My choice to speak in Hindi was also based on two other observations:

(1) All Dabbawalas spoke Hindi, as Hindi is one of the two official languages of India.
    Most of them could speak in three languages: Marathi (the language spoken by the people of Maharashtra), Hindi, and Gujarati, language spoken in the neighboring state of Maharashtra.
(2) Dabbawalas were required to know Hindi to communicate better with their customers.

Speaking and writing down the conversations in Hindi also helped me immensely, as I was able to *relive* many of the moments (in terms of certain expressions and associated hand gestures they would make) even after one year and even now, while translating and transcribing or referring to the notes in general. But what was fascinating to uncover, as a researcher, was that Mumbai Hindi dialect in some ways is different from New Delhi, capital city of India, Hindi dialect; for example, in the above sentence where Chotu expresses his feelings about my speaking in Hindi, he speaks the Mumbai Hindi—*Baath Kiyay*, or bAth kiYay versus Delhi Hindi—*Baath Kiyaa*; very similar to the distinctions we can make if someone is from the northern or southern part of the United States, just based on the drawl/accent in their speech. Despite the different dialects, what enables us to communicate with each other anywhere in the States is the commonality of language, English. Similarly, even when conversing with the Dabbawalas, despite the different dialects, I felt I was able to communicate with them on professional and personal levels due to the language commonality, Hindi. At times, it was the language familiarity that allowed the Dabbawalas to explain their everyday literacy practices in great detail. During some interviews and focus group discussions, I found myself drawn to the conversation, as it would be in Hindi and Marathi mixed with English words, a form of multilingual conversation. I felt

I was a participant rather than an observer. One of my research memos reveals this thought:

> I wish I had not been so rigid about following protocol. I wish I had been more non-intrusive and allowed them to talk while maintaining silence. Today, they were willing to talk to me about things that they did not discuss all these days. The group was actually at ease with me and discussed information about their religious beliefs, lifestyles, and about Lord Vittala, which they have not done so far! Have they suddenly realized that I am Indian born, speak the same language as they do, and I am a Hindu; suddenly what changed? Was it my concern that in the hot sun they were willing to answer my questions, or was it my gesture to buy them Fanta and soda (soft drinks)— that the conversation has become casual and reduced the interviewer effect on them? I wish I knew more! Welcome to ethnography and theory![1]

These notes were written based on the usage of native language and the advantages I had, as a researcher, in terms of taking up a study in the country of origin. I observed that their demeanor changed, and they were more relaxed and were able to have conversations ranging from their schedule to issues with one of their customers to even purchasing new crates in front of me.

Contrary to what Schensul et al. (1999) discuss as the issue/s researchers face in conducting investigations with natives of a different language, I felt privileged that the Dabbawalas were at ease with me and treated me as part of their group. Street (2001) describes this aspect in his own ethnography in Iran and why being one among your participants is important for qualitative study. It is only when you are an insider can you capture the "complex variations in literacy … happening in one small locale were (people of the village) characterized by outside agencies … as 'illiterate …' " (p. 6)

Note

1 In my memo, I have used the word ethnography, although at that point I should have mentioned it as case study, unsure why I wrote it.

References

Barton, D., & Hamilton, M. (1998). *Local literacies: Reading and writing in one community.* Routledge.

Gross, E. (1995). Deconstructing Politically Correct Practice Literature: The American Indian Case. *Social Work, 40*(2), pp. 206–213.

Heath, S. B., & Street, B. (2008). *On Ethnography: Approaches to Language and Literacy Research.* Teachers College Press.

Johnstone, B. (2008). *Discourse Analysis* (2nd ed.). Blackwell Publishing.

Krishnan, U. S. (2014). *A cross-cultural study of the literacy practices of the Dabbawalas: Towards a new understanding of nonmainstream literacy and its impact on successful business practices* [Doctoral dissertation, Kent State University]. OhioLINK Electronic Theses and Dissertations Center.

Maanen, J. V. (2011). *Tales of the Field: On Writing Ethnography* (2nd ed.). The University of Chicago Press.

Moss, B. (2003). *A Community Text Arises: A Literate Text and A Literacy Tradition in African-American Churches.* Hampton Press.

Sanjek, R. (Ed.). (1990). *Fieldnotes: The Makings of Anthropology.* State University of New York Press.

Schensul, S., Schensul, J. J., & LeCompte M. D. (1999). *Essential Ethnographic Methods: Observations, Interviews and Questionnaires.* AltaMira Press.

Street, B. (2001). Introduction. In B. Street (Ed.), *Literacy and Development: Ethnographic Perspectives*, pp. 1–17. Routledge.

Arriving at the Location: Bounding the Study

Ethically, research should never be undertaken lightly.

—Corbin and Strauss

Another important aspect the researcher needs to deliberate before traveling abroad and arriving at the site is to map out the terrain or geographical area of the study and the weather conditions during the time of the study and articulate that in the prospectus. For example, in my initial study, in the scope section, I noted that I will be following the Dabbawalas only on one railway route that they take the food to deliver in offices and return to their base. I wrote:

Location limited to the Western Railway route from Church Gate to Bandra/Andheri and back.

I did this as there were so many railway lines that my participants would take food to deliver, and I knew ahead of time it would be impossible to observe them on all the lines. Also, as the initial study was a pilot, I wanted to restrict my scope to one segment. This way the data gathered would be centered around one segment and replicable. Further, when I was writing my proposal, I had to explain all the different aspects associated with my travel to my committee members. This was mainly to make them aware of where I would be traveling and to ensure that I was adhering to the university protocols, as the study was international and not local.

I mention this as some universities have certain prerequisites or protocols, even health mandates, that need to be completed before the researcher pursues international investigations. Thus, I provided the following information to the committee members, including the fact that the Dabbawalas service industry was located in Mumbai, India.

Mumbai is one of the cities in the state of Maharashtra, situated in the Western part of India. It used to be referred as Bombay during the time of British Colonization, but the name change to Mumbai took place in 1995 to reflect the historical heritage. Further, Mumbai has always been considered a very cosmopolitan city in India, next to New Delhi, the capital. The three main spoken languages here are Marathi, Hindi, and English. Figure 1 below shows the location of Mumbai in the state of Maharashtra and its neighboring states

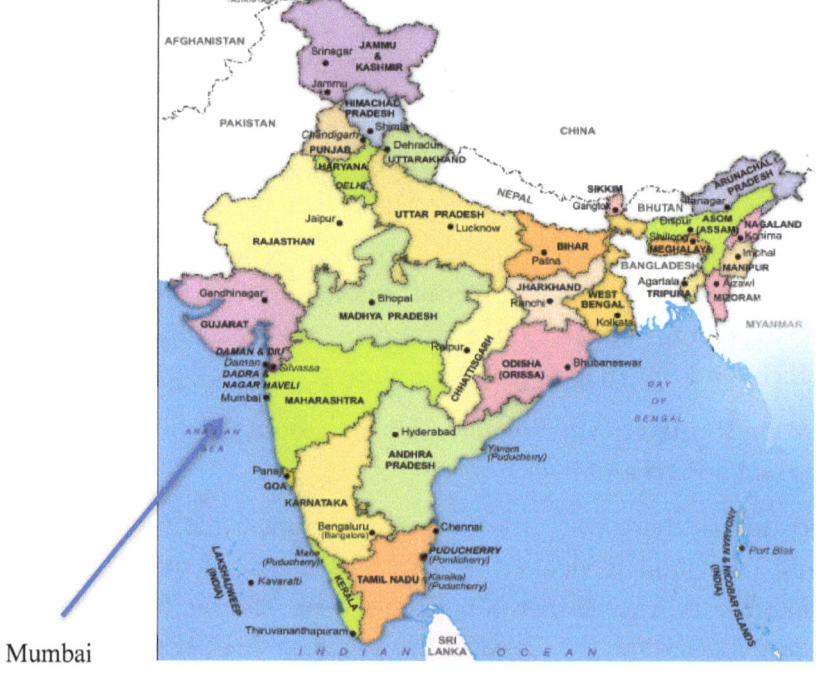

Mumbai

Figure 1. Map of India with Maharashtra highlighted in green (Google Images).

Gujarat (main dialect Gujarati) and Madhya Pradesh (main dialect Hindi). Mumbai, one of the four major cities in India with a population of 20 million as of 2011 with 233 square miles (UN Population Division), utilizes the train system to interlink all its suburbs. People of Mumbai refer to their "Railways" as their "lifeline of the city," as it transports close to 6.1 million people daily. It has three lines of operation: The Western, The Central, and The Harbor Line (Figure 2), running from 4 a.m. until 1 a.m. The Western Railway trains run between Church-gate and Virar station, but they also run express trains from Church-gate to Andheri to accommodate the commuters, including the Dabbawalas. Although there are other trains that stop at every station, I will

Figure 2. Mumbai Suburban Railway routing (Google Images).

be using the express train schedule (fast-orange grid), as the Dabbawalas who have been assigned to me use this railway route, and I will observe their literacy practices on this route (Figure 2).

Providing this background allowed me to showcase that my scope was narrow, due to the route the Dabbawalas would be taking and what I would be observing while traveling with my participants. It also allowed the committee to see how I was framing my study within a certain area of Mumbai. Further, bounding and providing such information about the geography of the region was important, given that many of them had never been India and to the location where the study would be conducted. Thus, providing details allows for the understanding of the context, geographical location of the case being studied, the language used, and the (cultural, religious) political, social, and traditional influences that play a role in the participants lives. In some ways, providing such details also helps future ethnographers to conduct their studies in the same location and enables them to gather replicable data and maybe discover something new.

Chapter Twelve

Designing the Data Collection

After being with the Dabbawalas for many days, observing their daily literacy prac-
tices, I realized that designing the data collection is one of the keys to understanding
and honoring our participants voices, stories, narratives, perspectives, and knowledge.
—Krishnan

Many colleagues and students, whom I met immediately, after my
return to the United States asked me how I started my journey in India
and how I arrived at the location and approached my participants.
One of the most memorable comments that still makes me smile came
from Kyle, a senior, an undergraduate at that time, "Given your passion about this study, did you unpack your bags, take your research
gear, and bam—start the investigation immediately or go straight from
the airport to the site of study—like they show in BBC documentary?"
My response was that I did start my field work the following day after
I arrived in Mumbai, as I was excited and emotional that I was conducting a study in my home country. In my daily memos I mention:

At last, I have arrived in Mumbai. All that I visualized and dreamt about in
terms of conducting this study is slowly taking shape. I realize this is just the

beginning and there is so much ahead of me. I hope and pray that everything goes well in the next few days. I am emotional and maybe having a cathartic moment in terms of my research work. I am also worried about the kids. Hope they are okay, as it bothers me that I have left them behind. Maybe this is why Behar appeals to me so much.

Ethnography brings with it what Behar (2003) addresses as "dislocation and relocation" factor (p. 21). She writes that by becoming an ethnographer she "acquired an intellectual and philosophical framework" for her study as it provided her an "exploration of identity, memory, home, and the crossing of borders." She defines the change in place and situation as "dislocation and relocations ... are at the heart of the ethnographic imagination, ... it was through the pursuit of ethnography that I was able to undertake the magical, and also politicizing, journeys into the everyday reality of people living in the Spanish-speaking world, the world I longed to reclaim" (p. 21).

In some ways, I realized to reclaim the everyday reality of the Dabbawalas meant a commitment to "bring back a story" of truth and honesty of what I saw and observed while on the site. What this also meant was that my data collection had to be very organized that anyone conducting later research on the Dabbawalas literacy practices could retell the same story but using—their own—personal touch. This further meant viewing scholars who had conducted and collected data for case studies. So, I referred to Yin (2009) and organized my data collection in five categories and placed them in the main folder that was marked with the date of the observation, such as June 25, 2011 and placed another set of five folders in June 26, 2011 and so on. These folders were colored and marked A-E, and almost all of them had subfolders and were categorized as A1, A2, etc.

Folder A: Direct field observations

Folder B: Individual (face-to-face) interviews and focus group discussions with candidates

Folder C: Field notes: Video recordings, written observations, and stimulated recall and memos

Folder D: Physical Artifacts, and

Folder E: Documents

The use of these multiple data streams are extremely important as they allowed me to obtain a deeper understanding of my subjects and their literacy practices, and later helped me with data triangulation. I used three types of procedures to analyze and triangulate the data, very similar to what Spinuzzi (2010, p. 373) suggests:

- Across data types: If a literacy event was being practiced by a Dabbawala, then I analyzed and cross-checked to see how it was being represented in two or more data types, such as observation and interview. Example of an observation would be: Dabbawalas greeting each other and their customers in different languages in the morning and during the day; the follow up to this observation was, did all the Dabbawalas in different groups greet each other and their customers the same way?
- Across participants: Any literacy practice or action that the Dabbawalas performed in their life: how is it represented in two or more participants, such as learning on the job, learning from others, and picking up English words.
- Across events and processes: If each Dabbawala followed a different route, how did they work as teams and replicate each other based on their actions? An example of this would be to observe them to see if they all follow a certain procedure, habit, time schedule in the way they exchange and deliver lunch boxes based on the script?

How to keep track of data: In the following paragraphs, my aim is to reveal how to keep track of the data collected, and how I assimilated the data for later analysis, coding, and triangulation. I provide details of how I wrote my field notes, interviews, and memos. I also provide tables of how I kept track of all the information in folders like a checklist. This, in many ways, will allow future ethnographers to follow the same procedure or tweak it to address their own situation and context. Although every person has his or her own method of organizing information, keep in mind that the data gathered in just one day can sometimes be overwhelming, unless it is appropriately placed in their respective folder.

Another aspect I realized was that this type of information is often missing in data collection methods leaving the researcher wondering about the process of gathering information and organizing the field notes and interviews. While reviewing this part, the question might arise, is it important to notate all the information as they are only meant for our own personal consumption, and the answer is—"**Yes, you must**." What is interesting is that during my defense one of the questions that was raised was, "If you spent only ten days following the Dabbawalas, how could you have theorized so much information about their literacy practices?" Fortunately, I was able to showcase and argue that as I had collected extensive data, recorded, written, and organized the information during my pilot study, I was able to theorize their literacy practices and validate that with my later visits. At that point, I listed out my visits to meet the Dabbawalas in person from the year 2012–2014 and provided the phone logs, pictures of my later site visits, recordings and transcripts of my conversations with my participants to my committee. *Showcasing the details of my visits allowed me to prove that the initial visit was enough to theorize information, and the later visits only helped me to reiterate and replicate my initial data findings.*

Folder A: Direct field experience and observation

This green folder had subfolders marked:

- A1—Arrival in India, Background literature and IRB
- A2—Being on the field, learning the everyday routine and flow diagrams—Interview with Mr. Medge
- A3—Memo/Observation day 1, 2, 3, … last day of my trip

Subfolder A1: Arrival in India, Background literature and IRB

In this folder, I placed my notes associated with my initial reaction and thoughts about arriving in India and notes related to the excitement and anxiety that I felt about my work. I also refer to the concerns I had and mention that in my memo:

Maybe I am a little scared about how things will shape up this week. Yes, I am a little anxious …again, hope and pray everything works out. I also need to

> read up on some materials and organize my folders for tomorrow. Hope jet
> lag doesn't hit me. I also hope Mr. Medge introduces me to the group.

I refer to this memo in particular as I was unsure about who would be introducing me to the participants, and I was unsure how the participants would react toward me, before starting my observation on the field. This insecurity was mainly due to the scholarship I had read on how and why an ethnographer should be introduced by a high-ranking person in the organization to the participants at the site; if not, the researcher may face challenges. Fetterman (1998) refers to this as the "halo effect." He believes that the participant dynamics changes if the right person introduces the ethnographer to the group, "The trust the group places in the intermediary will approximate the trust it extends to the ethnographer at the beginning of the study" (p. 33). This was true as Mr. Medge's introduction, as the President of the Nutan Mumbai Dabbawala Association, had a great impact in the way the participants of the group were willing to accept me as an observer and be themselves.

During the first two days, I was assigned a single unit of participants to observe, but on the third day, I was allowed to study another group. Both groups or unit of participants consisted of one Mukadam[1] (supervisor) and his team of Dabbawalas (eight members).[2] I was allowed to follow, observe, and record their practices. On the third day, I interviewed nine members from the second unit for focus group discussions. Other participants like Mr. Medge, Dr. Agrawal,[3] and Mr. Sawant, Principal of the Dabbawalas computer literacy program, a charitable trust created by Dr. Agrawal, were interviewed to provide additional information and perspectives about the organization. During my later visits, I didn't have to seek Mr. Medge's authorization to visit the participants, but I would call him and inform him that I was at the site with the participants. I would directly go to the site to meet Ahilum (Group I supervisor) and his group members and observe them. I also visited Dr. Agrawal to see how the Dabbawalas were progressing in computer literacy. On a side note, I feel fortunate that I have been in touch with him over the years and I have been able to converse and discuss with him the status of the Dabbawalas.

During these years, Dr. Agrawal had expanded his charitable center to three other locations to address the needs of the Dabbawalas, their children, and other members from the poor neighborhood, so that they can all acquire computer literacy.

Subfolder A2: Writing about being on the field, learning the everyday routine and flow diagrams

Van Maanen (1988) refers to ethnography as "the peculiar practice of representing the social reality of others through the analysis of one's own experience in the world of these others" (p. ix). This representation can only be conducted if the researcher is on the ground and observing the participants over an extended period of time. As Van Maanen suggests, it is "highly particular and hauntingly personal" when you observe your participants and interact with them throughout the day (p. ix). Emerson et al. (1995) refer to it as "deep immersion" into the field of participants (p. 10). In order to fully comprehend the practices of the Dabbawalas, their pathways and train routes, ways of conducting business, the challenges they faced, their regular and timely activities, I had to be fully immersed in their everyday routine from morning till evening. Being in the field not only allowed me to answer my research questions but also made me understand why they have a six-sigma rating.[4] It also helped me in representing their daily routine in the form of flow charts and process diagrams. In some ways, a visual representation of their everyday routine helped my dissertation committee to see the unique aspect of this business model and their literacy practices on the field.

The everyday observation was pivotal to my research, as the comments made by the Dabbawalas during their interviews corroborated their everyday physical work, team spirit, and peripheral participation[5] (Lave & Wenger, 1991). Some of their comments made while traveling or during fieldwork provided insight into other events happening in their lives, such as planning for the future generations, the role of literacy in their households, and their positions as literacy sponsors for their children. Some of them mentioned that as they had not received school education or couldn't complete their schooling due to

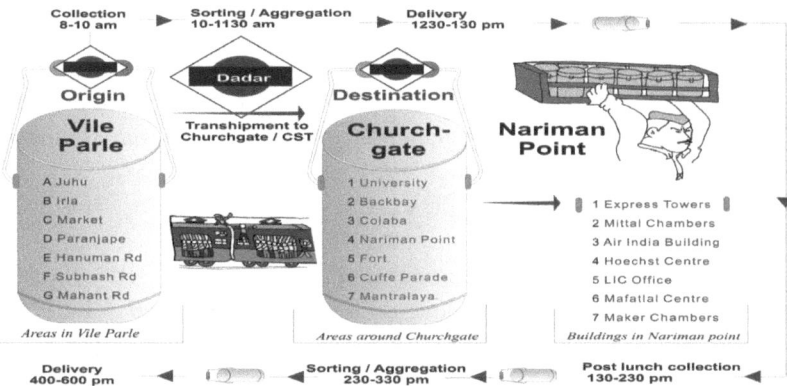

Figure 3 . Pickup and delivery of food. Flow chart used from Dr. Agrawal's book *Dabbawala of Mumbai: Masters of Supply Chain Management.*

circumstances, they were very keen to provide their children an education till high school. This type of thinking and planning for their children's future by setting short-term and long-term goals for themselves and for their family members provided me a glimpse of how even the *so-called* "illiterates" can plan for future events based on their own lifestyles. Further, what was interesting was a comment made by Mr. Medge, "Although we have followed the same business model for over a century, our ways of thinking about our children's education has changed." He continued, "We realize that even after high school education, someone can join our practice. Having a school or college education doesn't mean you can't own a Dabbawala franchise. Let me tell you, we are also into supply-chain management." Mr. Medge then explained what these practices were and elaborated upon the whole day's event as executed by the Dabbawalas, as a *process* involving collecting, carrying, sorting, picking up, and delivering of lunch boxes (pre- and post-lunch).

The above figure explains the process of pickup and delivery with timings on the top and destination marked in bold to show how a day's event becomes a systematic process to be followed from morning until evening, from the origin to destination and back to the origin; and how all the transactions take place among the Dabbawalas based on the script written on the lunch boxes. Table 4 describes the process

Table 4. Pickup and Delivery of Lunch Boxes

Events -Time of day	Process
Between 8 and 10 a.m.	• Dabbawala A carries about 10 to 30 (depends) lunch boxes from houses in an apartment complex to a meeting point in Vile Parle
Between 10 and 11:30 a.m.	• Dabbawala A meets many other Dabbawalas bringing in their customers' lunch boxes.
Scripts on the boxes allow for teamwork and deft exchange of lunch boxes	• Lunch boxes laid out, sorted, and placed into other crates or long rectangular wooden carts based on their destination: Dadar, Mahalaxmi, Church gate, etc.
Between 11:30 and Noon Scripts on the boxes allow for teamwork and deft exchange of lunch boxes for final destination	• Once sorted, Dabbawala A carries his crate to the railway station and gets on a train headed for Bandra station, which is his destination.
	• In Bandra, he downloads/places his lunch boxes at a common meeting place at the station around noon.
	• Exchange of boxes (bustling activity) takes place -based on the final destination of Dabbawala A, he picks up lunch boxes from other groups members that has his destination marked on the lunchbox, Bandra, a suburban district in Mumbai.
Between lunch hours of 12 and 1:30 p.m.	• Dabbawala A then carries his crate or cart filled with lunch boxes again, but this time to destinations with specific addresses in Bandra, as that is his designated area, where he needs to deliver his lunch boxes in certain offices or locations where his clients work.
	• Most of them walk to their destinations of a few miles, although some have bicycles to deliver the food.
Between lunch hours of 12 and 1:30 p.m.	• Given Mumbai's weather conditions, rainfall is a very common, but the Dabbawalas still deliver food on time, as many of the participants used the slogan, "come rain or shine."
	• Based on the script and the number of clients, ranging from 10 to 30, an individual Dabbawala will chalk out his route *mentally, like GPS,* of what his route should be for the delivery of food to the people in the final destination, who are waiting for their food—"to be efficiently delivered between 12 and 1:30 pm."

Table 4. Continued

Between 1:30 and 2:30 p.m. Post-lunch collection and sorting	• Dabbawala A starts picking up the lunch boxes from the previous or same day, depending on the situation • Brings the lunch box back to the station at Bandra for sorting.
Between 2:30 and 3:30 p.m. Dabbawala A boards the train for Vile Parle	• He again picks up lunch boxes that are marked for his final return destination, back to the original place, where he started in the morning; thus, Dabbawala A carries lunch boxes meant for Vile Parle, his original destination. • He brings them to the meeting place at Vile Parle. • Sorting again takes place dexterously and placed in crates or carts based on final home destination.
Between 4:30 and 6:00 p.m. Return lunch box to owner	• At this point, Dabbawala A makes sure his crate contains only empty lunch boxes meant for final home delivery (from homes he picked up lunchboxes in the morning)
Dabbawala A and his Unit of eight members	• All of the eight members operate the same way as Dabbawala A, having their original and final station as Vile Parle; so, they are considered part of one unit. • Based on the size of the suburb, there could be a few more units but the locations are all marked on the tiffin (lunch) boxes, so that there is no confusion between the destinations.

in detail about how communication and coordination are an intrinsic part of the Dabbawalas supply-chain business model.

Subfolder A3: Writing Memos and Observation of participants on day 1, 2 and 3(samples)

Emerson et al. (1995) in their discussion of writing field notes explain this aspect of research as the process of "understanding how an observer/ researcher sits down and turns a piece of her lived experiences into a bit of written text in the first place" (p. vii). This is sometimes considered a time-consuming process as it takes time to gather and pin down all the artifacts and thoughts, but it is worth every minute of your time. As Sanjek (1990) suggests, that although writing field notes vary from person to person, it is important for a researcher to keep all the writing that materializes from the observation, including scratch notes, personal notes, emails and thoughts written on pieces of paper as valid resources. According to Geertz (1973), "Doing ethnography is like trying to read (in the sense of "construct a reading of') a manuscript-foreign, faded, full of ellipses, incoherencies, suspicious emendations, and tendentious commentaries, but written not in conventionalized graphs of sound but in transient examples of shaped behavior … (p. 10). Thus, the ethnographer is instrumental in inscribing "the social discourse; *he writes it down*" (p. 19).

These resources, especially while conducting an international study, *really help to vicariously feel the sounds, smell, mental images of being there and relive through the past moments during the final stages of writing. And when you express them as a narrative, the images come to life and make the reader view the setting in their inner eye.*

As CNS would say, "When you create the visual effect by writing your narrative descriptively, you take over the mind of your readers for that moment; it is like viewing a movie; you are immersed in that action that you empathize or relate with the characters and the situation. The movie takes over your senses." This was true as I had referred to many authors before I started taking field notes; one such writing that took me to the place of the event was Geertz's (1973) description of a funeral held in Modjokuto, a small town in eastern central Java. Geertz, well known for providing thick description, provided subtle details about a burial situation that I felt transported to the town, and I could sense the controversy over the burial and the time period it took place. His references to how the wood for the ceremony was being chopped or how the mother insisted on seeing the body of her dead child before it was wrapped or how the political leader dragged Geertz into the conversation by saying, "Suppose this American (he pointed to me; he was not at all pleased by my presence) came up and asked you: what is the spiritual basis of the country? And you didn't know—wouldn't you be ashamed?" (p. 159-160). Just reading about it made these incidents come alive into the present. The details and the conversation were so real and vivid that I felt as if I was watching the whole scene and listening to the dialogues between the political leaders, government official, and the parents of the boy.

Reading such narratives also helped me to see how direct field experiences need to be natural and realistic. As my journalist friend would say, "Report the scene with all the details so that the audience can *see it live* and you, yourself, can *live and re-live* that moment later." Such comments only showcase what it means to be an ethnographer recording and observing an ethnic group and taking notes of their professional and personal lives; thus, allowing the audience to actually have a glimpse into the everyday life of these Mumbai Dabbawalas, their business and personal literacy practices. Glenn (2020) refers to this type of narrative as showcasing rhetorical feminism, in the sense that it showcases marginalized voices and their struggles. She writes, "The authentic voice of rhetorical feminism, which combines reason, emotion, vernaculars, and experience, speaks to a hopeful future of inclusive rhetorical practices that establish authentic connections with people like us, but especially with those who are not." Further, she suggests, "An emphasis on understanding rather than persuasion underpins much of rhetorical feminism, surfacing as it does in each of its features, explaining, as it does, the value of hope, of listening to and speaking from the margins, of engaging as equals in dialogue and collaborations, and of developing authentic, even if provisional relationships ..." (pp. 334–343) Thus, my focus was to show the literacy practices of these Dabbawalas in real light, as my equals in dialogue and collaboration.

In addition to my other data sources, observing the individual participants in the field provided me with a clear sampling of the Dabbawalas' work, including categories as mentioned in Table 5, and how all the Dabbawalas in group I followed the same routine. In this data collection section, I provide *only* pertinent details about my shadowing the Dabbawalas on three days: June 27, 28, and 29, 2011. In the following paragraphs, I provide a detailed (thick) description, as an example to reveal, how my participants perceived certain situations and spoke about their practices in their own words. This not only illuminated some of their beliefs but also provided validity to some of my interview questions such as "Why do you consider yourself illiterate?"

Table 5. Individual Participants in the Field and Their Work Routine

(1) Locations and routes for observation	From Andheri to Church Gate or Bandra/Virar to Church Gate
(2) Train stations and specific compartments where the Dabbawalas enter	Where they enter and depart
(3) Selected participants of eight members from group I and their daily engagement	first and second group
(4) Participants literacy practices used from morning till the day's end	Observing them on the train and off the train on the field
(5) Peer-collaboration among groups and conversation	Focus group discussion in the evening
(6) Dialogues as they were engaged in activity or writing the scripts	Observing participants write the codes on lunch boxes at railway stations at Bandra and Church Gate
(7) Language of thinking as opposed to writing on the lunch boxes	Discussion among the Dabbawalas at some of the stations
(8) Usage of symbols as codes to signify destinations	Observing the apprentices learning the codes to signify destinations

June 27, 2011: Day 1

Figure 4. Picture was taken after Mr. Medge introduced me to the Dabbawalas for the first time and was about to leave in his two-wheeler (so he is wearing a helmet) for a meeting in Andheri on June 27, 2011, to meet another group of Dabbawalas.

Observation Narrative: On June 27, 2011, I arrived at the site location around 9:15 a.m. Mr. Medge arrived at 9:30 a.m. to introduce me to the group leader, Ahilum, and the group members or my study participants. While waiting for Mr. Medge, I observed that some of the participants had already collected their lunch boxes from (their) assigned houses and were waiting for the other members to join them at the Vile Parle meeting point. As Mr. Medge had already explained to Ahilum and to the group about my study and informed them about the IRB, they were prepared to sign the forms, although some of them had questions. I went through the forms in detail as a group, explained everything in Hindi, mixed with English words, and informed them that they were under no obligation to sign the form or participate in the study as it had to be voluntary. I also informed them that if they didn't want me to use their original names, they could provide me with pseudonyms. Some of them didn't want to be identified, so they were given pseudonyms. Once they understood what the study was all about, they signed the audio and video formats. A few were hesitant about video recording; so, I assured them that I would not record them. I also informed them that they could, if they wanted to, see the video the same day or the following day, as I would be playing the recordings to validate some of their comments. A few of them wanted a copy of the signed form. Thankfully, as I had a few copies readily available I gave it to them immediately. Also, at that point, I showed them the interview questions, in English and Hindi, and explained how I would interview them. One of the participants was concerned that answering all the questions will disrupt their work as it ranged from 30 minutes to one hour. So, I assured all of them that I will work around their schedule, and they could speak to me whenever they had time, as I would be following them for the next few days. What is intriguing is a few of them asked me where I was from, as they had been interviewed by researchers from other universities like Harvard and Duke. They were also surprised to note that I was uninterested in their management system and interested to study only their literacy practices.

Once the formalities were completed and I had all the signed documents, Ahilum informed me that I would be shadowing him that day. He informed me in Hindi that I would be able to speak to some of the group members in the train, while traveling, "for the next 15 minutes." He also mentioned that I would be able conduct a focus group discussion in the evening "either at the railway station on our return back from delivering the lunch boxes or after coming here—our starting point."

After this explanation, he went back to sorting with his group members and started focusing and organizing the lunch boxes in his small crate.[6]

Once he knew he had all the lunch boxes and was ready to leave for the railway station, he looked at me and asked, "Are you going to videotape everything?" When my response was affirmative, he suggested that I should be careful while following him and while crossing the road till we reach the railway station "as there will be many vehicles on the road and water puddles due to the rain" and he did not want me to get "hurt or dirty." After making that remark, he placed the cart on his head and some lunch bags on his shoulder and started walking toward the station, and I followed him, the beginning of my first observation.

I started recording him from a distance of 10–12 feet, honoring Mr. Medge's request. When I questioned Mr. Medge about the necessity of maintaining distance between the researcher and participant, he explained that previously researchers were allowed to shadow the Dabbawalas closely, but they would ask too many questions during shadowing, which lead to a delay in the delivery of lunch boxes and thus hindering the timely process.[7]

His suggestion was to shadow Ahilum (or other Dabbawalas) in an unobtrusive way, so that it would allow him to work efficiently as he will not have to answer any of my questions, and he wouldn't be conscious of having an observer recording his every action. So, I continued to walk behind him throughout Day 1 and recorded as he delivered lunch boxes, picked them up in the afternoon, and returned to his group to sort at Church Gate, Bandra, and then back to Vile Parle at the end of the day.

Figure 5. First picture was taken after Mr. Medge introduced me to Ahilum. Second picture was taken during a later visit at the end of the workday.

While shadowing him, I was constantly commenting on my surroundings and what I was observing so that it would help me later to remember that moment and location. These comments ranged from thick descriptions of conversations with clients to impromptu murmurs that were later used for data analysis. One of the vivid memories that I have from the first day of following Ahilum was that in one of the crowded streets, when he made a right turn, I lost him as there were too many people walking in the same direction. I panicked and was unsure where I was, and my recordings indicate such moments:

> Oh! God! I am not sure where I am! I cannot find Ahilum or Yama[8]! I have no clue of where I am and what this place is all about! I wish I had at least asked him for the routing! If I am lost what I am supposed to do? What should I ask and whom? There are so many people here! This is like New York! God, what am I doing! I think it is jet lag! Why is my brain not functioning like the Dabbawalas?[9]

While I was contemplating on what action to take, Yama spotted me in the crowd and rescued me within minutes and I was truly thankful for being located. On the second day, noticing how I was getting lost in very crowded streets, Ahilum suggested that I walk with him and ask questions only during certain times, such as when we were on a quiet street or when there was no traffic. At one point, he even allowed me to converse with some of his clients. I appreciated the fact that he allowed me to converse with his clients and allowed me to walk with him. When I questioned him about it, while we were walking on the following days, he mentioned in Hindi:

> Sister! "Didi" Your quiet ways of walking behind and asking me questions yesterday about my activity assured me that you will not misrepresent us (*thik samjo-gay*); also, I want you to see what we are doing, as you are the first one who wants to observe our practice in a different way (he was referring to literacy; *saksharata—padhna likhna aur bolna*).[10] How come you don't think of us as *"unpad"* "illiterate" and why do you not want to know about our management system?

My response, as recorded on the camcorder:

> Bhaiya, (brother), it really upsets me that people consider all of you illiterates, when you are all conducting and running a successful supply-chain

management system. And, it is well known fact that top management schools across the world send their students to study your management practices, but none to study your literacy practice—as that is one of the key aspects of your business being so successful.

I continued to explain that these writers still believe in the autonomous model of literacy and don't think about the Dabbawalas practices in terms of the ideological model of literacy and the way it (literacy) works differently in ethnic communities. In response to this comment, Ahilum explained, "People educate (learn and study) themselves based on their job requirements; therefore, studying or education for every person is different (*padhai log apne apne dhandhay ke mutabit seekhthay or karthay hain—padhnay ka vichar dhara sab ka alag hotha hai!*)." In turn, I responded:

This is what I am trying to showcase. My research will present, and hopefully prove, that you are not illiterate by showcasing your successful literacy and management [11] practices; **it is because of and not in spite of**—using unique literacy methods and tools to facilitate your business that you are all so effective. Your success story is due to the use of your scripts, communication, and memory, which replaces many of the conventional forms of retaining information through writing.

This response made Ahilum smile and he nodded, as it was time to deliver another lunch box. Ahilum's questions about why I was uninterested in viewing their management practice was recorded, as it provided data on how the Dabbawalas were assessing outsiders.

My field notes reflect this observation as:

Ahilum's surprise was interesting to note on two levels: First, he observed that I was not shadowing him to write about the Dabbawala management system; and secondly, I did not think of him as *"unpad"*—illiterate. Why is he surprised? Is this because he assumes, he is illiterate as he does not know how to write in English or is he aligning with the societal norms and definitions and assumptions of illiteracy, as he didn't attended school? What really frustrates me is that everyone assumes that people who have not been fortunate enough to acquire school education are complete illiterates, reminding me of Debra Brandt. This seems to be a common understanding among all the people interviewed so far and is again being reflected in Ahilum.

Today's observation revealed that the Dabbawalas were unaware of any study conducted on their everyday literacy practices. It came as a surprise to Ahilum that someone was writing about their perception of literacy, as they had all along believed that they were illiterates due to lack of education and schooling. Comments made by Ahilum are significant in terms of data collection, as they shed light on the autonomous model of literacy and how the definitions appears to be the same—globally. It also proves that Goody and Watt's (1963) autonomous model of literacy still exists deeply within the different social classes in many parts of the world, where dominant groups define the term literacy for members of other groups. And secondly, Ahilum's and other participants' reference to educated people as people with a college education, working in high-raised buildings with knowledge of English, reveals how societal norms and assumptions have a huge impact on how a common man views the role of schooling, education, and English language in their lives.

What was amazing is that the so-called "illiterates or semi-literates" were not only polite but followed the rules of etiquette as applicable in any workplace environment. For example, if the trains were very crowded and too noisy, then we had to wait until the passengers got off the train to continue with the interview. If I was trailing behind while I was following him, Ahilum would stop and wait till I caught up with him. He never used my first name and always called me, "Didi" or sister or madam.

June 28, 2011: Day 2—Brief description

Figure 6. Vile Parle Station.

I started Day 2 at Vile Parle at 9:00 a.m. I was a little early, as I wanted to interview some of the other Dabbawalas in the morning before they left for the railway station. I followed the procedure of ensuring that

I had the IRB forms signed from the previous day, before conducting the interview. Ahilum arrived at 9:30 a.m. after collecting all the lunch boxes from his clients' houses. He started the conversation by wishing me in Hindi and as it was raining, he suggested, "It rains heavily during monsoon season in Mumbai; you need to be careful about water getting splashed all over your clothes." He also suggested that I should cover my video camera with a plastic sheet (similar to a disposable poncho), as the umbrella can turn over if the wind gusts are strong.

As it was raining heavily and windy, I heeded Ahilum's suggestion. When it was pouring heavily, I only audiotaped Ahilum's comments, as it was impossible for me to videotape and walk without stepping into a puddle. While I was facing such challenges, Ahilum kept walking with some of his lunch boxes in his hand and on his shoulders. As I walked along with him by his side instead of behind him, as I had the previous day, I noted that the paint marks remained on the boxes despite the heavy rains, and the water did not seep into the lunch boxes. Despite the rain and the wind, I was able to question him, while walking on a street that was quiet and had no traffic, about the paint not washing off from the boxes. Ahilum was very accommodative and willing to answer my questions on-the-go, while walking through narrow roads or maneuvering through traffic. When questioned about the paints, Ahilum explained that based on the weather conditions, the Dabbawalas have special emulsion paints that are used as non-washable markers on the boxes, and they sometimes use nail polish remover if an address needed to be changed immediately. His explanation for water not seeping into the lunch box was that every lunch box had an outer cover, "tiffin-dabba," as a supplement that protected the food contents inside from being exposed to dust or rain, and also provided a space for address markings to facilitate easy delivery.

June 29, 2011: Day 3—Brief description

On Day 3, I recorded one of the members from a different group, Shiv, at Vile Parle meeting place. The recording session was only for a short duration of two hours. Shiv explained that he was substituting for a member in Ahilum's group, as he was sick. I met Shiv at 9:30 a.m., provided the IRB forms for his signature, and explained my study and information about how I would be shadowing and recording him. Shiv greeted me, signed the form, and consented to being interviewed. But before the interview started, he mentioned that he did not want his name to be referred to. So, I asked him what he would like to be called for my research purposes and he responded, "Shiv." At the end of the 16-minute interview, he suggested that I follow him for a few hours until 11 a.m., as he would be using a bicycle to deliver the food for lunch after reaching the destination at Bandra. I consented and videotaped him walking to the Vile Parle railway station and taking the train to Bandra. After reaching Bandra, he got down from the train and slid his crate dexterously onto the station floor and placed it where the other Dabbawalas had assembled to sort their lunch boxes. After the sorting, when he was about to leave the station, he wished me again—*Namaste, didi*—and left, carrying his crate on his head to the area where the Dabbawalas park their bicycles every day. I also observed another member from a different group that day in the afternoon on the return route. I followed the same procedure as I did for the other participants.

Last day of my trip: Special day

On the last day, the participants were very relaxed and spoke about many things: information related and unrelated to their work, about their philosophy, their trip to their village, the long route they take walking and singing the names of the Gods, the importance of ethics in their life, recruitment of family members in the franchise, the sense of brotherhood in their business and other aspects related to their family life. There was no special order, it was just one topic leading to another as if they were relating their life stories to one of their relatives. In the evening when I had to leave, I was in tears and Chacha one of the senior members said, "Next time, you visit us, we will take you to our village and you can do another study there." Coincidentally, Mr. Medge when I met him later that evening mentioned the name of his village and mentioned that "there is a movie documentary about the travel of the Dabbawalas going home, during certain times of the year to Pandharpur, for religious festival." During the later trips, although I wanted to visit their village, I was unable to travel due to time constraints and the Dabbawalas schedule; it was hard to coordinate the trips. Further, during one of the later visits, I was informed that one of the senior members of the group with whom I had interacted extensively had passed away. I was teary and filled with grief and paid my condolences to the members while feeling a sense of loss. This is another aspect of ethnography that sometimes we will need to deal with—a loss of a human being—and still carry on with our work. Although, I continued my work that trip, I was in deep sorrow and gratitude for the help he had provided me and mentioned that to all the members.

Folder B: Individual (face-to-face) interviews and focus group discussions with candidates

This folder also had subfolders titled as:

B1: Individual Interview questions and Focus group discussion question
B2: Focus group discussions
B3: Comments pre- and post-interview

Subfolder B1: Individual Interview questions and Focus group discussion question

A crucial aspect of any qualitative study is the interview part. Yin (2009) suggests that the goal of research is to ask questions and not be necessarily focused on finding appropriate answers (p. 70). He claims that asking good questions is the key to unlocking a "rich dialogue with the evidence" as the participants have an opportunity to understand, interpret, and answer the question in a non-threatening way (p. 69). Based on this thought process, the questions I had prepared for individual interviews (Set I) were in three parts: Interview questions (IQ) 101, 201 and 301. The set 101 had subparts A, B, and C (Table 6). This categorization helped me to stay organized from the beginning till the end. I asked the participants as many questions as I could from the subsets 101 A, B, and C given their work schedule and the time they could allocate to answer my questions. I asked them question in Hindi mixed with English words, such as:

- *Aap mujhe apne business ke baare mein batha sak they hain?*
- How would you describe your business?

Table 6. Dabbawalas—Interview Questions—Individual Meetings—Set I—IQ 101A, B, and C

IQ 101 A: Questions Related to Work Practices—Everyday Schedule Questions

The Set 101A questions were asked if the participants had only 30 minutes or less to spare. If they had more time, then I continued with my list of questions from other sections (B&C), as it provided me an opportunity to produce a "Thick Description" (Geertz, 1973) from my collected data.

1. How would you describe your business?
2. Describe a typical day of work for you—as a Dabbawala?
3. What type of literacy tools (reading and writing) do you utilize every day? Can you define and explain literacy to me?
4. How do you accomplish the task that is set for the day?
5. How does the everyday schedule or routine help you to do your job a certain way, as you do not use any literacy tool or savvy technology that is available now?
6. How do you communicate with the other members of your team when you cannot see them in person?
7. How does the team relate to each other? How does a new member learn the practices of the community?
8. If one person is sick, how do you communicate?
9. Do you send a text or call and what do you write in it? Is it a detailed message or just quick information? Is there a sample that you can show me?
10. Do you think that you learn something every day by practicing this routine? Can you explain, how and why?
11. If you learn something or others learn something that can make the practice more efficient, how do you share this information?
12. Do you get to implement any of your suggestions that will enhance your practice? If yes, please explain? If no, why not?

IQ 101 B: Questions Related to Literacy and the Role it plays in Dabbawalas' lives and the role of Apprentice in the Dabbawalas Community of Practice

1. What is your definition of literacy?
2. What is your education level?
3. Why did you not continue your education?
4. Was it a lack of support system or did you just not feel the desire to study?
5. Why do you do this work, is it due to lack of school education?
6. Who prompted you to do this type of work: family, relative or friends?
7. What did you think this job was about when you joined?

(continued)

Table 6. Continued

---

8. How did you get trained? What kind of training did you get?
9. Were there any manuals for you to read?
10. Was it a field experience: like follow someone?
11. How did you keep track of everything?
12. What kind of mental notes does one have to keep to understand this unique business?
13. What do you expect from your job?
14. If there is a mistake, how do you resolve it?
15. What kind of reading and writing do you do other than at work?
16. What has changed for you in the course of your career?
17. What are your goals in terms of getting higher education?
18. How do you envision yourself in the near future?
19. How do you expect to survive in this age, if you don't use computers?
20. What role does education play in your life?
21. Do you expect your children to be educated?

IQ 101 C: Questions Related to Reading and Writing that the Dabbawalas do in Leisure Time

1. How do you spend your leisure time during the weekend or during the day?
2. When you read the newspaper or other subject matter (in your language), do you get an opportunity to discuss that with others?
3. Do you read any religious scriptures and discuss them with your family?
4. Do you attend discourses in the community? Why?
5. Do you participate in other community-related activities?
6. How does that help you in gaining anything, including customers?
7. Do you talk to them about your business model?

After my interviews, I ended my conversation by thanking them for providing me with information. I also asked them if I would be able to approach them the following day, if I needed clarification on something they were saying or working on. I also wanted to find out if I could get in touch with them later, once I was back in the United States, in case, I had questions.

DABBAWALAS—IQ 201 (Stimulated recall)

I termed IQ 201 as Stimulated Recall set, as they were based on clarifying information from the previous day's interview and recording. At the end of each day, I would view the recordings from that day's observation and if I had questions, I would write them down to ask the Dabbawalas the next day. The following day, I would conduct the stimulated recall by showing them the video from the previous day and ask questions correspondingly.

Table 6. Continued

DABBAWALAS—IQ 301 (Retrospective Interview)
IQ 301 was termed as Retrospective Interview as these were questions that
developed after I finished my starter, open, and axial coding and completed the
general analysis.

Another aspect that really helped me was I had typed out the questions
in Hindi underneath the English one.

I used the same set of questions for all of the group members.
I used iTunes and VLC recording software on my MacBook to transcribe the recordings. The software enabled me to rewind and listen
to the recordings repeatedly; sometimes multiple times, when I would
have a doubt with a word or phrase due to the background noise level,
dialect change, or simply due to the way the participant responded.

Focus Group (FG) discussion questions
I had another set of questions prepared for the focus group discussion
and categorized it as Set II—101 A and B consisting of 15 questions
(Table 7) related to technology and five related to past and present practices. I also had follow-up questions the next day, as stimulated recall,
and termed it as FG 201 and retrospective interview as FG 301, following the same pattern as individual interviews.

I recorded 21 interviews with the Dabbawalas and others, during
my pilot study, including those who had either conducted research
on the Dabbawalas like Dr. Agrawal, or those who were their literacy
sponsors in terms of providing them with basic computer training,
like Mr. Sawant. The interview questions were similar to the questions
in Tables 6 and 7 and were concentrated on finding responses to my
research questions.

Overall, the interview and focus group questions were a combination of close and open-ended questions. Some of the questions required
only brief responses of one or two words, such as: if you are sick, do
you text or call another Dabbawala? While other questions required

Table 7. Dabbawalas—Focus Group Meetings and Questions—Set II—FG 101A and B

FG 101A: Questions Related to Technology

1. What do you think of the technology, like cell phones?
2. What do you use it for?
3. Do you text?
4. If so, in which language?
5. Which aspect of the cell phone helps you the most: texting or calling? Why?
6. Recently you started a practice of placing literature in the Dabbas and delivering them to customers: how recent is this practice?
7. Who came up with this ingenious idea?
8. What do you think of the agency involved in doing this?
9. What are they (the advertising companies) benefitting from this and how does that benefit you?
10. What does that tell you about written information?
11. Do you read the information that you place in the lunch boxes?
12. If yes, what do you think of this method of advertising and reaching out to the audience?
13. If no, what stops you from reading them?
14. Do you think it is not beneficial to you?
15. Do all the Dabbawalas use this type of advertisement to propagate their own business? Why or why not?

FG 101B: Questions Related to the Past and Present Practices

1. Do you think your practices have undergone a change?
2. If so, what are they? Can you describe them in detail?
3. What do you believe to be the causes of these changes: technology, your group members or education?
4. In terms of technology, with so many forms of transportation available, why is that you have maintained the oldest form of technology; like carrying Dabbas on your head, using the bicycle, using metal tiffin boxes, etc.?
5. What do you think are the advantages or disadvantages in using these forms?

Thank you so much for giving me all this information. If I need clarification, would I able to talk to you tomorrow. Also, once I go back to U.S., if I have questions, how do I get in touch with you if I need to ask you more questions?

Table 7. Continued

DABBAWALAS—FG 201 (Stimulated Recall): Similar to individual interview, at the end of the day, I would view the recordings of that day and if there were some comments that were unclear or if I had doubts, I would write down my questions and ask them the next day. The following day, I would conduct the stimulated recall by showing them the video from the previous day and ask questions correspondingly to seek clarification..

DABBAWALAS—FG 301 (Retrospective): Questions that developed after I finish my starter, open, and axial coding and completed the general analysis.

---

more detailed responses, for example, how would you describe your everyday routine, or what is your definition of literacy? The set of questions from IQ and FG helped me to stay organized while interviewing the 21 participants and grouping their interviews as short, in-depth, or focus group, based on the availability of the Dabbawalas, the time they had at their disposal, and the number of questions I could ask them in one session.

- If they were able to respond to one set of questions from IQ 101, then I termed them as *short interviews*.
- If they were able to answer all of the questions from IQ 101—A, B and C and shed light on other issues about Dabbawalas' literacy practices, like Mr. Medge or Dr. Agrawal did, I termed them as *in-depth interviews*.
- If the Dabbawalas responded to all the questions as a group, I termed them as *focus-group (in-depth) discussions*.

Interview questions 101 were sometimes posed while traveling in the train or in short, sometimes narrow pathways while my participants were delivering food. The Dabbawalas would willingly respond and I would record them on my camcorder. Table 8 provides information about the interview categories. I followed the same procedure of asking questions with both the groups. If they could not respond to all the questions from the parts during the one-on-one interview session, as they were in a rush, then some of them responded to the questions during the focus-group sessions. This way, almost all the members responded to all the questions I had raised during my initial visit.

Table 8. Interview Questions: Individual and Focus Group Categories

Individual Sessions

Interview type	Sets and questions	Questions focusing on certain aspects of literacy
Set 1- IQ 101 Interview	A– 12 questions	Questions related to their literacy and everyday work practice
	B—21 questions	Questions related to their literacy in their lives, role of apprenticeship, and community of practice
	C—7 questions	Questions related to their reading and writing in leisure time
IQ 201 Interview	Stimulated Recall	Clarification of previous day's work—by showing them video from the previous day and asking for explanation
IQ 301 Interview	Retrospective Interview	Asking questions after coming back to U.S.—while translating, while coding the starter, axial code, and while writing the general analysis

Focus Group Sessions

Set II – FG 101 Interviews	A—15 questions	Questions related to technology
	B—5 questions	Questions related to past and present practices
FG 201 Interviews	Stimulated Response	Clarification of previous day's work—by showing them video from the previous day and asking for explanation
FG 301 Interviews	Retrospective Interview	Asking questions after coming back to the United States—while translating, while coding the starter, axial code and while writing the general analysis

Subfolder B2: Completed interviews/timings/ pictures/recorded tapes

In this folder, I kept track of all the people I had interviewed based on the day and created a table with columns for the type of interviews

I conducted, people I interviewed, and the total amount of time I spent with them (Table 9). There were additional columns in the table with names of the participants and the questions they responded to in detail, but that was removed later at the request of the participants. My everyday routine after observation would be to return to the hotel, have dinner, and meticulously arrange and place the data in their folders and work continuously for six to eight hours. To be honest, I was scared that I would lose focus and forget what I had observed or seen that day. So, every evening, all the interviews were handwritten and not typed, every other line, and transcribed into a legal pad of 8 ½ × 11 ¾ inch (21.59 × 29.85 cm) in Hindi. If there were questions that required explanation or description, I would highlight them on the notepad and mark the recording time in the margin, such as, "Interview with Mr. Medge—1 hr 17 min (unsure/ unclear /puzzling— ask for explanation)." The following day or whenever we were scheduled to meet, I would play the video from my computer or camcorder, from 1 hour 14 minutes through 1 hour 17 minutes and ask Mr. Medge or participants for clarification or further explanation. I did not have to rewind the recording too much to provide the context to their sentence, as many of them were able to immediately recognize and respond to their actions or comments from the previous day. This methodical practice of ending each day with the task of transcribing the day's events was helpful in two ways, as (a) it allowed me to seek clarification of their activities the following day by using stimulated recall and responses, and (b) it reaffirmed what I was transcribing and interpreting was correct. Once this was done, I would mark the Interview 201 (stimulated recall) as complete. This also allowed for the data to become more comprehensible and develop the aspect of trustworthiness among the participants.

At the end of the day, I also engaged in two other activities without fail: (a) logging the names of all the participants I interviewed or observed into a table to ensure that they had signed all the paperwork and received the IRB forms, and (b) I wrote what I classified as pre- and post-interview comments (samples provided in Tables 10 and 11).

Table 9. Type of Interviews, People Interviewed and Total Time (Sample Three Days)

Type of Interviews	People Interviewed	Time	Questions and Responses
Face-to-Face Interviews (10 individual)	10 interviews with different Dabbawalas; in the morning while the Dabbawalas were waiting for the other group members to join them	10–25 minutes (142 minutes total)	Set I— Interview 101— A and B
In-Depth Interviews (one-on-one) 5 sessions total	Mr. Medge Dr. Agrawal Mr. Sawant All three participants were interviewed in their offices.	45–55 minutes (165 minutes total)	Set I— Interview 101 A, B, and C. Other related information about literacy practices of the Dabbawalas shared.
Stimulated Recall 2 sessions	I approached some of the participants based on their ambiguous responses for clarification. I played the video and asked them to explain themselves further in the morning or in the evening.	10–15 minutes the following day of the interview (33 minutes total)	Interview 201
Focus-group discussions (5 sessions)		45–1:15 minutes	Interview questions and sometimes randomly posed questions

Table 9. Continued

Type of Interviews	People Interviewed	Time	Questions and Responses
Total—21 interviews between all four types of sessions, totaling up to approximately 582 minutes (9.7 Hours) of recording, but there were other conversations that were not video recorded. This was because the participant didn't want to be videotaped but didn't mind being audio taped. Total number of recorded information at the end of the week was close to 60 hours.	Interview examples All interviews were conducted in June 2011	Time ranging from 10–90 minutes sessions	Questions from all different sets

Subfolder B3: **Pre-interview, Interview, and Post-interview comments**

Entries before the interview and after the interview were placed along with the interviews as (a) pre-interview, (b) interview, and (c) post-interview reflective comments, in one folder. These three categories were placed together as one unit, such as *Interview with Mr. Medge,* record my assumptions or other impressions that I had, as a researcher, before and after the interview. The pre- and post-interviews were written by hand in English and were to be referred to later during data analysis. Table 11 provides a sample of how I documented my first conversation with Mr. Medge and how all three parts of one interview (pre-interview, interview, post-interview) were kept together.

Table 10. Forms and Signatures (Sample)

Interview No/ IRB forms provided	Date	Participant Name	Type of interview Single or group	Stimulated response (required –yes/no) if so, date when completed.
1. Yes—Signed	26 June 2011	Mr. Medge	Single, Set I— IQ101—A & B	Yes—29 June 2011
2. Yes—Signed	27 June 2011	Ahilum	Single, Set I IQ 101—A & B And focus group	Yes—28 June 2011

Table 11. Pre-interview, Interview, and Post-interview Sample of My First Interview with Mr. Medge

Pre-interview (Written in English)

Date: April 14, 2011, 9:45 p.m. US-EST (Around 8:00 a.m. in Mumbai, India)

Conversation: Mr. Medge (President of the Nutan Dabbawalas) preferred name.

Pre-interview: This is the first time I am calling Mr. Medge and I am not sure if I should speak to him in Hindi or English? I am planning to inform him about my study and need to make sure that this study is even possible, before I book my tickets to India and proceed with data collection. Questions to be asked:

- Can I do this study on the Dabbawalas' literacy practices?
- How many days can I observe the Dabbawalas?
- How many members can I interview?
- Can you provide me with literature material on the Dabbawalas before my arrival in Mumbai?
- Will you be able to introduce me to the group?
- What language/s do they speak?
- Do I need any specific permission from your organization?

Interview: Our conversation started in English but suddenly, rather unconsciously, it shifted to Hindi

Words Spoken in English (from the original conversation) highlighted in yellow:

UK: Good Morning, Mr. Medge! My name is Uma Krishnan. I had sent you an email in January and received a response last month from your office to contact you in this number. Thank you for taking my phone call.

Mr. Medge: You are welcome. Can you inform me more about your research?

Table 11. Continued

UK: I would like to study the literacy practices of the Dabbawalas. How do they read? Write? Carry on their business, etc.?

Mr. Medge: I hope you realize that they are not well (pause) educated, and some have gone to school only until third or fourth (3rd or 4th) "class pass" and can't speak English. What is your study related to? Business management? Other universities have already done supply-chain management studies on us? So, you are not interested in that aspect?

UK: I am aware that they don't speak English and have mostly primary school education. I am amazed (pause—in Hindi utter the word—*chonkit*) that they are able to carry on a six-sigma business without all the necessary schooling. As I said in my email, I am a PhD candidate/student, and my research is on finding more about their literacy practices.

Mr. Medge: Hm. (Clears his throat). Pause. You speak Hindi well, but you appear to have a South Indian name?

UK: (I respond back in Hindi) *Jee. Mein Hindi mai achee tarah baat kar saktin hoon* (Yes. I can speak very well in Hindi).

Mr. Medge: (Laughs)—*"Accha to phir*—Okay, then," I have no problem if you want to study them. *"Bhagwan ki marzi*—God willing," whatever will be, will be. You should be able to do it. I am visiting U.S. to speak to a business organization in Connecticut about 40 miles from New York. Can you come and meet me there? I will be there on June 12 and returning on June 16. Why don't you call me when I am there?

UK: I will certainly do that. Is there a number where you could be reached? Thank you again for talking to me.

Mr. Medge: Let me give you my number, and I will help you in any way I can.

Mr. Medge repeats *"Aap Aaiye" "Dekhlenge aur madad karengay"* ("Please come" "We will see and help you").

UK: Good day *(Namaste)*.

Mr. Medge: Good day *(Namaste!)*[12]

Post-Interview: Reflective Comments

Mr. Medge was very nice and willing to help me with my data collection. I was unable to ask any of the questions on my list. Looks like he was in a hurry and would be willing to answer questions during his visit to the U.S. He appeared surprised that I was not interested in their business model and wanted to study their literacy practices. Why did he mention that the Dabbawalas were not educated and only "3rd or 4th class pass?" Is he worried that I might not be able to gather anything from this research? Does he, too, have an autonomous view?

(continued)

Table 11. Continued

Appears God fearing, and his reference to "whatever will be will be" seems to be an interesting phrase for a first-time conversation. He also provided me with the name of the lady who is arranging his visit in the U.S. I am supposed to send her an email and if possible, set up a time to meet in New York on June 9 or 10.

To ensure that I had these three categories together, I made copies of the actual interviews that were transcribed at the end of the observation day from subfolder B2 and placed them in this folder.

Additionally, if there were some words or sentences that were spoken in English, then I wrote them down as they were spoken to maintain the originality of the conversation. These recordings were then translated into English after my arrival back to the United States, but the words in English remained highlighted. The sample in Table 11 reveals that as a researcher doing a cross-cultural study, I had apprehensions about collecting data on many levels from: addressing my participants, speaking in Hindi with them, relating the questions, interviewing them, to observing them on the field. The pre-interview was for listing my goals and concerns about conducting the interview; the post-interview was written to explain and clarify the doubts from the pre-interview and interview meetings, to reflect on the data gathered, and to write meaningful notes for later analysis. Also, in my interviews with other participants English words were highlighted and phrases or sentences referring to their literacy practices were bolded.

I followed the above procedure for all the other interviews. After each interview with the Dabbawalas, I would transcribe the recording (number each line in the margins) so that it would be ready for later translation, coding, and analysis.

Folder C: Field notes—video recordings, written observation, stimulated recall, and memos

I recorded the field notes in four ways and placed them in folders:

C1: Video recording and my intermittent observations and comments
C2: Written observation

C3: Stimulated recall interview (SRI) from the participants,[13] and
C4: Memos

Subfolder C1: Video recording and my intermittent observations and comments

As already explained, the Dabbawalas were videotaped on the field on all days they were observed, and the videos were viewed at the end of the day. Then, the whole day's events were written down and saved as Field Observations: Day 1, 2 and 3 and so on.

Subfolder C2: Written observations

While recording the Dabbawalas in the field, I also made comments on what I was observing, for instance: crowded streets or narrow pathways or raining heavily unable to record and audio turned on, and sometimes it would be, Dabbawalas climbing three sets of floors to deliver a lunch box; Dabbawalas having conversations in Gujarati or Hindi with clients, depending on the questions they were asked; how they greeted all their clients or discussed the weather like, *"Aaj barish bahut tej hai/ Bhari hai?* (Today the rain is pouring down rapidly/heavy?)."* Again, I wrote these observations at the end of the day into a chart as mentioned in Table 12 as *direct field observation, additional observation of the situation,* and *not sure (need clarification)—to be clarified as Stimulated Recall Interview (SRI).*

Column 1 consisted of a running account of events as I was observing the Dabbawalas performing an activity (such as getting into Vile Parle station—10:23 a.m.) or comments such as:

> The Dabbawalas are very polite and all of them are wearing topis (caps). Almost all of them are in white clothing. Yesterday's interview with Mr. Medge explains why they are in white. Already I can note the spirit of teamwork and discipline.

Column 2 consisted of notable short phrases or comments, as mentioned above, so that I was able to coordinate my notes with the video and audio recording (also usage of words such as stand outside, *"Bahar Khadayho"* and call another Dabbawala and inform him about space in a certain carriage like, *"Telephone lagao aur Bathaao ki train ka baxa khali*

Table 12. Field Observation and Writing Methods

Direct Field Observation	Additional observation of the situation and comments they make to each other	Not sure (need clarification)—SRI
Day 1: Ahilum getting into a train headed for Church Gate Day 2: Day 3:	*Bahar Kaday ho* (Hindi)—Stand outside on the steps when the train stops *Kutay? (Marathi)*	Why should one of the Dabbawalas stand outside when the train stops? For what? Why did the Dabbawala want to make a phone call and inform his colleague about space in the carriage 5; hasn't the Indian Railways allocated certain carriages for them?

hai"). I also noted any change that took place in audio or change in their routine, like when a Dabbawala would respond in a brisk, quick voice, *jee* (yes) to a question, or when they would respond to each other in Marathi (*kutay?*). Column 3 consisted of questions I wanted to ask the Dabbawalas the next day about their activity and comments they had made to each other or to their clients, etc.

Subfolder C3: Stimulated recall interviews (SRI)

After completing the first two columns from Table 12, if there were some incident or aspect of recording that needed clarification or observations, I was unsure of a comment, question, or practice, I used stimulated recall interview (SRI) the following day to seek clarification. For example, I was unsure why a Dabbawala would stand outside on the step when the train stops. The next day, when I questioned Ahilum, he explained that it is a way of communicating with other Dabbawalas about space in the compartment or other work-related information, similar to making a phone call.

I could only use audio to record their voices during *SRI*, as I had to replay the recordings using the camcorder from the previous day's observation, so that they could view the activity or comment requiring clarification. This ensured that my comments and their interpretations corresponded, rectifying discrepancies and misappropriation of contextual analysis.

Subfolder C4: Memos

After completing all the information in field information section, I wrote down memos, personal reflections or realizations with "aha" moments, right beneath it. These memos were based on continual internal dialogue that I was having with myself, bordering on data analysis (Heath & Street, 2008; Merriam, 1998; Strauss & Corbin, 1998). The main purpose to write down my reactions to situations, as I was observing the recordings, was I knew that I might be unable to recollect or feel these reactions later, especially after returning to the States. Comments included information about the day being productive, being fascinating, or even mind-boggling. These memos were written as the last piece of my work, similar to our daily journal, at the end of each day, and were to be read cumulatively along with my other data before I started my data analysis and coding. Table 13 showcases an example of a memo providing patterns and insights without modifying any of my feelings.

As I wrote down these memos at the end of each day, I realized that it became easier to pen down my thoughts and to see how the knowledge I was gaining would be useful for analysis and theory building for the findings chapter of my dissertation.

Folder D: Physical artifacts

As part of the data collection, I gathered some physical artifacts that supported my research questions, such as pictures of the Dabbawalas or a DVD that Mr. Medge provided me, which had information about the Dabbawalas' background and information about their supply-chain management. As the Dabbawalas refrain from using any physical artifacts other than dabbas or lunch boxes, I was unable to gather nor bring a physical lunch box with a script written on it, but I was able to take pictures. During my interview with Dr. Agrawal, he provided me with a small dabba or tiffin box as an example to use for my presentation. He

Table 13. Memos Reflecting the Day's Events

June 27: Memo

Intent: To reflect on today's activities and see what was important that
I observed and was noteworthy

Overview: Today was very productive, as I got five interviews completed. The
first one was with Mr. Medge, apparently he is now the ex-president of the Nutan
Mumbai Dabbawalas association, and his four-crew members. I was able to stick
to the questioning for the first one and then things changed as these people were
in the field and started conversing with me.

Patterns and insights:

Work being service oriented:

They are all very philosophical and talk about how they believe that being of
service is very important.

Interesting literacy practices:

- **Mind—CPU—GPS**—Remember, 40–50 addresses of clients in their heads;
  they commented that "people who are educated write, but people like us
  need to have a good memory" and "in some ways we are much smarter than
  others. No one can do this business as we do it. It takes a special kind of discipline, and this happens from only people coming from this ethnic group."

- **Role of education in their lives:** Keep reiterating that they are uneducated;
  when questioned, say they could not go to school. Their definition of education is a person who knows how to read, write and be successful ... *need
  to question them more on this.*

- **Role of next generation:** Some of them are being taught by their children
  to learn how to sign their names. Though they do not know how to read or
  write, they all recognize the English alphabet and can identify the codes.
  Some of them can sound out the letters and read English words. Chacha
  was amazing as I kept asking him to read words in English and put it
  together and he did.

- **Awareness of two or three languages:** Most of them know Hindi and
  Marathi alphabets and scripts though they have never been to school—*I see
  a gap here*—Reminds me of the Heath's ethnographic study and Vai literacy
  and how even a family friend can teach Vai and there is no certification
  needed to say, "You know Vai."

- **Role of Mr. Medge and how he developed the script:** Appears that Mr.
  Medge was the person who modified the present coding system; he seems
  to be very humble and uses a lot of similes and analogies to bring his point
  home. He has a Bachelor of Arts (B.A.) degree and has been in this business
  for close to 35 years. Learned everything from his father and grandfather.

NOTE: I have to remind myself that when I am coding, I have to fracture
the information, *otherwise I would be lost in rewriting all this information.*

also provided me a signed copy of his book, *Dabbawala of Mumbai: Masters of Supply Chain Management*. Also, the pictures I took were developed as artifacts and placed in the folder. These photos included Dabbawalas with celebrities, including the one with Prince Charles.

Folder E: Documents

In traditional qualitative research, data gathered from documents enable the researcher to repeatedly review the document and to use it to validate certain events, circumstances, or situations (Yin, 2009). Keeping this aspect in mind, I approached the Dabbawalas during face-to-face interview sessions and during focus group sessions, to see if they could share any physical document to showcase their literacy practices. Their response was that they avoid using paperwork, as all the transactions are followed up orally on the basis of trust. When I probed them further, one of them responded that once they establish a delivery service with a client, their immediate supervisor is informed about it and he in turn informs the head of the group, who records the information in his ledger (similar to an excel sheet but in notebook form). This information revealed that the Dabbawalas follow a centrally located ink-based database system; and although I was unable to view their ledgers, this was another way that the Dabbawalas used literacy to keep track of their clientele. They use ledgers—the old ink and pen method—documentation to facilitate their business practices although things have changed over the years.

When I questioned them about not signing contracts with their clients and having no paper documentation as proof for requiring their services, one of the senior Dabbawalas, who was aware of the legal system, explained, "Using paper documents is cumbersome and expensive, as we need to hire lawyers to write the legal document, and it also reflects that we are doubting our customers." He continued, "We have been in this business for a long time, and it is very rare to find a customer default on his payment. Even if they did, they will make the payment as soon as possible, as most of the customers are aware of the hardship involved in this business." Here, the hardship refers to the physical labor and weather conditions the Dabbawalas have to undergo every day to deliver the lunch boxes.

What was interesting was that senior members, like Mr. Medge, suggested that using paper does not make this a sustainable delivery model, as it becomes expensive. On the other hand, "it allows us to improve our thinking by using brain power, our CPU to retain information and helps in long term sustainable model—for the future generation" *(paper kay upayog se bahut din esa kaam nahin chalega; bahut karcha hotha hai hamare dhandhay mein. Is-say achha yeh hoga ki hum sab apni soch badayay aur apna dimaag kay CPU ki parivarthan kareke apne business ko aagay badayen—aagay ki pidi kay liyay).* This remark in particular suggested another unique practice of the Dabbawalas, involving paperless transactions based on trust and relying on memory, as opposed to having hard copies of all written documents between customers and Dabbawalas (although the head office maintains written records of all the clients). In some ways, these were characteristics of sustainable model with a philosophical approach (trusting another human being just based on what they utter). When I questioned them about it during SRI sessions, one of them said, "Didi, they trust us to carry their food from one place to another, don't they? This automatically means they have signed the contract. Developing clients also means trusting them and having faith in their integrity."

The Dabbawalas also mentioned that occasionally *they do use* paper pamphlets to convey an important message or to advertise their services to their customers or about raising the fees of the Dabbawalas or about holiday disruption of services, which they referred to as "when there will be no delivery service available." Usually, it is a one page 8 ½ × 11 inches (21.59 × 27.94 cm), or half a sheet with two to three scripts written on both sides of the paper, prepared by members in the main office and delivered to the local Dabbawalas through their supervisors. Keeping their clients in mind, the pamphlet has the same information repeated in three languages: Gujarati or Sindhi, Hindi, and English.

On June 26, one of the Dabbawalas gave me a pink memo they were placing in every lunch box, which revealed how the Dabbawalas use paper literacy to inform their clients about the upcoming rate and delivery changes. The Dabbawalas had received a physical document from the *Mandal*, or headquarters, to be placed in each tiffin box before

June 28, 2011. The document was titled "Appeal To Our Patrons," and explained why the Carrier Service is planning to raise the delivery charge by Rs. 50 = less than $1.00 beginning July 2011. The document stated that (1) due to "risk" (accidental traffic deaths) and "inconveniences" (weather) undertaken by these Dabbawalas on the roads and in the trains, and (2) due to "the high cost of living" and "non-availability of suitable persons for this kind of job," they intend to raise the "charges from the month of 1st July 2011 onwards." The document ended by thanking its patron. The front page of the script was completely in English, while the back was divided into two sections, top and bottom—half a page allocated to two languages, Marathi and Gujrati or Sindhi (I wasn't sure?), consisting of the English translation from the other side. As this came from the headquarters, the assumption was that someone who knew all three languages, including English, was writing this.

I asked some of the group members if they had read the pamphlet and their responses varied from: "It is the same information in three different languages, so we don't have to read all three" to "I read the Marathi one" or "I read the Gujarati one." One of them informed me that the script used on the back was Gujarati as I was unsure about the script. One of them said, "I read the English one" while another Dabbawala said, "My brother here let me know what the content was." One of the senior members commented that that he was glad this was being sent out "as we will be able to get our message across. After all, 50 Rupees might not be a big amount for some of our patrons, but it is for us." This document and some of the pictures from the DVD provided by Mr. Medge, corroborated the information about the Dabbawalas' literacy practices of being able to read in multiple languages. It also revealed how they use lunch boxes to communicate their concerns to their clients in effective ways.

At the end of all this data collection, I realized that I had accumulated lot of information/data material from approximately ten days of observation to transcribe and translate and to start the coding process. About three days before my journey was coming to an end, before returning to the United States, I asked the Dabbawalas three very specific questions:

- Would you be able to spare me sometime in the next few days for about one to two hours, so that I can showcase some parts of the video that need further clarification? Please give me a time, so that I can bring all the tapes along with me on that day (I made this request as I wanted to conduct the stimulated recall one more time and ensure that the information I had recorded and commented on aligned with their work and their interpretation of their work).
- Would I be able to call you and talk to you over the phone after my return to the United States and could you provide me with your phone number?
- If and when I visit you again, would you allow me to follow you during my next visit and not have any reservations about it?

The Dabbawalas consented to all my requests and were kind enough to let me know that they will help me in whatever way they can, so that I can succeed in my research. The day I asked them these questions, my daily reflective and subjective personal observation revealed:

I am getting tired of writing this every day and getting tired of asking myself the same question "How are they considered illiterates, when they have such a generous heart and want to help others?" (I should count the number of times I have asked the above question to myself– maybe use it as data— Haha!!). What is thought provoking is the comment Chacha made today with a smile, when I was about to leave, "*Jiyo aur sab ko jeenay kayliye sahayata karo, Namaste*" [14]—"Live and help others to live, Namaste!!" Also, why am I so emotional that this journey is coming to an end? Why did I cry in the car—back to the hotel today? I feel like I have a special bond with these people, unsure about it? The more I think about it, the more I feel there is some karmic karma that has brought me here to do this research.

How did every aspect of this research go like clockwork? When I look at the events that have happened in the past few weeks, I am amazed that everything had fallen into a schedule? Did all that planning help? Will I be able to share this with others?

If someone had provided me, an ethnographer who had conducted work like this, could I have saved a lot of time ... maybe? Well, it is a learning experience, but I will ensure that I will pass this along to others who want to do cross-cultural work. Although it is good to learn things on your own, I have realized that it really helps if someone provides you with a solid example to follow. I know I sound like my students. I used to get so annoyed when they would say, "Can you provide me with an example?" Now I feel like saying, "I wish I had an example to follow. A clear-cut method of seeing someone at work, gathering sources and showing how they got to collect nitty-gritty data in this type of study, could have certainly helped me. Maybe, mine is unique in that way; or maybe someone has done it and I have not been able to see it. But I have reviewed so many books, they all theorize, and it is like they are saying—you should do this, but none of them says, this is what I did. Maybe, I have not explored enough."

I have also added that "…maybe it is my fault, but I will share my experiences with others and say, 'These are the steps I followed and some of the mistakes I committed; now, you don't do that. So, follow this step or method.'"

Anyway, one thing is for sure, at the end of this journey, I want to provide all my peers down the road, a book that will showcase everything I did and wrote and followed, so that when they read my book, they will know what to do. I will also include these monologues, so that they know that they are not crazy to mull over thoughts like these. Isn't there a name for it—I think it is autoethnography? Need to include that in my data … ☺

Notes

1 The Dabbawalas hierarchy consists of the President (Mr. Medge) → Vice President → General Secretary → Treasurer → Directors (9) → group of 120 Dabbawalas, where each one is autonomous of the other. Each group in turn consists of four to eight teams working under them and each group consists of one Mukadam, who is responsible for five to eight Dabbawalas. This is very similar to the U.S. Government operations consisting of the President → Vice President → Secretary of State → Federal Chairman → House of Representatives → Congress and local legislators (governors representing each state) → mayors and group of councilmen.
2 As Yin (2009) suggests, as a single case study investigator, I had to think of myself as an independent investigator and not rely on a rigid formula to guide my inquiry (p. 74). Although I wanted to follow the other group on the train for replicating my data, I was not allowed to due to requests from higher powers (interview with Mr. Medge). I had to make intelligent decisions throughout my data collection process.
3 Dr. Agrawal's dissertation was on the Dabbawalas' management system (he provided me with pictures and his published book, *Dabbawala of Mumbai*).
4 Greg Brue (2002) refers to Six-Sigma "as hands on practice that gets results" (p. ix). The Six-Sigma story was developed and proven by Motorola in 1980s and defined as the need to create and operate a business model without defect and be error

free, "allowing only 3.4 defects per one million opportunities: products and ser-vices are nearly perfect (99.9997%). Eliminating defects eliminates dissatisfaction" (pp. ix–x).

5   Legitimate Peripheral participation refers to the process of how new members observe the older members in a given community, as apprentices or interns, to fol-low and emulate the seniors, that eventually, by virtue of practicing and following the leaders of their community, they achieve a level of mastery to become senior members themselves (Lave & Wenger, 1991).

6   *Crate*—it is like a wooden tray, usually having a dimension of, as a Dabbawala explained, "4 to 6 by 2 by 1–4 to 6 ft length × 2 ft wide × I ft depth. It is light yet sturdy for the Dabbawalas to carry the lunch boxes on their heads and easy to push it into the train during peak hours; it is also easy for them to stack one crate on top of another, if necessary.

7   It is interesting to observe that: (1) research inadvertently affected what the observer were trying to observe/achieve, and (2) the Dabbawalas efficient busi-ness practices made inefficient by researchers.

8   I am grateful to Mr. Yama, my taxi driver, who drove me around Mumbai; and at times, helped me with recording when I was with the participants during focus group discussions.

9   It is ironic that I made such comments, which I thought I would edit later but forgot to; what is intriguing about my comment is that I raise this question, "Why is my brain not functioning like the Dabbawalas'?" When I made that comment, I am unsure if I was associating it with their sense of direction or being able to maneuver through the crowds with their heavy loaded bags, or about their brain/ thinking being unique; this is not clear. Also, it reveals that I was an "illiterate" in their world, unable to function like the so-called "illiterate" Dabbawalas.

10 *Padhne, Likhne, aur Bolne/ ki yogyata—Saksharata means literacy.*

11 I used the words in English.

12 Using Gumperz (1958) *Conversational Analysis* I enclosed some of Mr. Medge's words in quotation marks like "Bhagwan ki marzi" to represent his emphasis of those exact words. Later he provides address specifications by providing informa-tion about the Dabbawalas education. Reiteration of words like "accha" or "Thik hai," which are very common words in India and basically indicating agreement or a way of listening and agreeing to the speaker—this is how I treated all the other interview data.

13 (Bloom, 1953, as cited in Calderhead, 1981).

14 Namaste—A salutation used in India that has a philosophical connotation and means, "I bow to the divine within you." Usually, people bring their hands together, bow or tilt their head forwards and greet the person across by wishing them, Namaste. Over the years, the bowing part has been reduced to a gentle nod and has become conversational like, Good day!!

References

Behar, R. (2003). Ethnography and the book that was lost. *Ethnography*, *4*(1), pp. 15–39. http://www.jstor.org/stable/24047800

Brue, G. (2002). *Six Sigma for Managers*. McGraw-Hill.

Calderhead, J. (1981). Stimulated Recall: A Method for Research on Teaching. *British Journal of Educational Psychology*, *51*(2), pp. 211–217. https://doi.org/10.1111/j.2044-8279.1981.tb02474.x

Emerson, R. M., Fretz, R. I., & Shaw, L. (1995). *Writing Ethnographic Fieldnotes*. The University of Chicago.

Fetterman, D. M. (1998). *Ethnography: Step-by-Step* (2nd ed.). Sage Publications.

Geertz, C. (1973). *The Interpretation of Cultures*. Basic Books.

Glenn, C. (2020). The language of rhetorical feminism, anchored in hope. *Open Linguistics*, *6*(1), pp. 334–343. https://doi.org/10.1515/opli-2020-0023

Goody, J., & Watt, I. (1963). The Consequences of Literacy. *Comparative Studies in Society and History*, *5*(3), pp. 304–345. http://www.jstor.org/stable/177651

Gumperz, J. (1958). Dialect Differences and Social Stratification in a North Indian Village. *American Anthropologist*, *60*, pp. 668–681.

Heath, S. B., & Street, B. (2008). *On Ethnography: Approaches to Language and Literacy Research*. Teachers College Press.

Lave, J., & Wenger, E. (1991). *Situated Learning: Legitimate Peripheral Participation*. Cambridge University Press. https://doi.org/10.1017/CBO9780511815355

Merriam, S. B. (1998). *Qualitative Research and Case Study Applications in Education*. Jossey-Bass.

Sanjek, R. (Ed.), (1990). *Fieldnotes: The Makings of Anthropology*. State University of New York Press.

Spinuzzi, C. (2010). Secret Sauce and Snake Oil: Writing Monthly Reports in a Highly Contingent Environment. *Written Communication*, *27*(4), pp. 363–409. https://doi.org/10.1177/0741088310380518

Strauss, A., & Corbin, J. (1998). Grounded Theory Methodology. In N. K. Denzin & Y. S. Lincoln (Eds.), *Strategies of qualitative inquiry*. Sage.

Van Maanen, J. (1988). Tales of the Field: On Writing Ethnography. In *Chicago guides to writing, editing, and publishing*. The University of Chicago Press.

Van Maanen, J. (2011). *Tales on the field: On writing ethnography*. University of Chicago Press.

Yin, R. K. (2009). *Case Study Research: Design and Methods* (4th ed.). Sage.

Part III

Develop

Decolonization is the process of deconstructing colonial ideologies of the superiority and privilege of Western thought and approaches. On the one hand, decolonization involves dismantling structures that perpetuate the status quo and addressing unbalanced power dynamics. On the other hand, decolonization involves valuing and revitalizing Indigenous knowledge and approaches and weeding out settler biases or assumptions that have impacted Indigenous ways of being.

—CULL ET AL. (2020)

In this section, I showcase how to unpack and develop all aspects of the field notes in a thoughtful manner, as longitudinal study notes. In this section, the audience will also be able to view the complexity and beauty behind coding. They will be able to recognize that simply coding and writing *are not* enough, as a researcher needs to cross-check every aspect of the field notes and ensure that ethical practices have been maintained—during and after coding. Further, I also share personal narratives of my joy at discovering information while analyzing the coded material, leading to findings and what Nabokov terms as *Upsilamba*.

Chapter Thirteen

Unpacking All Aspects of the Field Notes Including Transcribing and Translating

If you talk to a man in a language he understands, that goes to his head. If you talk to him in his language, that goes to his heart.

—Nelson Mandela

After my return back to the States, during the first week I sorted out all the materials and folders and rearranged them. I ensured all the IRB signed forms were filed in a proper way and numbered as participants signatures 1, 2, 3 and so on. I then developed all the photographs. All the documents in Hindi and other physical documents were assigned and placed in specific boxes for later coding. Thus, I had eight boxes labeled as:

1. IRB signed forms—copies
2. Observation field notes
3. Focus group discussion notes
4. Interview notes—All participants
5. Photographs and documents provided by the Dabbawalas
6. Video tapes

7. Memos—diaries
8. Secondary sources required for reference

This helped me immensely and my advice to all ethnographers is to follow a system/ organization that works for you, as organizing this massive data will help the researcher for decades to come. Over the years I have added few more boxes, transcription and translation, chapter rough drafts/reviews 1–5 and data rejected including dissertation copies.

Also, for those who are planning to conduct cross-cultural studies, it is important that candidates meet with their adviser to discuss their approach to transcribing and translating the data, as it helps in the transcription process and data coding. Ochs (1979) states that transcription is a "researcher's data" and it is a "selective process reflecting theoretical goals and definitions" of the researcher (p. 44). Interestingly, there is also an unstated view, in some literature, that transcription as a process is "theoretical, selective, interpretive and representational" (Davidson, 2009, p. 37). Further, research reveals that while transcribing information "researcher's make choices" and represent some actions in certain ways (Kvale, 1996, p. 37). Based on all the scholarly resources on transcribing materials, I had to make sure that I was being as objective as possible and not showcasing any bias while transcribing or translating the recordings. Also, for practical and theoretical purposes, I had to be selective about some aspects of my transcription. For example, although my recording showed that I walked in the pouring rain along with my participant for ten minutes in silence, I made a conscious decision not to write about the process of my walking for ten minutes, halting, crossing the road, then getting into the other side of the road as there was no need to refer to it in my data analysis. I would refer to it in the margin of my notes as:

- Walking 2:04 p.m.—2:14 p.m.,
- Train stopping 11:03–11:05 a.m., or
- Climbing staircase 3:04–3:10 p.m.

But if there were conversations or comments while walking, I would transcribe them as:

> Walking with … , 12:45–1:00 pm on narrow lane (greeted someone) *Namaste* or addressed a cab driver, *Bahut Barish hai bhaiya—gaddi dhire chalao! (too rainy brother, drive slowly!! He made the comment when the rainwater from the street splashed on us due to his fast driving)*

Such aspects enabled me to reauthenticate my transcriptions after my return to the United States. I had to diligently re-transcribe data from the videos and audio tapes of interviews, focus group discussion, and audio memos as accurately as possible. This was done for two reasons: (a) to carefully record even small details such as the train stopping at certain stations or passengers getting in and out, and (b) to ensure that words, phrases, or sentences were not missing in the transcripts, due to too many people occupying the compartment, or another train crossing, or an announcement on the PA. While writing the transcribing portion in Hindi, I would write on every other line of legal 8 ½ × 11 ¾ inches (21.59 × 29.85 cm) notepad so that if there were errors, I could correct them, similar to what I did when I was in Mumbai while working with the participants during stimulated recall.

Table 14. Example of Transcribing in the Notepad (Handwritten)

Date: June 29, 2011	Name: … . Category: Individual Interview—in the morning Time: 9:00 a.m.—9:30 a.m.
1	Namaste! Written in Hindi—आप मुझे अपने बिज़नेस के बारे में बता सकते हैं? (Aap mujhe apne business ke baare mein bata sak they hain?)
Dabbawala's response 2	हमारा बिज़नेस हमारे ग्राहक या कस्टमर को खाना/टिफ़िन देने का है!
Dabbawala's response 3	
Aap hamare saath chalengi?	

(continued)

Table 14. Continued

Date: June 29, 2011	Name: … . Category: Individual Interview—in the morning Time: 9:00 a.m.—9:30 a.m.
4	
5	
6	Had to skip question 2 as he said he follows the same routine like others.
7 He started sorting some boxes While talking to me	आप रोज क्या और कोन सी साक्षरता (पड़ने /लिखने) का उपयोग/इस्तेमाल करते हैं?? Aap roj kya aur konsi saaksharata (padne/likhne) ka upyog/istemaal karthey hain? आप मुझे "साक्षरता" की परिभाषा बता सकते हैं? Aap mujhe "saaksharata" ki paribhaasha bata sakte hain?

Table 15. Translation of the Above Example (Typed on the Computer)

Date: June 29, 2011	Name: … . Category: Individual Interview—in the morning Time: 9:00 a.m.—9:30 a.m.
	Namaste!
1	How would you describe your business? Can you tell/ talk/ discuss with me about your business?
response 2—Used English words—interesting to observe he uses or (ya) three times	Our business … is about delivering food or tiffin to our *grahak* or customers
3 Will you walk with us? 4	
5	

Table 15. Continued

Date: June 29, 2011	Name: … . Category: Individual Interview—in the morning Time: 9:00 a.m.—9:30 a.m.
6	Had to skip question 2 as he said he follows the same routine like others.
7 He started sorting some boxes while talking to me	What type of literacy tools (reading and writing) do you utilize every day? Can you define and explain literacy to me?

This also helped me to place numbers in the margins in a sequential fashion to corroborate certain categories with other forms of evidence (Krishnan, 2014). For example, in my second interview with one of the Dabbawalas, my notepad shows that the transcriptions and translations were kept together as a set, so that when I met with my committee I could showcase how I worked on them as a complete set.

Hindi language, translation, and code-switching: As my data collection was mostly conducted using the Hindi language, I needed to provide an explanation of how I transcribed and translated the information from Hindi to English, since any coding I constructed in English was dependent upon faithful interpretation from Hindi to English. Even before I started the coding process, I used Gumperz's (1982) approach for conversational analysis to transcribe and translate the data and for code-switching and contextualizing methods. I did this for two reasons as his study was mostly conducted in the northern part of India and was based on viewing the Hindi language and the different dialects used in that area. Also, his analysis of people using the Hindi language for rhetorical purposes and his analysis of people combining the regional dialects, village dialects, and standard Hindi in their daily life was very applicable for my study. This was especially useful in terms of how Dabbawalas used three dialects to converse among themselves, to interact with customers, and to carry out their administrative work. Further, sociolinguists Gumperz et al.

(1983) argue that sentences in Hindi can have a word order that is very flexible and can sometimes signal topicalization. This leads to emphasis being placed on certain words by the speaker based on "virtue of sentence position" (p. 32), making it impossible to directly translate Hindi to English.

Thus, based on their thematic approach and structure of how discourse progresses in Hindi conversations, I followed six code-switching functions:

1. Quotation marking by participants; for example:
   Humara Dhandha, "Business" Khana denay ka hai. (Our business is about delivering food.) The focus here is on *Dhandha* and how the Dabbawala stressed on the word *business* to categorically state that he is doing business and is not an employee.

2. Addressee specification; using the same sentence from above:
   Humara Dhandha, "Business" Khana denay ka hai. Here, the usage of the possessive noun *Hamara* (ours), symbolizes the whole group of Dabbawalas as being one group and outside members are being marked as *they*.
   Commentary: Pride in their business

3. Interjection; for example: *Aap hamarey saath chalengi?* (Will you walk with us?) Here, the Dabbawalas were surprised and not questioning me about my choice of walking with them the whole day and shadowing them.
   Commentary: Such expressions displayed that so far women had not ventured to follow them on their routes.

4. Reiteration: *Han! chacha ki baath sahi hay! Jaise chacha kah rahay thay, Kabhi kabhi bheed itni hoti hai ki humay aur thezi say kaam karna padta hai.* (Yes! What Chacha is saying is right/correct! Just like Chacha was saying, sometimes there is so much crowd that we are forced to work far more quickly.)
   Commentary: This repetition of the previous speaker's ideas is very common in Indian discourses, and it acts like a contextual reference, or segue to signal the development of new thought from the old one, and as a way to reiterate earlier thoughts.

5. Message qualification or tag question: *Ab apko samaj aaya ki hum itnay savery kaam kyon shuroo karthay hain? Samaj-gayeen na!* (Now do you understand why we start our work so early in the morning. You understood, right?)

   Commentary: Here, the Dabbawala was trying to make sense to me and wanted to make sure that I understood that the whole process of picking up and delivering lunch boxes is a whole day process and not just for a few hours. Here he qualifies his earlier remarks, by asking, "You understood, right?"

6. "Personalization versus objectivization" (Gumperez, 1982, p. 75): *Mein jaanta hoon ki Daftar mein kaam karne vale padhe likhay hotai hain, kyon ki vay college thak padhay hain aur in logon ko, angrezi padhna likhna aata hai.* (I realize that people working in offices are educated (can read and write) because they studied until/in college and know how to read and write in English.)

   Commentary: The Dabbawala was trying to objectify his personal observation and rationalize that education allows people to work in offices, along with the knowledge of reading and writing in English.

Such remarks and examples helped me to see why the Dabbawalas were self-justifying their literacy practices and in some ways providing rationale for thinking why they were considered *illiterates*. I have only provided a sampling of my translation here for the readers to showcase how contextualizing allowed me to stay as close as possible to the original meaning, knowing full well that "translation can never be exact" (Johnstone, 2008, p. 34). I mention this as there were times when it was impossible to directly translate Hindi to English due to the grammatical structure of each language and sentence construction being so different; the only thing that helped me to translate and transcribe the materials was keeping the context and situation in mind.

Further, ethnographic studies over the years reveal that translation involves a certain amount of interpretation. According to scholars in the field, the best way to remain close to the transcription under such circumstances is to adhere as closely as possible to the original meaning. For additional verification, it is better to have others proficient in the two (Hindi and English) languages to cross-check the work and certify that one has maintained the meaning and unity of the original structure. In my case, all the interview translations were studied and cross-checked using random sampling by two colleagues, one who taught Hindi to natives and one who taught Hindi to non-native speakers. I provided them the video and audio interview conversations and focus group discussion for them to see and hear. They would stop me at random and ask me about the transcription part on my notes, from the sets (Table 14) I had prepared based on the interview questions. I must mention here that the transcription also included information (placed in brackets like this) about certain body postures, emotions, pauses, or overlapping speech or conversations, voice modification, intonations, nail-biting, snoozing, singing, humming, monologues, and utterances. For example, my colleague chose one of the interviews from Set I with Chacha, one of the senior participants, from the collection of interviews and wanted me to play the video. While playing the video, he would stop me at random and request to see how I had translated the conversation or commentary. In another instance, while using a 50-minute recoding tape, he stopped the tape at 18.16 minutes, reviewed what I had written, then again continued to watch the tape till 18.18 minutes and correspondingly checked what I had written. There were times when both colleagues would rewind many parts of the video to listen to the Dabbawalas' dialect.

Given that these colleagues were teaching and involved in research, I was very grateful to them for patiently working with me, for a few weeks, to ensure that I had remained close to the original speech in my translation and transcription. If changes were necessary, they were suggested, such as replacing certain words or adding letters to words, like in the word *padhna*. I added the letter *h* to provide the stress in the sound *d* and modified my transcription. Once all the data had been reviewed, I started my coding process. What I didn't realize at that point was that this process was going to be truly time-consuming and exhausting, but it was worth every minute as it provided me with a strong basis for triangulation.

References

Davidson, C. (2009). Transcription: Imperatives for Qualitative Research. *International Journal of Qualitative Methods, 8*(2), pp. 35–52. https://doi.org/10.1177/16094069090 0800206

Ochs, E. (1979). Transcription as Theory. In E. Ochs & B. B. Schiefflin (Eds.), *Developmental Pragmatics*, pp. 43–72. Academic.

Gumperz, J. (1982). *Discourse Strategies*. Cambridge University Press.

Gumperz, J., Aulakh, G., & Kaltman, H. (1983). Thematic structure and progression in discourse. In J. Gumperz (Ed.), *Language and social identity* (Studies in interactional sociolinguistics, pp. 22–56). Cambridge University Press. https://doi.org/10.1017/CBO9780511620836.004

Johnstone, B. (2008). *Discourse Analysis*. Blackwell Publishing.

Krishnan, U. S. (2014). *A cross-cultural study of the literacy practices of the Dabbawalas: Towards a new understanding of nonmainstream literacy and its impact on successful business practices* [Doctoral dissertation, Kent State University].

OhioLINK Electronic Theses and Dissertations Center. http://rave.ohiolink.edu/etdc/view?acc_num=kent1416312472

Kvale, S. (1996) *Interview Views: An Introduction to Qualitative Research Interviewing*. Sage Publications.

Chapter Fourteen

Beginning of Coding (Fracturing and Reducing) from Data Dump to Data Saturation to Data Theorization

Clean code always looks like it was written by someone who cares.
—Robert C. Martin

One of the most stimulating aspects of an ethnographic case study or any study for that matter is the coding part. CNS would say, "If you are one of these people who loves to analyze and decipher patterns in anything and everything you see, then coding is your cup of tea. You will not only analyze for commonality but parse the data contents for anomalies, narratives, discourses, themes, philosophies, and the list goes on." The researcher after viewing all the data, in minute details, organizes and reorganizes them to place them in different categories to create a framework and build a theory around it. It is these microscopic evaluations that provide the macroscopic appearance. This reminds me of my photographer friend, who would suggest that it is the megapixels that allow the cameraman to zoom in or zoom out of a shot. Further, he explained that it is these pixels that allow him to decide what to focus on and frame, depending on the context or the situation, leading him "to showcase the smaller and larger picture and the nuances in between, and sometimes, even create the theme for the headlines in the newspaper." In some ways, the researcher's approach to the data collected and represented is like the cameraman trying to zoom in and out. It is how the megapixels are used to decide the angle to approach, then to organize, and then to build the theories that answer the research questions.

In addition, at this point it is important to make the decision about the approach the researcher wants to take to viewing the gathered data: should it be inductive or deductive? In an inductive approach or open coding, the researcher views the data material, analyses each aspect of the emerging information to see patterns to create smaller frames or codes and positions them appropriately—to fit the larger, already constructed, picture frame. While in deductive coding, the researcher first creates, rather predetermines, categories or codes and then reviews the data for information that aligns with the already created codes. Such as, if there a category created for "Dabbawalas literacy practices on the train" then I would try to find materials for that code from the assimilated data. While explaining this aspect to my students in an Argumentative Prose Class, a student suggested, "It is like the warrants we provide for a subtopic or paragraph in our argument paper. Both inductive and deductive have their pros and cons." I felt that for my case study, beginning with open coding or inductive approach was the best. I made this choice as there was so much rich data available for me to code that reviewing the materials to see categorizes was the best choice. As I started coding, my memo reflects my thoughts:

> There is something very intuitive about coding. I feel that there is a symbiotic relationship between the larger frame driving the smaller frames and vice versa, and this is the beauty of coding—one should be able to see and follow along. I am not struggling to see patterns—I feel they are speaking to me and emerging on their own. Someone would think I am crazy, but this is absolutely amazing!!

In many ways, using inductive and deductive coding is like constructing a house. The main plot is the whole house and would be considered the large frame. As my architect friend would say, sometimes based on the dimensions of the house we suggest different rooms or smaller

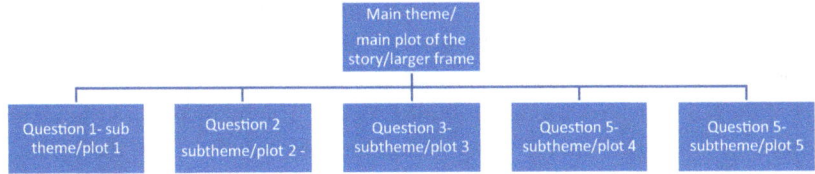

Figure 7. Hierarchical coding format.

frames to be built, "as it feels intuitive like inductive coding" but at times, there are customers who will dictate that they require "n" number of rooms with specific dimensions, very similar to what you consider as deductive.

Further, as Figure 7 reveals, I also chose a combination of hierarchical and flat codes, as I wanted see if the subplots related to each other and if I could place my data in different contexts and still create interconnections.

To be honest, once I had transcribed and translated all the data, I was still unsure how codes, in general, need to be properly constructed for theory building. This led to the realization that a good understanding of grounded theory is essential to developing theory. This led me to adopt the coding framework as suggested by Glasner and Strauss (1967), Strauss and Corbin (1990), Miles and Huberman (1994), Charmaz (2006), and Corbin and Strauss (2007) while completing my data analysis. Vollstedt and Rezat (2019)[1] provided a holistic definition of grounded theory that I referred to; they state:

> … There is no simple answer to this question as the term grounded theory adheres to different research elements. In the first place, grounded theory is a methodology, which is characterized by the iterative process and the interrelatedness of planning, data collection, data analysis, and theory development. Grounded theory further provides a particular set of systematic methods, which support abstraction from the data in order to develop a theory that is grounded in the empirical data. These methods include different coding procedures, which are based on the method of constant comparison. New data are gathered continuously, and new cases are included in the analysis based on their potential contribution to the further development and refinement of the evolving theory. This sampling method is called theoretical sampling. The iterative process of data collection according to theoretical

sampling, data analysis, and theory development is continued until new data do not contribute any longer to a substantial development of the theory, i.e. until theoretical saturation is achieved. The theory that is the product of this process is also referred to as grounded theory. The quality of a grounded theory is not evaluated according to the standard criteria of test theory, i.e. objectivity, reliability and validity, but according to criteria such as credibility, plausibility, and trustworthiness. (pp. 82–83)

Referring to scholarly work on grounded theory allowed me to focus on the research questions and data gathered from the field, rather than what type of action took place on the field that could be constructed into a theoretic model. I realized then that to construct a model, one must first begin with coding and placing all the data information into certain decipherable headings and subheadings (Figure 7). Strauss and Corbin (1990) refer to this aspect as *theoretical saturation,* and in my memo, I write:

I have exhausted all possibilities of viewing this data—Categories, sub-categories, sub-subcategories and more– I have exhausted viewing and reviewing every bit of this data that there is nothing left and I know new codes will not emerge out of it or that's what I think. I showed it to my adviser and his response was this is when you reach—saturation point!!I honestly feel like the data is like a large juicy lemon that has been squeezed out to the point that the skin has become dry. This has been an adventure in so many ways. I wish I could take pictures of my work to showcase it to my committee. What is fascinating is I started with inductive approach but looking back after all the coding, I can reverse it and make it deductive and looks like I will, when I start the second stage of coding as all my categories will be listed ...

Further, the strength of the grounded theory is that the coding emerges from the researcher's active and concentrated involvement in the process, allowing the researcher to stay focused on the data, and not rest their analysis on assumptions that prompted the study in the first place.
In other words, I felt that:

Coding is all about constructing a mechanism to reduce the corpus of collected data. It allows the researcher, you, to develop the best representation of collected data in a usable format; at the same time, coding allows you to retain and showcase the essential character and contributions of the participants, from the data collected in the form of primary research.

I specifically used this during my defense and was commended for summarizing the essential aspect of coding in any field.

Glaser and Strauss (1967; Glaser, 1999) refer to it as the breaking of data, where the researcher breaks the observation and other quantitative information into the smallest usable concept. Focusing on the data itself and reusing it to create thematic codes permits the researcher to see trends and patterns, from multiple data streams. Further, comparative analysis of data and replication allows the ethnographer to check and validate, "Is the fact a fact?" (p. 23). Charmaz (2006) argues that coding allows for a "move across" data of interviews and observations to "compare people's experiences, actions, and interpretations," leading the researcher to "condense the data and provide a handle on them" (p. 59). I must mention here that by the time I finished transcribing, translating, and coding, I had close to 6,600 pages of data, that had to be condensed to 200–250 pages or more for the dissertation.

Further, the purpose of coding was to move across data and systematically identify emerging themes related to literacy texts and tools that the Dabbawalas used every day during work and after work. As each datum could be assigned multiple codes, I started creating entries by using the following procedure: starter, open, axial, and selective codes.

Starter Codes

My first step to starter coding began with my reviewing the data methodically by creating an array of the different types of categorizations as showcased in Table 16.

The next step that I followed, after completing the categories mentioned in Table 16, was to take each one of the members I interviewed and list my conversation with them as shown in Table 17. As I couldn't list them in a horizontal way, I made it vertical as seen in Table 17. Further, once I had exhausted all the information and categorized them, I marked the last row as emergent literacy themes (Table 16) and used them to begin my open coding.

Once the initial inductive coding was completed, and once I had exhausted all the samplings, I started reviewing all the data again and

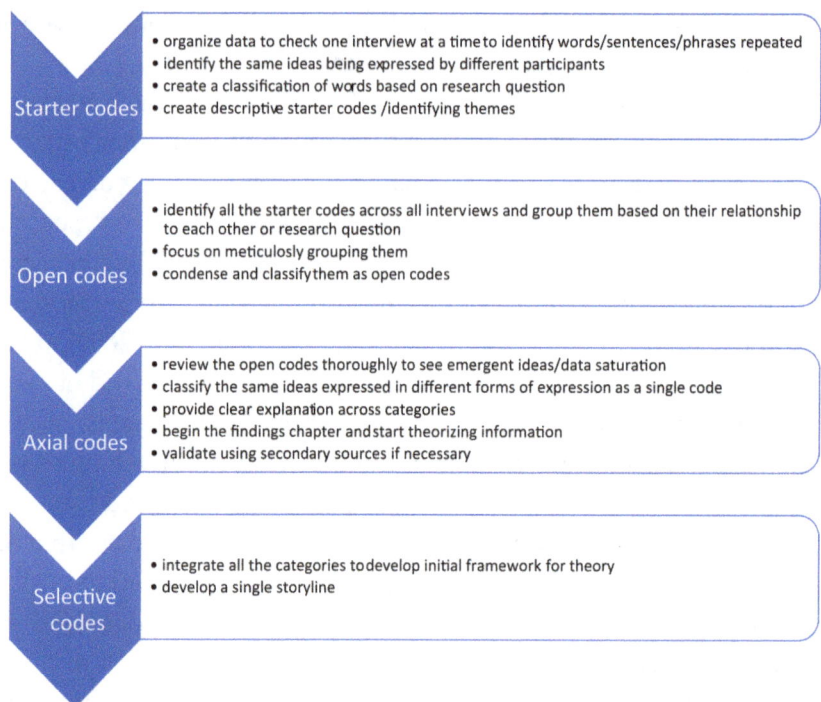

Figure 8. Grounded Theory Coding Process: Starter and open → axial → selective → formulating and writing theory.

started deductive methods to place them into descriptive starter codes based on my research questions about the literacy practices of the Dabbawalas (Miles & Huberman, 1994, pp. 56–58; Spinuzzi, 2010). By reviewing the interviews, focus group discussions, stimulated recalls, field observation, pamphlets and documents, I identified 56 categories related to literacy texts, tools, habits, and other references (languages they spoke, cultural habits, social behavior, and other recurrent actions) the Dabbawalas used or referred to in their lives. I used the same template for all participants and titled this folder as starter codes and labeled them by participants' last names or pseudonyms.

Table 16. Array Showing Methodical Categories

Data-Method	No. of Words Repeated	Sentence by Sentence-Ideas/ thoughts repetition	Paragraph by Paragraph	Emerging Literacy Themes	Important Information/ emergent liter-acy themes	Incomplete/ Complete
Interview with Mr. Medge—June 25/29, 2011						
Interview with Ahilum 25/26/27/28/29, 2011						
One-on-one						
Focus group						

Table 17. Organizing the Categories into Descriptive Starter Codes

Data-method	Interview with Mr. Medge—June 25 and 29, 2011	
No. of words repeated	GPS	Food Habits
	Memory	Knowledge
	Ethnic background	Routing
	Learning	Sharing
	Communication	Team Building
	Business	Health Issues
	Letters on the Dabbas	Texting
	English Words	Sensors
	Religion	FedEx
	Choices	Future of DBs
Line by line	Page 2—line 7 Important information referring to their literacy practice and their habits.	
	Page 3—line 18 Role of education in their lives	
	line 21 Who is an educated person according to the Dabbawalas?	
	Page 7—line 31 Revising the codes for all the Dabbawalas	
Sentence by Sentence		
	History	
	Mr. Medge's reference to their ethnic background and how Dabbawalas hire members from their ethnic group	
	Education and Dabbawalas lives—Schooling	
Paragraph by paragraph	Refer to second interview and the script he wrote in the restaurant for me—see the visual drawing	
	Page 21—Line 31–38 How he revised the codes so that all of them can understand and use it—*The color-coded script*	
Emerging literacy themes	Ethnic background and discipline	
	Education	
	Script and writing	
Incomplete/complete	*Interviews with Mr. Medge is complete and cross-checked for all descriptive codes*	

Open Codes

Once I had reduced all the data to 56 categories, I grouped them together again and condensed the 56 categories to 27 (Spinuzzi, 2010, pp. 397–399). By grouping them together, I was able to reduce the data and see the inter-related characteristics of what the Dabbawalas were trying to convey to me in terms of their understanding of their literacy practices and perceptions. For example, the first two codes in Table 18 (Starter codes and grouping into 56 categories) are: educated (reading and writing) and educated (awareness of English), and both codes relate to what the Dabbawalas identify as an "educated person." So, I grouped

Table 18. Starter Codes and Grouping into 56 Categories (Sample)

No.	Code	Description based on emerging themes	Example (line-by-line comments)
1.	Educated—reading and writing	People who work in offices are being classified as educated	"People who work in offices are educated (know reading and writing) but for us, our work provides us education."
2.	Educated—awareness of English	Assessing others based on their knowledge of English—reading and writing fluently	"Anyone who can read and write fluently and can converse with others in English." "People who can work in offices need to know English." "Well, even local newspaper journalists know English, though they write in Marathi."
3.	Speaking different languages, but not fluent in English	Assessing themselves—based on knowledge of three languages—Marathi, Sindhi and Gujarati	"I speak minimum three languages but know only a few English words and am not fluent in it like the people who work in offices."
4.	Habits related to literacy	Literacy related activity—reading papers while traveling	"I read the newspaper or magazine while I am traveling on the train. I also like to read short stories in Marathi."

(continued)

Table 18. Continued

No.	Code	Description based on emerging themes	Example (line-by-line comments)
5.	Tools that facilitate learning	Customers teach them new words to learn	"I have a customer who likes to teach me new words—he taught me the meaning of the word 'appreciate' as I delivered his food every day on time."
6.	Teamwork and learning	Learning from each other	"My young brother, who is in training, taught me the word 'delivery' on time."
7.	Ethnic background and influence on the business	Pride about their unique community and belief systems—discipline	"We belong to a specific community and have our own traditions. Our philosophy rests on serving others and this makes us disciplined as we have a goal, a purpose."
8.	Script and Writing	Outsiders view of their writing as codes and some letters and alphabets, but the Dabbawalas consider this to be similar to post office written address, but more cryptic	"You may think it is a simple script but what we use is what the post office uses. We are less wordy and more cryptic in our message."

them together as "Educated/literate person definition according to the Dabbawalas" in my axial coding.

The reduction of data from 56 categories to 27 (sample provided) in Table 19 revealed to me that coding is intuitive and when the researcher spends extensive time reviewing them, the easier it becomes to merge and group them.

As I continued coding, I realized that the open codes were "emergent and recursive" (Corbin & Strauss, 2008; Spinuzzi, 2010, p. 373) and were very useful for cross-comparison (triangulation) with the different data types. After completing open coding, I developed the axial coding, looking for the main emergent ideas/themes to group them together once again. Codes that appeared frequently were labeled as

Table 19. Open Codes Sample and Description (56 Categories Reduced to 27)

	Open code—27 categories	Description	Starter codes—56 categories
1.	Educated/literate person definition according to the Dabbawalas	The Dabbawalas are trying to compare themselves to the people working in offices and trying to measure the difference in work environment and economics. The role of literacy and importance of being proficient in English.	Educated person—"People who work in offices are educated (know reading and writing) but for us, our work provides us education." Awareness of English—"Anyone who can read and write fluently and can converse with others in English." "People who can work in offices need to know English." "Well, even local newspaper journalists know English, although they write in Marathi." "If I were educated in English, I would be doing a desk job."
2.	Reading	The Dabbawalas find reading the script to be easy and think that information on the lunch boxes should be concise and brief for an effective delivery. Comparing their codes to modern-day scanning, address location, and delivery	"The information on lunch boxes is simple, but enough to provide information to deliver the dabbas—Sentences are not required for delivery of actions." "I know how to read the scripts on the lunch boxes. It is pretty simple. It is all letters and numbers, like math." "I know addresses when I see them or when the customer tells me." "These days people use barcodes to scan and know the address, but they too have numbers and letters like we have. They don't have complete addresses."
3.	Writing	All of them know how to write scripts, and they are trained on the job to learn how to write and color code according to the station.	The written information on lunch boxes is simple, but enough to provide information to deliver the dabbas—Sentences are not required for delivery of actions Beauty (*Khoobi*) is you can learn it on the go and repeat it until you learn it thoroughly.

a single code to express the relationship among them and to represent a particular type of literacy text (oral or written), and as tools and acts performed by the Dabbawalas to execute an action.

Axial codes. Charmaz (2006) explains axial coding as a way of synthesizing the fractured data into a coherent whole (p. 60). She suggests that "axial coding relates all the sub-categories, specifies the properties and dimensions of a category, and reassembles the data you have fractured during the starter or open coding to give coherence to the emerging analysis" (p. 60). Strauss (1987) argues that axial coding provides the researcher a "dense structure of relationships around the 'axis' of a category" (p. 64). I created seven and later nine axial codes and provided specific descriptions for that code, so that each piece of data would fit one of the nine descriptions.

Referring to the grounded theorists and closely following their parameters to measure causal relationships and other categories helped me to see the connections in the axial codes. At one point, as I could not categorize some of the sentences or phrases into the seven categories I added two more categories that Lincoln and Guba (1985) refer to as "filling in" when the researcher finds that there are new insights emerging from the information that has been gathered. Finally, the nine axial codes (Table 20) led me to a fourth coding scheme—selective coding—that related all nine categories to one core category or findings and enabled me to narrate one single story that I explain later in the next chapter.

Table 20. Nine Axial Codes

1. Acquisition of literacy as a child—history and background—Causal conditions
2. Literacy and culture—ethnic community and their practices
3. Literacy and strategies used to be successful at their business
4. Literacy and business model—audience awareness—six-sigma achievement
5. Literacy and sustainability—business model—supply-chain management—service oriented
6. Literacy and mind-mapping—using the scripts to hone new skills—harnessing brain power—mind mapping to succeed in their business
7. Constructing or acquiring new literacy tools based on the actions and reactions from the society and clients/customers
8. Literacy and world recognition—consequence/s of their hard work
9. Literacy and Dabbawalas' future—outlook for themselves, their business, and their children in the future.

These categories provided me with the steps to construct an in-depth data analysis, and guided me in addressing my research questions: What are the literacy practices of the Dabbawalas (in general)? What type of literacies do they use in their daily lives to maintain their business practices? How and why do they write the scripts in English without being schooled in it; how do they interpret the codes (scripts written on the lunch boxes) and translate it in their minds? And although the Dabbawalas consider themselves literate, *they feel* others who observe them *think* they are illiterates. Why?

Further, what I realized was that the first three axial codes enabled me to understand some of the literacy practices the Dabbawalas follow in their daily lives and in their business. They attribute these literacies to habits they acquired at a young age, due to their traditional and cultural upbringing, and at times, to their social environment. The fourth and fifth axial codes enabled me to see how the Dabbawalas use specific literacy practices, from writing the address seen as cryptic codes by people (researchers, viewers on the train, members at large), to translating the addresses/codes, and to mind-mapping a route quickly and efficiently as strategies to maintain a successful business practice. The seventh and eighth code of acquiring new literacy and world recognition revealed the Dabbawalas' goal of satisfying their customers' needs and the extent they are willing to change, learn, and adapt to a given situation. The last axial code revealed the challenges the Dabbawalas face in terms of maintaining their business in the future and the steps they are taking to overcome such challenges, despite the society's assumptions about their illiteracy.

Note: I have provided in the following pages the axial code description only for the first one, the rest of the axial codes are in the tables (in brief) and provide information that reveal how patterns emerged from coding and categorization of information.

For the first axial code: **Acquisition of literacy as a child: history and background—casual conditions**, I reviewed all the data that related to the early literacy conditions of the Dabbawalas, such as not being able to go to school as children, the environment they were raised in, the school systems and economics pertinent to the city, family conditions, and cultural influences and placed all of these subject matters related to their past and background together in terms of acquiring certain types of literacy. Their comments showcased that they were all related to the social environment that the Dabbawalas grew up in and provided a rationale for why they joined their current business.

- "Did not study due to family situation."
- "Did not study as there were no schools."
- "Necessity made me come to this job and it is a business that has continued in our family—old tradition."
- "We followed mostly what our elders told us to do and came into this business. As you know, in our culture, we don't argue with the decisions made by elders in the household, we implicitly followed."

By using interpretive social science understanding of the situation, I was able to create meaning without assumptions (Charmaz, 2008) and categorize their comments as: (a) followed an ancient tradition; (b) needs and conditions induced certain practices; (c) denied opportunity and literacy. These references, causal conditions, when grouped together meant that environment, social circumstances, and literacy acquisition play a huge role in the way a person acquires and develops certain habits of reading and writing as a child (Brandt, 1998).

Table 21. Axial Code—Acquisition of Literacy and Sponsorship (Sample)

Axial code—acquisition of literacy	Interpretive social science with emphasis on creating meaning without assuming	Participants' comments
Causal conditions: *What led members of the Dabbawala community (within a family) to join this business?* Environment, social circumstances, and literacy acquisition play a huge role in the way a person acquires certain habits of reading and writing	Ancient tradition—business started by forefathers and so wanted to continue with it Necessity—due to family situations Denied opportunity and literacy development	Did not study due to family situation Did not study as there were no schools Necessity made me come to this job and it is a business that has continued in our family—old tradition We followed mostly what our elders told us to do and came into this business

Table 22. Axial Code—Literacy and Culture (Sample)

Axial code—literacy and culture	Interpretive social science with emphasis on creating meaning without assuming	Participants' comments
This section consisted of all the information related to the Dabbawalas ethnic background, habits, religious practices, traditions, literacy practices, and values that allow them to follow a certain routine and work together as a team. This shows—how in an ethnic community, members of a group help each other to succeed.	Varkari community—Family members of a certain ethnic community Unique members of this community Religion, an intrinsic part of their belief system and business—karma theory Reading Pothis—religious texts in their language	"Many people like our system, as they know the food they are eating has been made by their wife or mother or sister." "Coexisting as family—people who are traditional and conservative like the Jain people prefer this, as opposed to outside 'fast food.'" "People with diet or health restrictions prefer our delivery system." "Our ethnic group makes us who we are." "Our food and our God keep us going. We read scriptures at home or listen to religious discourses" "During certain times in a year, we all go to our village to celebrate religious functions and pay homage to our God, "Vittala" and read our pothis."

Table 23. Axial Code—Literacy and Strategies (Sample)

Axial code—literacy and strategies used to be successful at business	Interpretive social science with emphasis on creating meaning without assuming	Participants' comments
Being purposeful and goal oriented has enabled them to bring changes to their work and to their own literacy skills—becoming digital	Texts and tools used by the Dabbawalas, directly or indirectly, are based on the scripts, including the aspect of learning English—this is mainly done to help some of their customers and to build clientele.	"Our system is unique— We all know how to write addresses in English on Lunch boxes." "I speak minimum three languages, such as Marathi, Hindi and Gujarati." "Disciplined, Timely, conscious habits–do not drink or smoke during business hours or eat meat." "We deliver 30–40 lunch boxes sometimes. Do not take off from work unless very sick." "Our work is hard."
	Family is important but "Work is worship"; if customers want us to learn, then we will; therefore, learning to text through cell phone and learning English words.	"We are very strict about following our principles." "Delivering food on time is the most important job." "We visit our families back home when we have time, otherwise we work six days a week depending on customers' requests."

Table 23. Continued

Axial code—literacy and strategies used to be successful at business	Interpretive social science with emphasis on creating meaning without assuming	Participants' comments
		"Though we don't know English fluently, we can write alphabets and read simple words. Some in our group can read sentences and pages; and there are others who have studied till college."

Table 24. Axial Code—Literacy and Business Model (Sample)

Axial code—literacy and business model	Interpretive social science with emphasis on creating meaning without assuming	Participants' comments
Unique business model due to the setting of Mumbai city layout and due to the railways requiring a unique script; and thus, becoming non-replicable. Context of the business model not replicable due to Indian railways and ethnic background	*Not replicable* due to site location. Script cannot be replicated, as the stations and addresses are interrelated to the script being created a certain way. Their ethnic background helps them to undergo hardships—end result is that they deliver the food to hungry customers in different parts of society—on time.	"This business cannot be replicated as the railways and city layout is unique to the city of Mumbai." "Our Industry is about doing service—if our business was about profits, we would not be charging Rs. 500 per month." "Our customers depend on us about delivery of their food, which is a big responsibility—so we cannot drink or take breaks—we have to be goal oriented." "If you see, almost all of us are like that and the Gandhi topi really helps us in our work, reminding us that we are here for a purpose."

Table 25. Axial Code—Literacy and Mind-Mapping (Sample)

Axial code—literacy and mind-mapping of business routes	Interpretive social science with emphasis on creating meaning without assuming	Participants' comments
Script serving as a Mnemonic device	Six-sigma and how a business must be run based on low-cost, high efficiency, and cost sharing	"So far as there is a need for fresh food, our business will survive."
Role of the brain in decoding script		"Our memory is the most powerful aspect of our business."
Script also requires a certain type of reading and writing skills	Role of peripheral participation in terms of training on the job—why literacy manuals are not required	"Following certain routes and doing the same activity helps us in solving problems and do things effectively /efficiently."
	Literacy as being able to impart education and knowledge	"The addresses serve as memory devices to prompt us to go from point A to point B."
		"Based on the address on the lunch boxes, we plan our route."
	Role of memory—mental aptitude and development has nothing to do with literacy	"We plan and assign the route for all our Dabbawalas as we have to deliver food in a timely fashion."
	-Brain potential verses learning acumen	"The information on lunch boxes is simple but enough to provide information to deliver the dabbas—Sentences are not required for delivery of actions."
		"It is because the language is simple that I can teach 15–20 people—I can teach you and you will understand—communication and information is the key not writing like long sentences."
		"It is like calling someone on the telephone—we get the message and acquire new clients."

Table 25. Continued

Axial code—literacy and mind-mapping of business routes	Interpretive social science with emphasis on creating meaning without assuming	Participants' comments
	-Human Memory equivalent to a computer chip—role of language to initiate and execute commands -Sensory verses motor skills -Sustainable model for food industry	"Beauty (Khoobi) is you can learn and repeat it again and again till you learn it: -We use cell phones to acquire new business -I know addresses when I see them or when the customer tells me -Some customers SMS or email their addresses -Though we don't know English fluently, we can write alphabets and read simple words -Business helped us to learn a lot of words and due to meeting customers who want to teach us new words -Might be illiterate in education but not in work -We calculate mostly mentally our money matters." "Animals use their five senses to navigate to places—humans in America use GPS—we use memory." "What is unique about our memory is we are like the computer brain with a computer chip; it keeps things stored; when customers, after a few years call us, we know them and we go back as they were our old customers."

Table 26. Axial Code—Literacy and Limitations (Sample)

Axial code—literacy and limitations in terms of external conditions to their business	Interpretive social science with emphasis on creating meaning without assuming	Participants' comments
Decentralized form of work—team work Dabbawalas can create their own scripts based on customer calls They can't perform an action until they find a solution to their current problem "*Samasya aur suljav*" But *suljav*/solution is right there on the script	Location and direction—use outside resources to gather information and execute work.	"We ask others if we don't know the address and strangers/others will help us."
	Finding means for substitution and solution building when sick—intervening conditions allow them to think ahead of the problems and find solutions—teamwork and humanity	"If we are sick, we need to find a substitute immediately, otherwise the customer will suffer." And, in our team, we find others who will immediately take up the extra work to deliver food.
	Teamwork enables them to solve problems, thus there are no limitations per se due to lack of high school education or not being proficient in English	"Carrying heavy loads was a problem in the beginning, but we are now used to it as we have found ways and means to carry heavy loads. Now we have crates that can compactly accommodate lunch boxes. If it is a very heavy load, other Dabbawalas will immediately reach out and help us load quickly. We believe in teamwork."

Table 27 . Axial Code—Literacy and Constructing or Acquiring New Literacy (Sample)

Axial code—constructing or acquiring new literacy tools based on their actions/performance at work, as individuals and as team members, and based on the reactions of clients/customers	Interpretive social sciences with emphasis on creating meaning without assuming	Participants' comments
Strategies devised to manage, handle, carry out, respond to a phenomenon; under perceived conditions people can do things on their own, but why do they involve others and how? **Literacy is how you construct it and not what others say about you!**	Customers' wants and needs must be met; therefore, even if you have to learn something, learn it; it is part of business development—like software updates Philosophical outlook—sense of gratitude toward life. In terms of people commenting about their illiteracy—their reaction was: *Dabbawala padhna likhna apne mutabit say kartha hai. Log to bol thay rahengay ki hum unpad hain; tum bhi unpad ho sak thay ho par mehnat aur kamayee karna zaroori hai* "Dabbawala reads and writes as per his desire and limitations; people will keep saying, we are uneducated; you can be uneducated, too—but striving hard and earning a living is a must!"	"As standard of living has gone up, we would like to charge more but *customers will not like it—reaction of customer.*" "We believe in joint family—living together help all of us save on rent, food and cost of living—action performed by DB to sustain his lifestyle." "Action taken by DB—low-cost industry so helps in maintaining less cost—walking, bicycling, using train saves money and keeps you healthy—no obesity issues!" (Reacting to Customer's needs) "Customer is like God, and to please them we want to learn English." (Reacting to comments made by the others) "We feel we are better off than many people who are jobless."

(continued)

Table 27 Continued

Axial code—constructing or acquiring new literacy tools based on their actions/performance at work, as individuals and as team members, and based on the reactions of clients/customers	Interpretive social sciences with emphasis on creating meaning without assuming	Participants' comments
		"People say we are illiterate as we don't know English, but we are better off than many of them working in offices."
		Focus group members—"Some of us feel sad that although we do not interfere with other people's business, they call us names as illiterates -*unpad gawar!*"

Table 28. Axial Code—Literacy and World Recognition (Sample)

Axial code—literacy and recognition	Interpretive social sciences with emphasis on creating meaning without assuming	Participants' comments
What happens when they have achieved something?

Does recognition really matter? | Noteworthy Recognition

Proud of their work

Lead examples of logistics and supply-chain management—play hard | "Only rarely I wish I was doing something else on days when it is very hot or raining heavily or when sick."

"We are proud that our business is getting recognition."

"We never thought this job would get us recognition; after all we are into delivery business." |

Table 28. Continued

Axial code—literacy and recognition	Interpretive social sciences with emphasis on creating meaning without assuming	Participants' comments
		"It is all about learning the job and executing it properly based on the information provided on the lunch boxes and also about having a good team to work with."

Table 29. Axial Code—Literacy and Dabbawalas' Future Outlook (Sample)

Axial code—literacy and Dabbawalas' future outlook	Interpretive social science with emphasis on creating meaning without assuming	Participants' comments
Children's education is important as they need to survive in the global world—increase in literacy rates Health literacy—food and sustainability	Preparing children for the digital age Literacy is empowering, but our business is the best model—it is empowering in terms of providing food for long-term living—*sustainable healthy living* Fast food might be great for present generation, but so far as there is a need to eat a healthy home prepared meal; we will survive	"Children are studying English, Hindi, Marathi, and few other languages." "How would you define literacy? People who work in offices are educated (know reading and writing) but for us our work provides us education." "Literacy is empowering, but our business is the best model—it is empowering in terms of providing food for long term living—*sustainable healthy living*." "Fast food might be great for present generation, but so far as there is a need to eat a healthy home prepared meal; we will survive."

Axial to selective coding. After completing the nine axial coding and writing about it, I still felt that I didn't have one cohesive statement that could amalgamate all the data I had collected, and this led me to the final selective coding. This coding involves the integration of the categories that have been developed so far to form the final theoretical framework. This is also the last step in grounded theory and is like creating a thesis after all the research work has been completed. As Strauss and Corbin (1990) suggest, "The core category must be the sun, standing in orderly systematic relationship to its planets" (p. 124). They suggest that selective coding is like developing a single-story line, where all other categories aid in developing the initial theoretical framework; selective coding, as discussed in the next chapter, is about finding the driver of the story.

Note

1 Kaiser and Presmeg (Editors) Compendium for Early Career Researchers in Mathematical Education. Springer Open access https://link.springer.com/book/10.1007%2F978-3-030-15636-7; Part of the ICME-13 monograph book series.

References

Brandt, D. (1998). Sponsors of literacy. *College Composition and Communication, 49*(2), pp. 165–185.

Charmaz, K. (2006). *Constructing Grounded Theory. A Practical Guide Through Qualitative Analysis.* Sage Publishing.

Charmaz, K. (2008). Constructionism and the Grounded Theory Method. In J.-A. Holstein, & J.-F. Gubrium (Eds.), *Handbook of Constructionist Research,* pp. 397–412. Guilford.

Corbin, J., & Strauss, A. (2007). *Basics of Qualitative Research: Techniques and Procedures for Developing Grounded Theory* (4th ed.). Sage Publishing.

Corbin, J., & Strauss, A. (2008). *Basics of Qualitative Research: Techniques and Procedures for Developing Grounded Theory.* Sage.

Corbin, J., & Strauss, A. (2015). *Basics of Qualitative Research: Techniques and Procedures for Developing Grounded Theory* (4th ed.). Sage Publishing.

Glaser, B. (1978). *Theoretical Sensitivity: Advances in the Methodology of Grounded Theory.* Sociology Press.

Glaser, B. G. (1999). Keynote address from the fourth annual qualitative health research conference. *Qualitative Health Research, 9*(6), pp. 836–845.

Glaser, B., & Strauss, A. (1967). *The Discovery of Grounded Theory: Strategies for Qualitative Research*. Sociology Press.

Lincoln, Y. S., & Guba, E. G., (1985). *Naturalistic Inquiry*. Sage Publications.

Miles, M. B., & Huberman, A. M. (1994). *Qualitative Data Analysis*. Sage Publications.

Spinuzzi, C. (2010). Secret Sauce and Snake Oil: Writing Monthly Reports in a Highly Contingent Environment. *Written Communication, 27*(4), pp. 363–409. https://doi.org/10.1177/0741088310380518

Strauss, A. (1987). *Qualitative Analysis for Social Scientists*. Cambridge University Press.

Strauss, A., & Corbin, J. M. (1990). *Basics of Qualitative Research: Grounded Theory Procedures and Techniques*. Sage Publications.

Vollstedt, M., & Rezat, S. (2019). An Introduction to Grounded Theory with a Special Focus on Axial Coding and the Coding Paradigm. In G. Kaiser & N. Presmeg (Eds.), *Compendium for early career researchers in mathematics education*. ICME-13 Monographs. Springer. https://doi.org/10.1007/978-3-030-15636-7_4

Chapter Fifteen

Recognizing the Complexity and Beauty in Coding Through Personal Memos and Overcoming Frustration

Rhetorical feminism employs and respects vernaculars and experiences, recognizing them as sources of knowledge. And rhetorical feminism also shows us ways to reshape the rhetorical appeals, including a reshaped logos based on dialogue and understanding, a reshaped ethos rooted in experience, and a reshaped pathos that values emotion.
—Cheryl Glenn

When I started writing this book, I went back to reviewing all my data including personal memos and journal to see what my thoughts were before, during, and after my visits to Mumbai, India. To this day, I have a habit of writing journals and expressing my thoughts on paper at the end of the day, as my friends call it, "an act of feminism" but for me, they are "sources of knowledge" (Glenn, 2018, p. 4). They vary from a few lines to few pages, depending on my experiences on that day. But what is interesting is that all my writing few months prior to my journey to Mumbai, during, and after my return to United States are quite lengthy and reveal my thoughts in great details. They express my feelings ranging from amazement to vexation to restlessness to confidence. While reading them recently, these memos generated such emotions that I felt I was reliving my visit, similar to viewing a photograph that brings back deja vu memories.

I am providing this information as personal notes play a very important role in an ethnographic study (as already mentioned in the data collection section). Miles and Huberman (1994) refer to it as "fodder for deeper reflection" as they strengthen coding and they point toward the "underlying issues that deserve analytical attention" (p. 66). Sadly, it is often overlooked as being subjective and often neglected, instead of researchers capitalizing on this type of natural reflective data (Clarke, 2005). Glaser (1978) argues that it preserves the ideas of that moment, which might be lost otherwise. For example, on June 28, 2011, I write:

> *Overview*: Today was a mind-boggling day as I witnessed the Dabbawalas writing new scripts *in front of me* based on just phone calls they had received during the day.
>
> *What an experience*!! This is the opportunity I had been waiting for to show the groups' literacy practices. It reveals not only team collaboration, but also the type of writing the Dabbawalas use to facilitate their business.
>
> *Patterns:* All three Dabbawalas wrote the script with basic information being that was given to them by Ahilum, their supervisor. They were aware of what needs to be written and where, without details being provided by Ahilum. There was no paperwork to be followed or directions to refer—to write the new addresses. They manipulated the script based on just three different phone calls.
>
> *Insight:* What does this mean for me in terms of my research?
>
> *It is clear that this business model is decentralized where the Dabbawalas can acquire new customers, change old orders, change routes, and manipulate the script to facilitate delivery.*

In another incident, when I had just started my initial starter codes, my journal reflects what I was feeling, as I felt it was a time-consuming process and I question my dedication to my study:

> *2/14/12—This is nightmarish!! I am going crazy. I have completed coding information from scripts from only two participants and it has already taken me twelve days, and I have not completed my work. I am restless and having sleepless nights and my acid reflux has increased. I am physically feeling ill thinking of how long this will take. At this rate, I am unsure if I will be able to even complete all this work in one*

year. I know I will soon get into a panic mode as I have hundreds of pages to interpret. Ridiculous that I have reviewed only 51 pages of these copious notes!!

BUT, on another note, I am loving this aspect of my research and recognizing that this is very time consuming. I am fascinated as I can see something but unsure. Having mixed feelings about this; did I do the right thing by taking on this journey. Preaching is easy but practicing is difficult with life constantly throwing curve balls at you. (Mei poori pagal hoon—I am fully mad!!)

Did I do the right thing to take on this project!! I am also emotional about the Dabbawalas. They work so hard in the heat and rain. Reading all that they shared with me is making me emotional. They are an amazing group of people—dedicated, good, kind, and service oriented. Will I be able to represent them properly? Why is this coding so hard? Now that I have visited them over the years, they feel comfortable to talk to me about their personal issues. I wish I could help them more. I don't know! I don't know; how?

2/16/12—Going for a walk really helped me, as I was able to mull over my work and see the bigger picture, but ...

... I love Charmaz and I am so glad I read these guys on grounded theory. OMG, I am so happy that I read Clarke as memoing is considered to be an intellectual capital ... I don't feel I have any capital now—while I am writing this. I feel dull-witted!! Will I ever be able to see what these scholars are saying as selective coding and stream-lining ideas; looks like this isn't happening for years to come—the way I am going!! I am lost in this maze and there seems to be no one to help me. My inner self says, "Be methodical." Even speaking with dad is NOT helping me. Dad and mom always act as my anchor, but this is not helping. I have not spent any time with kids. Sk feels that I am neglecting everything and wants me to take time away from this. IS he having hubby syndrome? Does anyone understand what I am undergoing? There is a tornado brewing within me. I feel I don't have time for anyone and want to get this done. I don't even feel like teaching. A job that I love to do. Maybe cooking will help. I feel down and my head hurts.

Gerry (my colleague) said jokingly today that if I want to commit suicide, I better leave a note and blame myself as being responsible for my actions; she said I am crazy to teach five courses, write my dissertation, and take care of my family; looks like everyone can see my listlessness. She suggested that I take a break from work for a few days. That was nice of her. I want to take a break from everything and just focus on coding but life and duties????Sometimes, I feel this everyday routine is overrated. No wonder the sages in India went to the mountains to retreat. I might just do that one of these days—tired!! I am so tired that I feel every bone, no, no, every cell in my body hurts.

What such paragraphs reveal are many aspects that I would term as "researcher's chagrined moments." On one side, I felt this love for coding and on the other, there was this realization and feeling about lack of time, frustration of failing in terms of completing daily tasks, disassociation with work and family, and increasing health issues due to stress. All these were stemming from not knowing if I was headed in the right direction in terms of coding and the feeling of despair that "no one can help at that point." Over the years, I have joked about Gerry's comments and assured many graduate students that they are not alone in feeling frustrated or feeling like a failure in their attempts, but I always assure them that help is only an email or phone call away.

One thing that needs to be stressed in graduate programs is the need for graduate counselors, who can work with the candidate/researcher before and during qualifying exams and while writing the dissertation. I have talked to many such students and realized that it really helps them to share their concerns, discuss their work, and showcase their progress to someone who can help them in their journey; sometimes, they say, "It just helps to talk about our frustration about the whole process with ourselves and with others." My suggestion to all of them is to seek help from people within or outside the program, who are supportive and willing to listen to their issues and help them on some level/s.

Contrary to this memo, there is another memo that was written at the end of all the coding, which appears to be very jubilant and has seeds sown of writing a book down the road.

1/28/13 -Today, I am so happy that I really understand what it means to "be jumping with joy." What all these scholars have been saying is true. I LOVE CODING! LOVE CODING!! LOVE CODING!!! I completed the selective coding today and (OMG) I can see that it is all coming together.

One year!!Close to one year of just coding!!! One year of work on just this process!!! Will people think I am crazy if I say this! Do people really spend that much time on coding? My God—I am glad I didn't give up, although last year this time, I was frustrated and ready to throw in the towel!! I vividly remember meeting with Huot, as it was such a disaster, and I was so close to arguing with him, which I have never done before, … and inform him that he should have never encouraged me to take on this monumental, voluminous task …

1/28/12: Looking back from the journal entry from last year:

I was in tears today as my advisor returned my methodology section, the first draft, saying it was a "data dump and nothing made sense." What bothers me even more was it was all in red and green!! He has never done that—did I really give him just raw data?? He is not providing any clear solution but wants me to work on coding but how? If he shows me one sample, I will be able to comprehend the coding process. Also, I don't understand his handwriting, not that I don't scribble. I am very frustrated and unable to organize this data to make sense out of it. There is so much to discern. How do I go through these 4000 or 5000pages or more? I don't want to even see the page numbers as I am scared. They are voluminous; did I REALLY write and type out all of them. WOW! I need to admire my patience and work, but I don't feel anything close to that. I think all these notes are my contribution to the Dabbawalas and their work, but will I be able to showcase them in proper light? What if I don't? What if I become too clinical? What if I don't know how to code?

Just saying "work at it and organize it"—doesn't help. I really wish there are people to guide during coding process. He is very supportive but … I am unsure. The fault is all mine. Really! I don't think I can blame anyone but myself.

Today, I called home. Thank you, dad, for keeping me on course and talking to me. Mom, I don't know how to thank you for all your prayers and encouragement. Love you both; if I ever write a book, it sure will be dedicated to both of you!!

Close to one year later:

1/21/13 Something interesting—What I recognize is that these researchers are truly scholars and they have proved that this coding is very streamlined, and one has to keep at it like a woodpecker. Glaser and Strauss, Bless you! Charmaz, Glenn, and Spinuzzi, you guys are all genius as far as I am concerned. I am just so grateful and thankful, as you filled me with hope. What is clear is that as a researcher, one needs to be patient while working with the starter codes and then the rest follows easily. I will write this in my book. ☺

… Whenever that happens and if it happens … Ha, I have not finished my dissertation but thinking about my book. What wild imagination I have—Reminds me of Beetles—they may say I am dreamer, but I am not the only one. I hope someday you can join us … imagine … What I also realize is that maybe sometimes talking to someone, a peer or mentor, helps in the long run but why do we not have people that we can talk to when we are direly in need of just consulting … especially in grad school … maybe they should have one-on-one consultation or workshops to help people like me write, as we are not traditional students.

2/1/13—Wow—this is what they mean by reducing data from 6,600 pages (references not included) to close to 660 pages! My advisor saw the typed pages from page 1 to 660 and there was a smile and a sense of disbelief that I had reduced and condensed the data…His suggestion was that I reduce it further to about 50–60 pages. At this point, I need to be focused on one thing and that is my writing. I am celebrating today for sure as it is also Nims, my little son's birthday.

The above memos reveal contradictory emotions mainly due to what I was facing as a researcher. Sometimes having such moments—a sense of achievement and exhaustion combined with annoyance and admiration for coding, and a sense of anxiety and calmness combined with the level and lack of commitment—can change the course of path for researchers as they get depressed and decide to stop working on their seminal work. In the memo, there is also a sense of how others should not undergo what I underwent and how help should be provided to graduate students in ways that will help them to stay on course. I showcase how holding workshops help students voice their issues, form/develop writing groups, and seek graduate mentors, an idea that could be implemented across graduate schools.

Overcoming Frustration While Coding

In 2013, during another one of my visits to India, I was frustrated that I was not progressing with my coding and went to meet one of my spiritual gurus as he was giving a lecture on life and philosophy. I refer to it here as it made so much sense to me then and even now. He referred to life as a journey and suggested: "… while pursuing truth and transcendental liberation, one needs to stop at times to look at the larger picture and then pause for some time; then, again, get back on to the course we are pursuing. Stopping and viewing the bigger picture, reaffirms our goal and motivates us to continue walking on our path. Remember what Gandhiji said about the future being dependent on what you do today." Interestingly, his suggestion motivated me to continue working on my coding. I went back to the drawing board and asked myself, why was I frustrated and why did I want to pursue this journey in the first place? I also went back to meeting my participants, and Ahilum made a comment that stuck me, "Didi, our business will never grow if we were to stop and think about the weather, about the rain or wind, we just keep walking and doing our job, things fall into place." This really stuck a chord in me and after my return to the States., I committed myself to doing just that "Keep walking" and "let things fall into place." Also, viewing my research questions gave me hope that I will find answers to my questions at the end of my coding. Somehow what Ahilum said also made me think of pregnancy and childbirth, and how a pregnant woman undergoes changes on so many levels and continues to live her life, despite all the inconveniences, just to see her child being born. I felt that my study was also like that, and I must undergo some or many inconveniences and trepidation to see my research findings being born.

A few years later, after I had completed my dissertation and won the Toerne Outstanding Dissertation Award from Kent State University, and received Honorable Mention, James Berlin Outstanding Dissertation Award from Conference on College of Composition and Communication, I was asked to conduct a workshop at Kent State for nontraditional graduate and doctoral students consisting of married, pregnant, and women in their late forties, who were working on research and coding. What I didn't realize then was that using my earlier pregnancy analogy would make a lot of sense to my audience, as one of the graduates, mother of three children, emailed me to say that I should refer to this analogy in workshops that I conduct henceforth, especially when it consists of nontraditional students:

> When frustrated and you are at the tip of giving up everything, literally you feel this is the last straw, STOP!! Go back and review all the work you have done and accomplished over the years. Look at the bigger picture. Get a perspective of why you wanted to pursue this in the first place and why you need to get back on course. Think of yourself as a pregnant woman giving birth to a child. When you see the baby, you forget all that you suffered while being pregnant including the labor pains. The child brings you so much joy that you feel all the previous months of pain were worth it—to see that bundle of joy in your life. This is the same euphoria you feel on the day you complete your dissertation and prepare for your defense. Unless it is impossible to continue due to certain extenuating circumstances, get back and commit yourself—but this time—200% to reach your goal.

After the workshop, the email I received from April:

> Uma, Thank you so much for your talk today. It really helped me as I was close to giving up on my work as I have been feeling overwhelmed, mainly due to all the life commitments—family, home, work pressure and teaching. I felt that I just didn't have it in me to continue. You showed me that there is

meaning to what we do. Looking at the big picture and analogy of giving birth to a child was classic. I have new hope, and believe me, I am now 200% committed. Just wanted to send a quick note to say, "Thank you."

And, also, please use this analogy in all workshops you conduct, especially when you have students like me, nontraditional mothers, often out of place in all these classes, and trying our best to compete with these young grads ...

Another colleague few days later, mother of two, hugged me in the corridor and said, "Thank you!! Childbirth analogy worked—you nailed it, 200% commitment has given me a newfound understanding—I love it!! I am back on track!!"

References

Clarke, A. (2005). *Situational Analysis: Grounded Theory After the Postmodern Turn.* Sage Publications.

Glenn, C. (2018). *Rhetorical Feminism and This Thing Called Hope.* Southern Illinois University Press.

Glaser, B. G. (1978). *Theoretical Sensitivity: Advances in the Methodology of Grounded Theory.* Sociology Press.

Miles, M. B., & Huberman, A. M. (1994). *Qualitative Data Analysis*: An expanded sourcebook. Sage Publications .

Chapter Sixteen

Cross-checking and Ensuring Ethical Practices: Triangulation and New Discovery—Triangle Becomes Cyclical

… our research should illuminate and enhance our practical wisdom, and our disciplinarity should be guided by the complexity of our subject rather than the limits of a small range of method.

—Charles Bazerman

The memos from the previous section showcase that they were subjective and personal, representing one set of data that focused on the internal feelings that a researcher undergoes when dealing with a situation that is beyond one's control. The question then arises, how does one use the memo for comparative analysis and yet remain objective in data representation. Behar (1996) refers to it as a dilemma that ethnographers face while transcribing, coding, and writing about their data findings. By referring to Geertz (2000) and the dilemma he faced as an ethnographer, Behar draws attention to three questions: what should an ethnographer do under such circumstances, should they become clinical and not use the data, or should they add it as observation of a vulnerable observers to the data pile and see how the world will read their text?

She states:

> But just how public an activity is the work of the anthropologist? Yes, we go and talk to people. Some of these people even have the patience and kindness and generosity to talk to us. We try to listen well. We write field notes about all the things we've misunderstood, all the things … will seem so trivial, so much the bare surface of life. And then, it is time to pack our suitcases and return home. And so begins our work, our hardest work—to bring the ethnographic moment back, to resurrect it, to communicate the distance, which too quickly starts to feel like an abyss, between what we saw and heard and our inability, finally, to do justice to it in our representation … we lack the language to articulate what takes place when we are in fact at work. There seems to be a genre missing. (p. 117)

What Behar suggests was true in my case. Although the data I had collected was well organized, I was unsure at the beginning on how to interpret the data I had brought home, and I was unsure about how to include the memos in my theory development. What I realized was that being an ethnographer and writing memos works to one's advantage. Interestingly, while unpacking the gathered data, the researcher views all the material as an objective observer yet thinks like a subjective participant (emic and etic perspectives). The question then arises, how can this be possible—to be objective yet subjective at the same time? Is it possible? My response based on my work is "it is possible and necessary," especially when you are observing ethnic groups like the Dabbawalas, and the best way to walk on both sides of the fence is to use the triangulation process.

The triangulation process consists of three aspects: the observer, observed and observation. These three parts keep us centered on the context and subject matter that is central to our work.

Triangulation as a method *creates an opportunity for the observed to correct the observer on their observation. At that point, the triangulation becomes a cyclical process and becomes authentic or real; a process every ethnographer or researcher should aim for and achieve. Role reversal between the observer and observed dissolves many of the uncertainties, and thus, the data that emerges is true and closely resembles the observation and interpretation.*

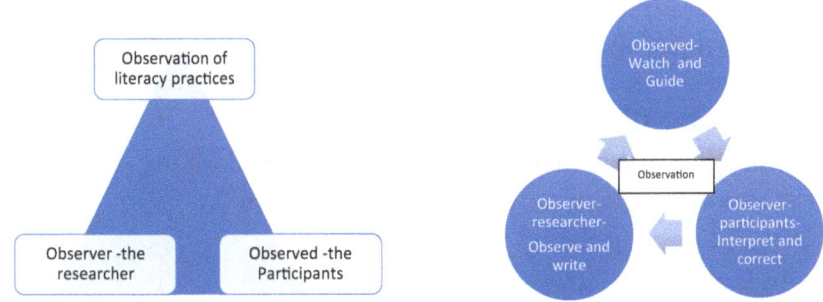

Figure 9. Ethnographic texts and interpretation: Process of triangulation and cyclical writing.

In addition, this type of three-way association provides an ethnographer tool/s for real time interpretations and cross-examination leading to findings that are valuable resource materials not just for one field but across many fields. Triangulation across datatypes for this research was based on: (1) what I had observed as a researcher and written, (2) how my observation or viewing of the participants and their actions taking place in real time—was also being observed back by the participants (how I viewed the Dabbawalas and how they viewed me), and (3) how the observed-participants were correcting the observer-researcher. It is the symbiotic observation that enables the data information to remain *objective* as the observations made by the researcher are cross-checked for correct interpretation by the observer-participants through the process of stimulated recall. Thus, the observer's research work and observation of the participants changes during stimulated recall, as he or she becomes the observed—a participant in front of the participants; there is a gentle role reversal as the participants watch, interpret, correct the researcher's work, making the triangulation a cyclical process. This continues till all the data streams have been checked: across participants, across data types and incidents, and across different actions taking place during certain times of the day. On the other hand, the observer by using personal memos interprets the observation for his or her personal use, which in turn provides the observer-researcher a subjective interpretation, an opportunity to relive certain aspects of what was observed to be able to write about it later, as viewed in the previous chapter. The cyclical process, as show-cased in Figure 9, consisted of:

Observation (Data Collected)
- Being in the field with my participants and taking notes
- Recording them on video and audio tapes
- Interviewing them
- Having focus group discussions

Observed (My participants)
- Performing literacy-oriented action
- Using certain tools
- Following certain directions as stipulated by their franchise or organization
- Working as a group
- Recognizing the division of labor and working with the group members
- Showcasing their short-term and long-term goals and outcomes
- Reacting to their community needs
- Following ethical principles
- Maintaining traditions
- Reading and writing codes that are specific to their business
- Negotiating with new customers
- Using digital media to gather new clients

Observer-Researcher (on and off the field)
- Maintaining clear log of all that is being observed
- Ensuring ethical practices
- Recognizing the complexity in the work of participants
- Checking the participants and asking repeated questions
- Seeking constant clarification—through stimulated recalls
- Using personal memos and understanding the situation through reflection; a different awareness about certain aspects that need to be interpretive and subjective to capture the intensity of the moment.

Observer-Participants (on and off the field)
- Checking to see what the researcher is writing about
- Asking researcher questions about their work

- Assessing the researcher for their work and behavior on the field
- Accommodating the researcher on their observation
- Answering questions based on their observation of the researcher
- Expecting that the research work will be showcased in a proper and ethical way

After reviewing all the coding, I placed these categories in columns and started the comparative analysis, which enabled me to cross-check the data every step of the way. For example, the first column refers to cross-checking information across columns. What this meant was that all the data I had gathered after coding were pointing toward the same direction, so that I could articulate my findings.

What is intriguing about this study was sometimes toward the end of the day or during stimulated recall, during my first visit and later visits, the Dabbawalas would ask me interesting questions about my data gathering and about my writing. I felt that this process was indeed a role reversal. At certain points, I, as a researcher, was under scrutiny and the participants were observing me to see what I had written about them and would comment about certain things.

During my first visit, while having a focus group discussion during one of the days in the evening, the Dabbawalas saw I was tired, so they purchased and brought tea from one of the tea stalls at the railway station. As I sat down with my interview questions, recording devices, and notepads to write down the conversation, one of the youngest members asked me, "So, what will you do with all this information? What will you write? People think we are illiterates, so how do you prove that otherwise?" For a minute, there was a pause as all the participants were watching me—I stopped writing—as I had never thought about this question in my quest to gather data. I finished my tea and thanked them profusely for their thoughtful gesture. I also informed the participant that I will respond to his question in my next visit. This was truly a thought-provoking question, "Truly, how will I prove otherwise?" It made me mull over it till I returned back to the States, as I was unable to answer that question at that point, as I had never reflected on that question.

Table 30. Comparative Analysis and Cross-checking Method

Triangulation	Observer: Data consisted of	Observed: Participants	Observer being observed—by participants
Cross-check information across columns Allows for rich data to emerge through comparative analysis Provides enriching information, refuting, confirming and explaining (Carvalho and White, 1997)	Being in the field with my participants and taking notes Recording them on video and audio tapes Interviewing them Having focus group discussions Creating categories of observation Using personal memos	Performing literacy-oriented actions Using certain tools Following certain directions as stipulated by their franchise or organization Working as a group/ Recognizing the division of labor and working with the group members/ Reacting to their community needs	Checking if I was maintaining a log of all the actions that was taking place. Ensuring ethical practices Discussing and asking me if I recognize the complexity in the work they are doing? Participants checking with me and asking me questions
	Using memos and understanding the situation through personal reflection; a different awareness about certain aspects that need to be interpretive and subjective to capture the intensity of the moment.	Showcasing their short-term and long-term goals and outcomes— Following ethical principles Maintaining traditions Reading and writing codes that are specific to their business Negotiating with new customers Using digital media to gather new clients	When I sought clarification, patiently responding— through stimulated recalls

Although, I tried my level best to answer him, I felt hollow within as I was unable to provide a concrete answer. I responded by being honest and informed him that all the collected data will be first analyzed, then coded by me to develop a theory about their literacy and their practices. I also informed him that during one of my future visits, I will provide him the right answer; unfortunately, I couldn't showcase my work to him till my visit in 2015 after my defense, although I had visited them after my initial visit in 2011. At that point, when I did show him my work and what I thought of them and their literacy practices, his reaction was a beaming smile and a comment that made me smile, *"Accha-hua, koi to hamay unpad nahi samjtha.* (Glad at least someone thinks we are not illiterates)." I also thanked him for being such an amazing participant and for asking that question.

Another incident worth mentioning in terms of the cyclical process is during the stimulated recall sessions, I would first explain one aspect of their practice and then show them the tape recordings of what I had observed; sometimes they would agree and at times they will correct me by saying, *"Nahin, Didi; wo to galat hai!"* (No sister; that is incorrect!!). They would then point to the video recording and properly translate their actions into words and wait till I wrote it down. If I missed something, they would comment by suggesting, *"Aap bhool raheen hain hum yeh bhi karthay hain*—You are forgetting that we do this, too." Some would ask me to rewind the tape and pinpoint some clip that I thought was unimportant and ensure I wrote it down. At such points, I was truly thankful and grateful for their patience and guidance, as they were willing to view the video tapes and see the corresponding Hindi notes written by me. Such moments also made me realize that a simple thank-you was an inadequate word to express what I was feeling, and my personal memos reflect my thoughts:

> *Once again, I am in tears as they spent so much time with me today to clarify and explain all the tapes and my Hindi notes. I didn't even buy them a cup of tea!! And instead, they bought one for me!! How can these people be so generous and kind. What is it with them? How many literate people will do this? They will probably shun me for bothering them for such long hours. Today, it was late in the evening when they all went home after speaking to me (third day in a row). I realize they have to be early at work tomorrow. I am indebted to them for sharing their time and wisdom— generosity of a different kind.*

Also, Chotu's question threw me out of my wits today. Will I really be able to write about their literacy practices in new light and how am I going to write it? I am so unsure about this; but what I do know for sure is that I didn't think about this question till he asked me. And, the world calls them "unpad???" Interesting.

References

Bazerman, C. (2011). Standpoints: The Disciplined Interdisciplinarity of Writing Studies. *Research in the Teaching of English, 46*(1), pp. 8–21. http://www.jstor.org/stable/23050587

Behar, R. (1996). *The Vulnerable Observer: Anthropology That Breaks Your Heart.* Beacon Press.

Carvalho, S., & White, H. (1997). *Combining the Quantitative and Qualitative Approaches to Poverty Measurement and Analysis. The Practice and the Potential* (Technical Papers 366). World Bank.

Geertz, C. (2000). *The Interpretation of Cultures.* Basic Books.

Chapter Seventeen

Findings Based on Selective Coding and Deciphering the Larger Picture

Selective coding is like the locomotive driver; once the driver is in the front, he or she directs the train towards its destination and the carriages follow suit.

—CNS

One of the key aspects of triangulation, based on axial coding, is that it leads the researcher to understand the central aspect or nucleus of the study; and this in turn, helps in developing and articulating the findings. Viewing, analyzing, and creating the nine axial codes led me to create the final selective code—the core thesis—enabling me to theorize and answer the five research questions. Thus, my research thesis was:

The Dabbawalas are successful "not in spite of being illiterate but because of their literacy practices." In some ways, such ethnic and indigenous groups teach us that given the context, situation, cultural practices, personal situations and circumstances, members of the group adapt, adopt, and acquire skills through different modes; from observing, reading, writing, communicating in different ways to using peripheral participation, and practicing their work in their own ways—allows them to sustain and live in successful ways within their means and within their communities.

Once I was able to frame the final selective code, "once the driver was in place," as CNS suggested humorously, it was easy to answer the research questions. The key five findings that appeared were based on (1) face-to-face interviews, (2) focus group discussions, (3) fieldwork observation, (4) stimulated recall, (5) memos, and (6) analysis of pertinent document that the Dabbawalas placed in the lunch boxes. Thus, in the findings chapters, I addressed each question and provided a detailed response to each one of them. Here, I have provided a short response for questions 1 through 5 and provided an example of the longer version for just question 1.

> **Finding 1:** What are the literacy practices of the Dabbawalas in general?
>
> Dabbawalas read and write every day, from morning till night, and use these two modes to communicate with others, depending on contexts and situations. All the participants mentioned that they read and write every single day, "work or no work."
>
> **Finding 2:** How and what type of literacies do they use in their daily lives to maintain their business practices?
>
> The majority of the participants expressed that literacy should not be measured just in terms of reading and writing, but as skills that you acquire from being in school or from outside agencies, to communicate your thoughts effectively to others in *multimodal and multilingual forms/ways*. The terms they associated with literacy as a skill were:
>
> 1. *Yojan:* cognitive thinking
> 2. *Kushal:* smartness
> 3. *Upaay:* solution
> 4. *Kaushaltha:* clever enough to deal with problems
> 5. *Vidhi:* method and an appropriate way to follow a method; and
> 6. *Prayog:* utilize, apply or the application process.
>
> **Finding 3:** How and why do they write the scripts in English without being schooled in it?

The majority of the participants suggested that they learned to read and write the English alphabet after joining the Dabbawala business—from their peers. Many of them also suggested that learning the sounds associated with the alphabet and watching their team members write the letters on the lunch boxes enabled them to learn it quickly, "on the go." All participants agreed that in a successful business practice, the information that is communicated among the team members is streamlined, efficient, and effective. For this to happen, as one of the senior members commented, "The employees need to follow certain procedures and policies of the company and adopt it as part of their lifestyle; and for us Dabbawalas, learning the English language, following a certain writing procedure, wearing a white uniform and *topi* (The Gandhi cap), or learning languages are all part of that adaptation." He continued to say, "You really don't go back to school to learn or adapt to a company's policies. You learn on the job and that is why 'we call it training and not schooling' *(isi liyay hum isay training kah thay hain, aur school nahin).*" Most of the participants could read and write the scripts in English; all of them could speak words in English, as they knew the meaning of the words they uttered, while a few could speak and read complete sentences.

Finding 4: How do they interpret the codes and translate it in their minds?

All the participants suggested that writing the codes using letters, numbers, and colors were a part of their everyday business routine; and, over a period, the habit of performing an activity "led to mastery" that "we don't really pay attention to how we do it." Majority of the participants suggested that the script being so clear and precise helps in understanding the code, that translating hardly takes time. One of them commented, "The coding and decoding the scripts are so clear that we can do it on the go, and it is all due to the information being brief, important, clear, and uniform *(mukhya, spasht ya saaf aur ek samaan, uniform).*" Almost all of the participants commented that this was the way of future communication, as it appeals to the visual senses and provides a clear method for routing the paths in their minds.

Finding 5: Though the Dabbawalas consider themselves literate, *they feel* others who observe them *think* they are illiterates. Why? Although the majority of the Dabbawalas believe they are literate, they are forced into thinking they are illiterate due to societal values (Western) and certain (Eastern) beliefs, in terms of defining the concept of literacy and its association with schooling.

For each finding, I provided a detailed rationale so that my committee members could understand how I came to that conclusion. I have provided a sample of the first finding that showcases how theory was built based on the axial codes. I used the same pattern to respond to the other four questions.[1]

Finding 1: What Are the Literacy Practices of Dabbawalas in General?

The main finding of this study was that the Dabbawalas read and write every day, from morning until night, depending on context and situations. Their reading depends upon where they are at a given time, and how the location and circumstance mandate or voluntarily allow for certain types of reading. The readings could range from viewing a script for two minutes, to reading a pamphlet for five minutes or more, to even reading a novel or newspaper beyond ten minutes, to reading messages on their mobile or cell phone.

The Dabbawalas business activity is dependent on writing and reading the script during different times of the day. The pickup and delivery process begins with writing the scripts (addresses) appropriately on the lunch box. Once the script is written, the box can be exchanged in many stations between the Dabbawalas before it reaches its customer. For the exchange to take place correctly and to maintain and facilitate the delivery in a linear fashion, the address or script is read many times as Dabbawalas exchange boxes, allowing us, the observers, to see that writing and reading the scripts are an intrinsic part of the Dabbawalas' daily routine and their impeccable business model.

The box reading is usually done a few minutes before sorting and placing the boxes into different crates. New appointees or apprentices take slightly more time to decipher the codes, but experienced adults read the scripts, translate it within seconds, and quickly place the lunch boxes in appropriate crates in an efficient manner. This difference between experienced and inexperienced Dabbawalas illustrates that while the script might be considered as a simple graphic form of characterization, it takes time to become a skillful user of the script. The reading of the scripts begins in the morning when they all meet and sort out the lunch boxes; then, read again when they sort the lunch boxes at different stations based on destination, and repeated during the time of delivery at the customers' offices. Interestingly, this process of reading and distribution is repeated and followed post-lunch or reverse cycle when lunch boxes from the previous or the same day are collected from the customer's offices. At end of the day, the scripts are read again at different stations during sorting and exchanging of lunch boxes as they reach their original destination. Once the lunch boxes are back at the starting point, home station, they are again read and sorted out to be taken back to their clients' homes. While on the job, when Dabbawalas are not reading or writing their business scripts, many of them read magazines or books. Some participants also mentioned that they do not read while traveling in the train due to poor eyesight, dizziness, or lack of time.

Almost all of them participants (82%) mentioned that they read the newspaper in Marathi or Hindi in the morning, even if it was to quickly glance at the sports page to know the cricket score, while 18% said they did not have time in the morning as they had to drop their children at school or had other work; so to compensate for not reading in the morning, they would read in the train or at the station while waiting for the train to arrive. Some of the Dabbawalas read magazines or storybooks on the train, as they said, "That is the only time to catch up on mystery novels or gossip columns," revealing a different use of literacy.

While discussing the Dabbawalas' reading practices, Savan (one of the participants) mentioned that all of them were required to read the pamphlets (documents received from the head office) before placing them in the lunch boxes, as they needed to know the content. He also said that any form of advertisement placed in the lunch boxes has to be read: (a) to make sure that the content was appropriate and "did not offend the customers' sentiments" and (b) to explain the pamphlet to their customers "who did not read any of the languages" on the pamphlet. Though the companies provide pamphlets for distribution, the Dabbawalas are involved in communicating and negotiating with their main office, on what to say and include in the lunch boxes for their customers, highlighting their ability to use literacy for managing a successful business practice. Savan also suggested that reading texts received on their mobile phones was also part of a day's work "as some of the new customers would send their addresses or current customers would want some change in their delivery schedule." Overall, the 18 participants whom I interviewed, (100%) read scripts during the day, at different times, interpreted them in their minds and delivered the lunch boxes to their clients on time. Although I was not able to observe all the Dabbawalas after work hours, based on focus group discussions and individual interviews, 4 of the 18 participants, mentioned that in addition to reading at work, some of them would return home to: read with their children, read religious texts, read texts that would scroll on their television screens, or read with technologies (mobile phone) that would help them with their business practices.

Writing practices. As far as writing *at work* was concerned, the Dabbawalas could write and complete information to fulfill their business transactions and could write other notes for personal purposes. Discussion with the initial set of 18 participants revealed the different types of writing the Dabbawalas use during a workday, which includes: (a) writing the script on the lunch boxes or making changes on the script, (b) writing notes or annotations as a response to their own reading some magazine or religious texts, (c) writing information for themselves on their hand, which acts as mnemonic tool to remember to perform an activity once they leave work, and (d) texting back customers after they receive an order.

Writing the script or code on the lunch box—as a complex symbol system—involves team collaboration and communication, as they all need to ensure that the Dabbawalas who pick up and deliver the lunch boxes at clients' sites and return it back home are aware of that particular routing. The other writing activities, like sending a text (based on the Dabbawala who owns a mobile phone), is done individually and collaboratively depending on the request of the customer. For example, if a customer wants a lunch box to be delivered to a different part of the city, then the Dabbawalas discuss the request with their group members and locate the person who follows the route where the customer is requesting delivery. Then, they text the customer back saying, "Will be done (*Ho jayayga*)." As many members of the team do not have cell phones, the common practice is that the member owning a mobile phone shares the information within the group to locate the appropriate person for lunch delivery. I refer to this aspect of team collaboration among the Dabbawalas specifically to highlight that writing the script extends to other modes of communication.

From my tally of writing behaviors, it was evident that:

1. All 18 participants (100%) could write the scripts using the English alphabet.
2. All 18 participants (100%) could make changes to the script based on customer's request including new hires and apprentices who are trained to learn "how to write the scripts."
3. 8 out of 18 participants (44%) responded in writing to the texts they received from customers either in Hindi or Marathi. Though 10 out of 18 (55%) did not respond to texts due to various reasons (not owning a cell phone or the mobile phone does not have texting facility), they were aware of the contents of the text received by others, mainly due to the open communication among the team members.
4. 12 out of 18 (65%) interacted to books they were reading by writing comments on the side, while 6 out of 18 (35%) said they preferred not to write while traveling.
5. All 18 participants (100%) mentioned that they would write something on their hand, book, or diary to remind themselves of

what needed to be completed later during the day, which acted as a mnemonic device/tool to recollect thoughts; and

6. All 18 participants (100%) mentioned that they discussed the information related to their writing with others in their team for effective collaboration. (Krishnan, 2014)

Analysis of finding 1. Analyzing the information based on their reading and writing habits reveals that across participants and across their activities, Dabbawalas use different types of literacies during the day. In reading, it ranges from reading the daily newspapers to other types of readings in three or more languages, usually in Hindi, Marathi, and English. In writing, it ranges from writing the script and other information in at least two languages (English and Marathi) to communicating their thoughts in writing to their teammates during the workday.

This type of communication or literacy practice begins from the time the lunch boxes are collected and brought to the common meeting place till the end of the day when they are brought back to the same place. As this communication extends to other Dabbawalas with whom they exchange lunch boxes, these variable forms of literacy practices allow them to maintain timeliness and successful delivery. Contrary to popular belief prompted by journalists and researchers that the Dabbawalas are "illiterate or have low literacy," my findings and data reveal that they constantly read and write depending on the circumstances and the time available for them. During work time, they not only use literacy to successfully operate their business, but if time permits, such as when they are traveling on the train or during lunchtime, they read what interests them.

My study documents that Dabbawalas not only read and write for professional purposes but also for personal use. Further, it is important to note that the Dabbawalas read in multiple languages, and they use the English alphabet, another language skill, in the lunch box script. As Street (1995) suggests, local perceptions and uses of literacy must be considered to understand the literacy experience of local community practices as they may differ from dominant culture. He argues that we cannot ignore the local literacy practices and measure literacy based on dominant culture or based on the autonomous model. Further, if we allow such statements to pervade our ways of thinking then statements such as Dabbawalas are "illiterates," or "semi-literates," or "cannot read or write," are made possible. Street's argument is that people with this type of "dominant viewpoint" should observe how the local groups "perceive different literacies to which they are exposed and how they make pragmatic adaptations to serve their particular interests" (p. 42). This is certainly visible in the Dabbawalas' developing a specific use of literacy by creating and adapting a concise writing system to facilitate accurate and timely transportation of lunch boxes from one location to another in a workday. *Just as this business can only operate in a city having a distinct railway system, so, too, is the script and the literacy practices of the Dabbawalas—as it is only relevant to them. This is mainly followed here as it supports their business operation and allows them to execute the transaction successfully in a city like Mumbai. This script, though concise, taps into all of the technologies available to them, from reading, writing, and texting, to using different languages to communicate with each other as a team and to their customers. The Dabbawalas' usage of multiple modes of literacies, including switching languages to read, write, and communicate effectively and appropriately with others, reveals a crucial mantra of the business world, "Keep customers happy and they will come back."*

On another level, the Dabbawalas have realized and harnessed the potential of face-to-face communication or effective oral communication to the use of graphic representation for enhancing their business (Kuiper & Clippinger, 2013). As the business world harnesses digital tools such as Microsoft Teams, Zoom, Web-ex, Skype, FaceTime, and other video conferencing platforms, and gravitate toward more oral forms of communication, the Dabbawalas have already adapted their business to fit their site and resources available to them. What major corporations like Starbucks are promoting as a successful supply-chain aspect "creating an atmosphere of collaboration where cross-functional teams can meet and work together towards success" (Supply-chain 24/7)[2]—the Dabbawalas are already practicing this in their workday through oral communication and meetings. These meetings are held in a convenient location for each group member to attend in the morning and evening. What the Dabbawalas are practicing, illustrating, and advocating is way ahead of their time, leading to their achieving a six-sigma rating and a sustainable model of supply-chain management that is used in the business world. Further, the aspect of using different modes of communication highlights that literacy for the Dabbawalas is not just reading and writing, but a complex web or network of social activities where even juggling languages becomes a part of their workday routine (Barton & Hamilton, 1998).

My main research question for this study was to investigate why the Dabbawalas are being considered illiterate *in spite of* their literacy practices, and how this perception about literacy *still exists* in many parts of the society, within India and across the world, based on the autonomous model (Goody, 1968). Again, I found Street's (1984) explanation to be the most appropriate as to why this perception continues to exist, as it is disguised in "neutral and universal" terms, advocating that introducing literacy to people in "villages, urban youth, etc. will have the effect of enhancing their cognitive skills, improving their economic prospects, making them better citizens, regardless of the social and economic conditions" (p. 63). Over a period, when the educated masses in any community enhance their economic status, they tend to attribute their success to their schooling and education, leading other members of the society to believe that these two aspects do improve the socioeconomic status of an individual. As this belief establishes itself, the norm to evaluate the *haves and have nots* is based on their economic status and their level of education, leading to some individuals, certain groups, and even specific communities, being classified as *literate or illiterate*.

Despite the Dabbawalas being termed as illiterates, they continue to operate the same way, never heeding the value system that the society places upon them. As Nath, one of the participants, explained, "Being steadfast in our ways has led us to be who we are, and we are not going to change our system, as people think we are illiterates." He continued with a smile, "It is these *illiterates'* coding that has gotten the world's attention, so literate or illiterate, people come to see us and learn from us; so, you tell me if we are literate or illiterate (*tho didi, aap bathaiyay ki hum padhay hain ya unpad hain)?"*

Analysis and Answers to the Five Research Questions: Findings and Theory Building

Based on my observation and data collected, the first finding revealed that the Dabbawalas can read and write and use literacy practices available to them to be successful in their business. The findings also revealed that the Dabbawalas are literate, given Street's (1984) definition of ideological model of literacy. *Decolonizing the Dabbawalas literacy practices validates my argument that imposing a Western concept of literacy onto another culture or ethnicity like that of the Dabbawalas and calling them illiterate, based on their schooling and technical skills of reading and writing, is morally inappropriate and pejorative. More importantly, this finding enabled me to see that calling the Dabbawalas illiterates or semi-literates and focusing on their English proficiency ignores their rich cultural, historical, and traditional background, and their extremely versatile ways of using languages to suit their audience and occasion.*

The second finding was categorized into three parts based on how the Dabbawalas use their literacy skills every day in their business practices. This finding made me realize what Street refers to as local people defining their literacies and having their own method of explaining their language and literacy uses. In a country like India, where there are at least 20 official languages, knowing at least three fluently—is by itself—a feat in many ways and speaks volumes about the aptitude of an individual. In addition to knowing these languages, all the Dabbawalas are capable of reading and writing the English alphabet, and some of them even know how to read words and sentences in English. Another important aspect is that almost all of them use English words constantly as part of their conversation and code-switching of languages, which is an integral part of their everyday lifestyle. The amazing fact that they are constantly willing to improve their vocabulary in English along with other languages and acquire digital skills reveals that they are very cognitive of their audiences' needs and are willing to adapt and adopt to their environment.

The third and fourth findings revealed that the Dabbawalas method of adopting their cultural values to establishing a successful business venture has allowed them to carve a name in the business world, that even Prince Charles who came to observe them, complemented them on their successful business methods and strategies. The world is fascinated with their script and how they, as a team, utilize the script to transport 200,000 lunch boxes everyday throughout the city of Mumbai in very effective and sustainable ways. The addresses written on the lunch boxes are often considered as "codes by the social media" when they write about them in newspapers and magazines. *What is considered a code—numbers, letters, and colors—is actually a complete script written in a cryptic form to maintain accuracy and conciseness, two important aspects to execute a business transaction efficiently and effectively.* Again, all these practices of the Dabbawalas challenge the "literacy myth" as explained by Graff (1979) that literacy per se does not lead to social improvement or civilization or social mobility. Graff also states that literacy itself does not make a difference in occupation or wealth as compared to the impact ethnic or class origin has on a group.

The fifth finding revealed that stigma associated with illiteracy—unfortunately, still continues and exists—and why more studies need to be conducted in terms of viewing local practices on their own merits and what *we*, as members of the outside world, can learn from them. Based on the Dabbawalas' literacy practices and their lifestyle from the past to the present, it is evident that they define literacy more in terms of reading, writing, and using oral modes/methods of communication. According to my participants, it is the combination of the three modes that leads to complete communication. This establishes that literacy depends on not just the context but also the speaker, the audience, and the appeals used as in the rhetorical triangle. Though the Dabbawalas never completed schooling, they are aware of such concepts based on their practical experience in the field, raising the issue—*does schooling necessarily raise the cognitive and logical reasoning in a person?*

Finally, all these findings allowed me to conclude, based on my ethnographic case study and the data collected, that the Dabbawalas are indeed not illiterate or semi-literates, but fully literate in ideological ways, given the social context and milieu of their practice.

What I also realized at that point was that all researchers at the end of their seminal work should address the implications of their study and how the study will provide further opportunities for other types of explorations.

In my conclusion of the dissertation, I discuss what Dowdy (2008) suggests as making the "invisible visible" in literacy studies. Conducting this ethnographic case study enabled me to expose and make the Dabbawalas literacy practices visible, what was originally invisible to the world. This also provided me an opportunity to challenge the autonomous model perceptions allowing for new perceptions and perspectives to emerge. Further, my study addressed the overall implications of such a cross-cultural study in the field of literacy and business, especially supply-chain management, and Street's (1995) call on how:

> International literacy work should be used to help open up this debate (about literacy itself promoting cognitive abundance, social mobility or progress) and establish clearer concepts and frameworks on which practice can be based, not to reiterate worn clichés and patronizing stories about "illiteracy." (p. 24)

Notes

1 What my study further revealed was the Dabbawalas, in addition to their unique literacy practices, are also business leaders, communicators, and future thinkers. I say this as many of my participants mentioned that researchers from other universities and Ivy league schools had visited them to see how they were leaders in the "service-oriented-food-industry." When questioned about it, they mentioned that "the phenomenon of interest for all the researchers," who visited them from all over the world was to comprehend their unique business model. Mr. Medge suggested, "What was of great interest to them was that this business that started in 1890s has been functioning and existing and still continues to operate on its traditional principles." Further, he believed that the achievement of six-sigma by the

Dabbawalas had created additional interest among the researchers, as they felt the members consisted of men: (1) who were "uneducated in English," and (2) who had "not attended elementary or middle school," who were basically "considered illiterate" were conducting a complex business—without using modern methods of communication and without having a complete written script or manuals written in any language. Further, Mr. Medge mentioned that the Dabbawalas were aware of this unique aspect about their writing script and were willing to communicate about it to others, "despite being considered uneducated." He commented that people from academia are "fascinated that we are thinking about our future as we are aware of the challenges placed on us and our business, given the digital and technological progress." But what people need to realize is that "we were taking steps to find solutions for it, just like corporate businesses are acquiring and updating their hardware and software to help their employees" (Krishnan, 2014).

2 Information provided appears from a website on Supply-chain 24/7, where they refer to how the CEO of Starbucks, Howard Schultz, has built a success story based on seven principles of supply-chain management, where one of the key principles to be followed is communication and team building. The article is titled "What Your Supply Chain Can Learn from Starbucks."

References

Barton, D., & Hamilton, M. (1998). *Local literacies: Reading and Writing in One Community.* Routledge.

Dowdy, J. K. (2008). *Ph.D. stories: Conversation With My Sisters.* Hampton Press.

Goody, J. (1968). *Literacy in Traditional Societies.* Cambridge University Press.

Graff, H. (1979). *The Literacy Myth: Literacy and Social Structure in the Nineteenth Century City.* Academic Press.

Krishnan, U. S. (2014). *A cross-cultural study of the literacy practices of the Dabbawalas: Towards a new understanding of nonmainstream literacy and its impact on successful business practices* [Doctoral dissertation, Kent State University]. OhioLINK Electronic Theses and Dissertations Center.

Kuiper, S., & Clippinger, D. A. (2013). *Contemporary Business Reports* (5th ed.). South Western, Cengage Learning.

Street, B. V. (1984). *Literacy in theory and practice.* Cambridge University Press.

Street, B. (1995). *Social Literacies: Critical Approaches to Literacy Development, Ethnography and Education.* Pearson Longman.

Chapter Eighteen

Writing the Ethnographic Case Study and Feeling: *Upsilamba*

Every major work that we accomplish in life is followed with a celebration—to remember that moment—but, never forget, they are also gentle reminders that there are many more to conquer and achieve. Never rest on your laurels.

Kamala

The day I completed writing my dissertation, there was a unique feeling, a sense of joy combined with gratitude and a sense of relief that I had represented the Dabbawalas' literacy practices in honest and ethical ways to the best of my abilities. I felt that my final selective code said it all. It was like everything had fallen into place. There was this sense of gratitude for all the scholars like Street, Heath, Scribner and Cole, Glenn, Moss, and many others, as I realized that indigenous and ethnic communities, in general, learn to adapt and adopt to changes that are placed on them and harness tools that will help them in the future to be successful. I was able to see that the Dabbawalas were no exception to the rule, rather it was their approach to the whole business practice that had made them unique and famous, a model to emulate in many ways. It is at that moment I felt the word striking me, an unexplainable feeling of light-headedness, *"Upsilamba."*

If you are wondering, why would I use this word in specific to gauge my emotion, the reason is related to my teaching Nabokov over the years in some of my literature classes. The word *"Upsilamba"* and its association has always been associated with a sense of joy. But, it was only when I taught Azar Nafisi's *Reading Lolita In Tehran* that it took on a different meaning that I associated with at that moment—not just joy but with a new sense of revelation—something her students' feel, as she writes:

> The truth was that *Upsilamba* was one of Nabokov's fascinating creations, possibly a word he invented. I said I associate *Upsilamba* with the impossible joy of a suspended leap. Yassi, who seemed excited for no particular reason, cried out that she always thought it could be a name of a dance—you know, "C'mon, baby, do the Upsilamba with me". Manna suggested that the word upsilamba evoked the image of small silver fish leaping in and out of a moonlit lake. Nima added in parentheses, Just so you won't forget me, although you have barred me from your class: an upsilamba to you too! For Azin it was a sound, a melody. Mahashid described an image of three girls jumping rope and shouting "Upsilamba" with each leap. For Sanaz, the word was a small African boy's secret magical name. Mitra wasn't sure why the word reminded her of the paradox of a blissful sigh. And for Nassrin it was a magic code that opened the door to a secret cave filled with treasures.

Thus, **Upsilamba**, at that point, became "the impossible joy of a suspended leap," "a Blissful sigh" "a magic code opened" that "I wanted to do the dance" with my study. A feeling that I experienced after I had completed writing all the findings, answered all the research questions, provided explanations about my findings, and theorized the concepts and realized that I "might" have added -my ethnographic case study on the Mumbai Dabbawalas—to the field of literacy. What my study did was to showcase and validate that literacy must be viewed in ideological ways and in terms of multiliteracies, as developed by the New London Group (NLG). It revealed, as Street (1984) suggests, that context, situations, and social milieu dictate the literacy practices of a group and that schooling does not necessarily raise the cognitive or logical reasoning in a person; and in this case, it was the local situated practices that enabled the Dabbawalas to be successful (Krishnan, 2014, pp. 130–133).

In short, the study proved that the Dabbawalas are indeed not *illiterate* or *semiliterate* but *fully literate in ideological ways* (Krishnan, 2014).

References

Krishnan, U. S. (2014). *A cross-cultural study of the literacy practices of the Dabbawalas: Towards a new understanding of nonmainstream literacy and its impact on successful business practices* [Doctoral dissertation, Kent State University]. OhioLINK Electronic Theses and Dissertations Center.

Nafisi, A. (2003). *Reading Lolita in Tehran: A Memoir in Books.* Random House.

The New London Group. (1996). A Pedagogy of Multiliteracies: Designing Social Futures. *Harvard Educational Review, 66*(1), pp. 60–93.

Street, B. (1984). *Literacy in theory and practice.* Cambridge University Press.

Part IV

Demonstrate

Decolonization is an ongoing process that requires all of us to be collectively involved and responsible. Decolonizing our institutions means we create spaces that are inclusive, respectful, and honour Indigenous Peoples.

—CULL ET AL. (2020)

In this part, I address the steps that need to be taken before the researcher sends the final revised chapters to the committee members. I explain: how and why the researcher will need to address and review the rhetorical aspect in their thesis, how to involve and work with the thesis director at this stage, why discuss the format of the defense with the director, and how to prepare for potential questions and answers. It is important to address these steps as you, the researcher, are at the final phase of your dissertation journey.

I also provide suggestions on how to prepare a slide deck (using PowerPoint or other presentation formats) for the defense and how to develop confidence in defending your brainchild. I conclude with why congratulating oneself on a job well done is very important and necessary. Then, I discuss how to submit the thesis for national repository based on the format, and requirements, and how to decide on whether to embargo the thesis or not, depending on personal choice/s. This section also includes a chapter on how my ethnographic case study, a small contribution, adds to the large field of literacy studies.

Chapter Nineteen

Sending the Chapters to the Committee

Writing your dissertation chapters for the committee members and writing for a journal are way different—as you are working with different types of audiences.

—Takayoshi

This is the final stretch of the dissertation or thesis process, where the researcher sends their revised and edited chapters for review to the committee. Before sending the chapters, the thesis director might suggest that the candidate review other dissertations, as it helps the researcher see how others have formatted and presented their work and adhered to the department and university requirements. Another helpful tip that came from CNS when I was planning to send my chapters to my committee was "now that you have finished writing, do a backward study and see if the findings and claims you make in chapter 4 and 5 (conclusion chapter of your dissertation) have been addressed in chapter 1. Your first chapter are like the seeds being placed in the soil. They germinate and grow into a big plant or tree by the end of your dissertation." This is a suggestion I have passed on to all my undergraduate and graduate students over the years that once they have completed writing their essay or thesis, "to flip it to see if the claims made in the conclusion are being thoughtfully addressed at the beginning and throughout the essay."

Further, at this stage, the already chosen defense committee members are aware of the candidate's work, the timeline to review the chapters, and provide feedback. Usually, this process takes one or two months and sometimes more, depending on the type of study, and complexity involved in understanding, critiquing, and providing feedback to the candidate. I say this as my methodology and findings sections were thoroughly scrutinized leading to my rewriting, providing details, and editing some parts. Additionally, depending upon the department policies, when the chapters are sent for review the committee members are aware that they must complete the review process for undergraduate thesis within 4–6 weeks, graduate 6–8 weeks, and doctoral about 8–12 weeks or more months. If the committee members review and send their feedback promptly, then it is important to work on their suggestions and discuss those changes with the thesis director before sending it back for a second review.

Although there are some directors who will suggest sending individual chapters as you complete writing them, as separate single documents, there are some who will suggest that you send the committee members the whole draft as one complete document. Some graduate students have also mentioned that there have been requests made by committee members to print the document and send them a hardcopy, as the members prefer to make notations while reading the document. So, my suggestion to my students is to be prepared to send the copy the way the committee members want as this whole process is time sensitive.

In my case, my advisor was not in favor of sending the whole document together for a reason. He felt that an ethnographic study like mine cannot be read in "one complete sitting—as a whole." He suggested that "in your case, your study provides a different perspective when it is read in pieces as opposed to a complete work." Therefore, initially I send my committee members the individual chapters and once they were revised, I sent them the complete document to see if there is a definite flow and continuity. This was a great piece of advice to follow; as and when he received reports from the committee members, he would provide me their feedback and their expectation in terms of the changes I need to make on the chapters.

I must pinpoint here that there have been cases where the committee members have made suggestions on the first draft and were not keen on viewing the second draft with changes. This is mainly due to lack of time, as all of them had many other responsibilities, and they trusted the candidate to make the changes/edits and send them the final draft before the defense. Also, please note that in some cases, the reviewers will ensure that the changes have been made, some may pose their questions from the suggested changes, and some may even refer to those pages during the defense. This happened in two of the defenses I attended. In the first one, the committee members were happy that their suggestions were incorporated. In the second defense, it was clearly pointed out, during the deliberations, that unless their suggestions were incorporated, they will not sign-off on the project/ thesis. Either way, it is better to make the necessary changes, as the committee members are the first set of readers to critique and enhance the thesis work. Although, it is a humbling experience and time-consuming, my suggestion to my students has been to view it from a rhetorical perspective as it prepares the candidate for their defense and later publications.

Chapter Twenty

Preparing for the Defense

Your defense is your first step towards showcasing your scholarship to the public.
—Joanne Dowdy

While the candidate is preparing for the defense or viva, as termed in some countries, the director usually coordinates with the other committee members to schedule a date for the final defense. Of late, across universities, depending on the department, candidates are asked to prepare a set of questions that they would like the committee to consider, in addition to the questions the committee members might pose on their own during the defense. The questions are then presented to the director, who then emails it to the other committee members before the defense.

Although this differs in every field and departments, in most cases the defense is a public event within the university community, allowing for graduate students and family members to attend the thesis defense. Attending a few defenses prior to one's own is very advantageous, as it prepares the candidate for what to expect in their own session. You will learn everything from dress code, presentation, defense format, question-answer responses, and other protocols, including interactions that takes place between the committee members, family, friends, peers, and colleagues. It allows you to see what to expect, what to do and what not to do? I must mention that attending a few defenses prior to mine made me realize that there was nothing to fear or to be nervous about, as everyone in the room was interested to know about the presenter's research and how it was conducted. It also enabled me to be well prepared for the big day.

Please find below a list of important aspects to work on, prior to the defense, that I have shared with my students:

- Prepare a slide deck using PowerPoint, or any application that you are comfortable with, that takes the audience on a journey of your dissertation or thesis presentation (time restrictions apply and is dependent on the departmental protocols and stipulation) before the Q&A session starts. Most of the time it is the director or the graduate or undergraduate faculty representative, chosen by the department, who orchestrates the whole event and provides guidance through the process. Use the PowerPoint slides as cues for talking. Things to follow: Avoid being wordy; don't read from the slides; don't show your back to your audience. Please maintain eye-contact with all members of your dissertation committee. If possible, add visuals and few videos. This not only breaks the monotony but keeps the audience interested in the topic.

  Note: An important aspect to keep in mind is to ensure that all the sources are cited in the presentation and at the end. In one of the defenses that I attended before mine, a committee member asked for references for quotes while the candidate was presenting, and when the candidate was unsure and caught off guard, the member loudly commented that "references should be made appropriately; if you are unaware of the study, then don't refer to it; ... this showcases to a certain extent lack of thoroughness." Although an embarrassing moment for the candidate, her director came to her rescue and explained that it was an oversight.

  Also, end the presentation by thanking your committee members and audience. This will act as a cue for the director to move to the next phase of the presentation.

Further, rehearse your presentation thoroughly the day before and time yourself.

- Set up a time to meet early with your director in the place where the defense will be held and have a pre-run session. This mock defense is very helpful. In case, this is not achievable, at least have a meeting and chalk out all the questions and appropriate responses with them. Please note that the director is your best ally in that room on that day; so, work with him/her and ensure that their suggestion/s are being followed.

- Have a notepad, extra pens, and a hardcopy of the thesis/ dissertation with the revised suggestions highlighted on a separate piece of paper. If there are some artifacts or written pieces of evidence from participants that you want to present to the committee members, make copies ahead of time so that all the members have a copy for themselves. If they are physical artifacts, ensure that it is presented. In my case, I had small lunch boxes, as samples, to showcase the meaning of the word *tiffin* or lunch boxes and *topis* (Gandhi cap) that the Dabbawalas used every day while conducting business.

- Transfer the presentation, dissertation, videos, or pictures on to an external hard drive and take the flash drive, in case there are technical issues, such as connecting the computer to the internet or to the projector. Being prepared is an instant score with committee members.

- Wear professional attire for that day. Often this goes unmentioned, as it is assumed that the presenter is aware of the professional setting and dress code. But, attending defenses over the years, I realized candidates should be made aware that having a blazer/ sweater/vest always comes in handy, as they can get nervous based on the question. In one of the defenses, the candidate became so nervous that one of the committee members had to provide his blazer, to stop her from shivering. Keep in mind, the committee members understand the situation and work with you.

- Ensure the phone is completely charged or any other digital recorder plugged into an outlet, if you want the defense to be recorded completely; also, ensure that the digital device used for recording the defense has enough data storage. The only reason that people suggest the defense should be recorded is to help the researcher, as he/she will be able to refer to the committee members' questions or refer to the changes they want to see in the defense. Also, as Dowdy suggested that "having a recording helps as the committee or audience might ask questions that can be used as materials for writing articles later." Unfortunately, in three of the defenses that I attended including mine, our cell phones lost power halfway through the defense and none of us had chargers to plug the phone into the outlet. To this day, I regret what happened. One of the grads after her defense said, "I wish someone had reminded me or given me a heads up on this, as there were so many things to remember for that day and this slipped my mind."

Chapter Twenty One

Developing Confidence and Delivering Your Brainchild

A morphological analysis of the dissertation will showcase that it is truly like a child, born from the deep grooves of our brain.

—Joanne Dowdy

Few weeks before my defense, I worked on my PowerPoint and practiced my presentation. I even recorded some portions to see if I was on time and on my delivery. There was a checklist that I followed based on other defenses: nod; smile; provide eye-contact; look around the room but be focused on the committee members as they are the most important people to be addressed; begin some of your responses with "thank you for asking me that question"; slow down if you are unsure; if there is a three-part question, write down the question in a cryptic way on your notepad—respond methodically and address all aspects of the question. Other things that I made a conscious effort to work on were the following:

- If you digress, come back to the question, and begin with, "Again, going back to the question;" sip water if you need to; be poised and not nervous.

- If unsure, be honest and say, "I might have to look into it, or I am unsure as it was beyond the scope of the study, or maybe I might have overlooked that part, but I will certainly revisit that aspect (write it down on your notepad)."
- If there are questions on citations and references being too old or not pertinent or lack of recent publication included in the thesis or dissertation, ensure that you address it properly; during such instances, cite the major contributors in your field, the year their work was published and their influence in that field, as it important to either showcase them in the presentation or refer to them while responding to their questions.
- If there are questions as to why other works or publications from the same author have not been mentioned, the researcher can suggest that given the scope the project, some of the references would have been outside the framework of the study; the candidate can also defer the question and suggest that after consulting with their adviser, they will include it in the final revisions.

Remember, the committee and other members attending the defense are there to seek answers and ensure that the researcher is presenting the work in a successful manner, by showcasing all the research that was conducted and the knowledge they gained through the process. Therefore, it will be incorrect to assume that they remember every page of the dissertation during the defense. Therefore, it is necessary to be patient and if necessary, repeat in brief, a few aspects of the study or draw attention to the page where there is a reference to the question that is being posed. Respond to all the questions that are posed, including from the audience, in a thoughtful manner as responses to others are also gauged.

At the end of the two or three-hour defense session, depending on the type of thesis or department, the candidate is often asked to step outside the room along with the audience, as the committee deliberates the outcome of the dissertation and presentation. The members usually make up their mind during the defense as they would have taken notes on many of the responses. This usually provides them ammunition to pass or fail the candidates or pass with reservations. One of my friends emailed me with suggestions, about her own experience and what to expect during the defense. She even suggested that I should use the information in my book (Kiara, 2010).[1]

> They were the most discomforting minutes in my life as I unsure of what to expect. I reminded myself that I had done everything that was necessary to complete the dissertation. Walked the walk and talked the talk … I walked into the room after 25 minutes of deliberation and I could feel something wasn't right. I could see it in their faces. And when they said, we have made a decision, I could hear the ominous music—dah dah, daah—you have failed, and we want you to revise the whole darn thing. I thought I will faint as all my family members including my kids were all there.
>
> Uma, my suggestion to you after my defense, don't have family members; but then, I leave it to you. Okay, I digress. Wish you were there!
>
> Anyway, it was not like what I had expected. I passed "but" with reservation. They suggested they liked all aspects of my study, but there were changes—that had been specifically requested that I didn't work on—so they were giving me a week to make the changes and send it back to them. Based on the changes they will sign the forms, which meant that my defense was still incomplete. Yes, you can use this in your book, as I want people to heed … work on the changes! I looked at my director and she nodded and said she will talk to me. At the beginning, I was mad with my director that she hadn't insisted on the changes, but I realized it was not her fault as she had mentioned it during one of our meetings, but I thought it was not pertinent … as I felt it added a completely new perspective to my study, which will take it in a different direction. Finally, I ended up adding all the suggestions the committee members suggested; and now, a week later, I have all the signatures. I could have avoided all this agony had I done the darn thing right at the beginning. Something that you should mention to your readers!!

Similar to the above email, I received another email from a graduate student after her defense.

Few weeks before her defense, I mentioned to her that the last stage of our dissertation is like "delivering a brainchild." I suggested this based on my own research work, on the development of a concept that grows and develops over a period and on how it is actually invisible to everyone for a long period of time, other than the candidate and the director. When I texted her, and wished her saying, "Go, deliver your brain child!!" her first reaction was to mock me, with a text "lol" and suggest that I am using the "analogy of childbirth again??" She was clearly irritated that she said, "What is wrong with you? I know you love babies, but this is too much." But, a week later, she emailed me, after her defense, "Delivered my child. Ha! Ha! Absolutely a beautiful feeling, all the brain pregnancy pains I underwent vanished, ☺. I just wanted to showcase to the committee my writing, my participants, my students', and their work. I wanted to show how proud I was of my participants' work. I was like a mother being proud of her children. I wanted to prove something and when I heard, 'You passed. Congratulations.' What you said was so appropriate. Take back my laugh and on board with your reference."

A morphological analysis[2] of the dissertation will showcase that it is truly like a child that is born from the deep grooves of our brain. *A dissertation in many ways is a unique creation, a synergy of thoughts and writing, based on the candidate's research and quest to learn something about a topic that hasn't been thought of before, specifically in the angle that the researcher wants to pursue, very much like a newborn child that has a unique identity, a unique personality, and a unique characteristic in every way.*

Notes

1 S. Kiara (2010). Personal email.
2 Here the association to morphology is to show the exploration of a literacy practice from a multi-dimensional and ideological perspective.

Chapter Twenty Two

Succeeding in Your Efforts: Congratulating Yourself on a Job Well Done

True satisfaction comes from the effort we put in, not just the result.
—Mahatma Gandhi

On the day of my defense, I was an hour early as I wanted to ensure that all the technology tools worked in the conference room—projector, computer, flash drives, and audio files, etc. I also wanted to make sure that there was internet connection available, as one of the committee members was joining us through Skype. I had about ten copies of the handouts I was planning to give out to the committee and other members of the audience. Also, Kiara had sent me an email with some suggestions that I have mentioned in the earlier section, "Remember to seek permission from your department personnel, if you want your defense to be recorded, as some departments prohibit recordings. Also, please have a printed copy of your dissertation, as the committee might ask you to refer to a certain page and it is much easy to refer to the hardcopy in front of you, rather than maneuvering the laptop and losing the earlier setting or information that you were presenting." As per her suggestion, I did print out a draft and take it.

She also suggested that I ensure that there is enough power backup and space on my recording device for three-to-four-hours of recordings, which I forgot to heed. Halfway through the recording, my phone stopped working due to lack of space and power, but I am thankful that the audio recording device was on, and I was able to record almost half of my defense.

After I completed my defense, a colleague and dear friend from my department, congratulated me and sent a personal note saying, "How was the experience as it looked like, based on what I am hearing, you were enjoying your defense and not at all nervous. Heard yours was a myth-buster? Let me know or call me when you have time. Congratulations!!" As we had a habit of writing short letters or notes, I wrote a letter back to her a few days later. Looking back, I am glad that I copied what I wrote to Elizabeth, as she will be remembered very fondly for her support. I have added it here as it showcases that the defense hinges on how confident we are about presenting the researched subject matter, what are the audience expecting from viewing the presentation, how are they going to judge the content and presenter, and what does it mean to leave lasting impressions. I wrote:

> I was nervous initially when they all walked into the room but once I started presenting, I felt I was showcasing my work, my research on the wonderful Dabbawalas to my audience and to the world. The defense started with Huot welcoming everyone and letting them know why they were here. He provided the format for the defense, and how it will be conducted. He suggested that I will begin with my presentation for 20 minutes, followed by individual round of questions from each of the five committee members for one hour or more, till I have answered their questions. Then, questions will be posed by members as a group followed by question-and-answer session with the audience. The back row was full of graduate students and colleagues; it was a blur at that point. I was praying I wouldn't black out. I took a deep breath and started.
>
> The first thought that came into my mind was a sense of calmness and a recognition that I was going to be revealing the literacy practices of the Dabbawalas, *hidden behind an opaque window*. So, everything was about presenting them, their work, and their literacy practices. As I shifted the focus from *moi* to them, it was like a natural process to take my audience on an ethnographic journey with me. And, in terms of the myth-busters of

being nervous—I was not at all nervous!! All the prep work came in handy; my initial thoughts were here are scholars attending my defense to see what I can add to the field, and I am just sharing my work. I went to great lengths to prove that the Dabbawalas were literate in terms of "nonmainstream and ideological" approach. *And, yes, brought in decolonizing indigenous studies and aspect!!*

I must say, they liked the video clip that I showcased of Chotu speaking in English and Chacha reading English sentences and ending his final statement saying, "You are from Kent State University." Thanks for editing those clips for me. I felt, based on their questions, they were fascinated with videos of how the Dabbawalas wrote their script in real time, their conversations with their customers and methods of communication, how they read, what they read, how they got on the train, how the exchange of boxes and delivery took place and the whole process. They were interested to know how my study adds to the field of cross-cultural literacy, the methodology I used, non-mainstream business practices, and international study of literacy practices and ethnic studies.

Although I was unsure about a few questions, I felt I answered all of them to the best of my abilities. One of the members asked me about language skills and about translation. She also suggested that I should write a chapter on code-switching and language skills as we need more articles in that field. Something to think about for future!! The members from the audience had a few questions about my presentation, as I had used an example of hypothetical delivery system (if Dabbawalas were in US having a railway system similar to one in Mumbai, India) from my home to Kent State University. As we were towards the end of my defense, everyone was relaxed and started discussing how it will be interesting to start a business like that in U.S., and I was then asked to leave the room for committee deliberations.

At the end of 15 minutes, I was asked to enter the room along with the audience; and the committee members reaction was, "Congratulations!!" And, they were all clapping when I entered the room and stood up for me. I felt so humbled and grateful that I became teary. One of them said, "After a long time, I have attended a defense that was just amazing and powerful that I want to meet these Dabbawalas now." Another, suggested, "So, what is inside those lunch boxes. Where is our tiffin?"

The best part was to hear the committee members say different things at the end. One thing that stuck me was what Takayoshi said, "This is unbelievable that I didn't doodle once in the three and half hours you were presenting. I was wrapped in attention, and I was fascinated to see that everyone was looking at you to see what the next magic word you were going to spin on us."

I will send you some clips as Jen recorded the presentation for me on my phone. Looking back, I am grateful for her patience as the phone died half-way through my presentation; she tried to use her own charger, but it didn't work. The last part about their views on my diss is on the audio file. At the end, after everyone had left, Huot gave me a nod and said, "You did great. My 20th was a tremendous success story!!" At that point, I was done with my dissertation! *Voila! C'est Fini!!* I truly felt a sense of joy and fulfillment that my cross-cultural study will play an important role in measuring nonmain-stream literacy and literacy practices of indigenous groups, and—yes—I have added a small pillar to the literacy field.

After I sent her the letter, I realized that I had forgotten to mention one of the key questions that came from Dowdy, one of my committee members. She asked me about why I had not titled it as "ethnographic study or ethnographic case study" as I had visited the Dabbawalas so many times after my initial visit. My response, based on my recording reveals, "This study was based on the initial data that I gathered through my first visit, and all the later visits were used to validate the first set of data gathered—to concretize my findings." I added that my later visits not only established they were literate in ideological ways, but also "enabled me to see that they (the Dabbawalas) had more new narratives to share with me based on their experiences, but the main concept of literacy practices remained the same; my findings remained the same."

The main takeaway from my dissertation as I ended was:

My main purpose for this study was to prove that literacy is amorphous and changes shape depending on situations and contexts. And, only when we view the invisible literacies of indigenous groups like the Mumbai Dabbawalas—are we able to judge them on their own merits and understand that literacy is ideological in so many ways.

And if we are to apply the definition of literacy, as suggested by UNESCO (2004, 2017),[1] on the Dabbawalas, then *they are literate in their own contexts and in their community of business practices:*

Beyond its conventional concept as a set of reading, writing, and counting skills, literacy is now understood as a means of identification, understanding, interpretation, creation, and communication in an increasingly digital, text-mediated, information-rich and fast-changing world. Literacy involves a continuum of learning in enabling individuals to achieve their goals, to develop their knowledge and potential and to participate fully in their community and wider society.

And if we are to apply the definition of literacy, based on National Council of Teachers of English (NCTE),[2] 03.23.20 statement, on the Dabbawalas, then *they are literate in their own contexts and in their community of business practices:*

> … So what does this mean for our definition of literacy? At its simplest, literacy is the way that we interact with the world around us, how we shape it and are shaped by it. It is how we communicate with others via reading and writing, but also by speaking, listening, and creating. It is how we articulate our experience in the world and declare, "We Are Here!"

And, I firmly believe, the Dabbawalas and their literacy and business practices are here to stay and it is time for the world to understand that ideological literacies and practices change from culture to culture—across the globe. As the authors,[3] appropriately suggest in *Pulling Together: A Guide for Indigenization of Post-Secondary Institutions:*

> Decolonization is the process of deconstructing colonial ideologies of the superiority and privilege of Western thought and approaches. On the one hand, decolonization involves dismantling structures that perpetuate the status quo and addressing unbalanced power dynamics. On the other hand, decolonization involves valuing and revitalizing Indigenous knowledge and approaches and weeding out settler biases or assumptions that have impacted Indigenous ways of being. For non-Indigenous people, decolonization is the process of examining your beliefs about Indigenous Peoples and culture by learning about yourself in relationship to the communities where you live and the people with whom you interact.

Notes

1 https://en.unesco.org/themes/literacy and http://uis.unesco.org/en/glossary-term/literacy.

2 https://ncte.org/blog/2020/03/literacy-just-reading-writing/.

3 Cull et al. (2020). https://opentextbc.ca/indigenizationinstructors/.

References

Cull, I., Hancock, R. L. A., McKeown, S., Pidgeon, M., & Vedan, A. (2018). *Pulling Together: A Guide for Front-Line Staff, Student Services, and Advisors*. BC Campus. Retrieved from https://opentextbc.ca/indigenizationfrontlineworkers/

Cull, I., Hancock, R. L. A., McKeown. S., Pidgeon, M., & Vedan, A. (2020). https://opentextbc.ca/indigenizationinstructors/

Submitting to the National Repository: Official Completion of Thesis or Dissertation

Focus on taking the right actions, regardless of immediate outcomes, as the act itself is what truly matters.

—Mahatma Gandhi

On a final note, one of the comments from the committee members after they had congratulated me and signed the forms (completion of oral defense) was that after taking a break for few days, I should start working on adding my dissertation to the national repository. I had never thought about this process, and it came as a rude shock that there were still a few more steps required to complete the whole process of dissertation. So, I asked the graduate secretary about when was the "repository submission" due and her response was "usually, two weeks after the oral defense." In my mind, this meant spending many hours back on the computer and getting frustrated with the formatting. This also meant that candidates coming after me need to be informed about it.

When doctoral candidates or graduate students begin writing their thesis, it is necessary that they are strongly encouraged to review the *Style Guide and Instructions for Preparing Dissertations and Theses for Electronic submission* to the "National Repository."[1] Almost all graduate advisers and secretaries have this format and are willing to provide it to the candidates. Also, some universities and departments have a website dedicated to the formatting and submission, and students should access this as soon as they begin their writing. This document is a long checklist that provides information about formatting from the first blank page to the last page of the Appendix. I wrote my dissertation following the APA format but realized that the formatting was different for the submission process. I made the mistake of working on this for a few days and became extremely frustrated that I realized that outsourcing this and spending money on formatting was worth every penny. So, like some of my predecessors, I met with this individual and handed over her my dissertation with the submission format and left her office knowing it will be done. After one week, it was all formatted and the only thing left was to file it electronically.

Fortunately, the electronic filing is a straightforward process of uploading the thesis or dissertation for the public to view. Once the dissertation has been uploaded, it is necessary to ensure that it is visible online as candidates have had issues and unable to graduate on time; in some universities, until the thesis is published and can be viewed on the national repository, the dissertation is considered incomplete. Also, those who plan to write articles or publish their manuscript need to consider an embargo on publishing the complete dissertation and might want to speak to their director or concerned people about it. As there are different views on embargo, it is at the discretionary power of the writer to make that decision.

Once this process is complete, be ready for the final walk, *Dr ...!!*

Note

1 I would rather mandate this, as right from the beginning of writing the Honors thesis/dissertation it helps with the formatting and citations.

Appendix

This is a list that will be of great help while writing your dissertation and will help you to stay on track.

Task Numbers	Tasks	Tentative Date to complete	Final Date when task is completed	Comments/ Thoughts
	Part 1—Dream			
1.	Visualizing the research topic/project			
2.	Providing rationale for choosing a specific topic.			
3.	Choosing a dissertation director			
4.	Formatting the research question			
5.	Developing a rough sketch of methods section			

Task Numbers	Tasks	Tentative Date to complete	Final Date when task is completed	Comments/ Thoughts
6.	Passing the Citi Test and Writing the IRB			
7.	Preparing the pro- spectus or proposal for submission to the committee			
	Part 2—Design			
8.	Understanding the methodology			
9.	Choosing the location and participants			
10.	Chalking out other aspects of the study– including writing field notes			
11.	Arriving at the location			
12.	Designing the data collection			
	Part 3—Develop			
13.	Unpacking field notes including Transcribing and Translating			
14.	Beginning of Coding- fracturing and reducing			
15.	Recognizing the com- plexity and beauty in coding through personal memos and deciphering the larger picture			
16.	Cross-checking and ensuring ethical prac- tices: Triangulation			

Task Numbers	Tasks	Tentative Date to complete	Final Date when task is completed	Comments/ Thoughts
17.	Findings based on selective coding and deciphering the larger picture			
18.	Ethnographic case study and *Upsilamba*			
	Part 4—Demonstrate			
19.	Sending the chapters to the committee			
20.	Preparing for the defense			
21.	Developing confidence and defending your brainchild			
22.	Succeeding in your efforts and congratulating yourself on a job well done			
23.	Submitting to the national repository—Official completion of thesis or dissertation			

Index

Printed by
CPI books GmbH, Leck